They Created Us

Special Education, Medicaid
Waivers, EPSDT, Independent Case
Management - A family's journey
through a bureacratic maze!

Denise Mercado

Bloomington, IN Milton Keynes, UK
authorHOUSE®

AuthorHouse™
1663 Liberty Drive, Suite 200
Bloomington, IN 47403
www.authorhouse.com
Phone: 1-800-839-8640

AuthorHouse™ UK Ltd.
500 Avebury Boulevard
Central Milton Keynes, MK9 2BE
www.authorhouse.co.uk
Phone: 08001974150

362.4
MER
4/08

First published by AuthorHouse 11/3/2006

ISBN: 1-4259-7070-2 (sc)
ISBN: 1-4259-7069-9 (dj)

Library of Congress Control Number: 2006909327

Printed in the United States of America
Bloomington, Indiana

This book is printed on acid-free paper.

The following individuals provided permission to use
materials within the content of the book.

Brian Burwell, Vice President – Thomson Medstat
Charles Broadwell, President & Publisher – The Fayetteville Observer
Dave Richard, Executive Director – The Arc of North Carolina
Jane Perkins/Sarah Somers – The National Health Law Program
Barbara Trader, Executive Director – TASH
Steven L. Mason, Executive Director – Parent to Parent of Vermont
North Carolina Parents of Children with Disabilities referenced throughout the book

This book is dedicated to the thousands of parents who battle bureaucracies on behalf of their children with disabilities.

Acknowledgement

There are many people who have contributed to my life and the creation of this book. The list is endless. But there is only one person who has faithfully walked beside me, led me, and followed me through this journey. My husband, John is a dedicated husband and father. He has been from the beginning my very best friend, my mentor, my soul mate. I thank him beyond words for his love and affection and most importantly for his gentle and kind spirit. Many times, when the journey was unbearable and I wanted desperately to throw in the towel, it was John's encouraging words that simply said, "We can do this. You can do this. God is with us. We are not alone." His unwavering faith has enabled tremendous spiritual growth in a woman who has relied so heavily on his love and affection. Together, John and I embarked on a journey that was not planned. And together, as a team, we continue to face battles and make hard decisions on behalf of our children, especially our son, Daniel. I thank John from the bottom of my heart for honoring our marriage vows and being there with me through all the good times and the bad times.

I love you always and forever – thank you, John for everything!

Table of Contents

Introduction

Parents of American children with disabilities grew up in a land of freedom. In our school systems, we learned the words of our Constitution, the Bill of Rights, and the Emancipation Proclamation. We read over and over that all men were created equal and that Americans – All Americans – had a right to freedom, life, liberty, and the pursuit of happiness.

Growing up in the 1950s and 1960s, we soon realized these words were not reality for many Americans. In the 1970s and 1980s we became parents of children with disabilities and realized these basic American freedoms did not apply to our children. As parents of children with disabilities, we began our journey, innocent and naïve of the intentions of the bureaucracy to help our children and our families. We learned from experience the reality of the human service system and its many flaws. We are now clothed in armor and approach every meeting with a battle plan in hand to obtain what is vital to the health and welfare of our children.

Chapter 1

Hit Below the Belt

It is amazing to me that the day this story begins, even though it took place many years ago, feels like it was yesterday. I remember every detail of the day, the weather, the TV program, and even what I was wearing.

It was Columbus Day 1982. I was in my kitchen baking bread and enjoying my family. Six months prior, I had given birth to our second son. Our family started out with just the two of us and grew to be the typical American family of four, complete with Toby the dog. Little John, our oldest son, was three years old at the time and was watching his favorite TV program, *Sesame Street*, with his new little brother, Danny. I had just put the bread in the oven when I heard a noise. Little John was quick to announce, "Mommy, Danny got sick!" I immediately ran to the living room and picked Danny up. He had vomited all over the blanket I had laid him on, and when I looked at him he smiled. I noticed, however, that he was very warm, and since I was now an "experienced" Mom, I did not panic, as I had done so often with my oldest. I looked at little John and said, "It looks like brother might have one of those famous ear infections."

Since it was a holiday and the Aviation Family Practice Clinic we were assigned to at Madigan Army Medical Center was closed, I knew it was off to the emergency room. I bundled Danny up in a blanket, wrote a quick note to my husband, grabbed my purse, and buckled the boys in the car. Once in the emergency room, I signed in at the front desk and then waited to be called. After a short time, they called our name for vitals to be taken. Danny's temperature was 103. There was no runny nose or any other indication that he might just be fighting a cold. Luckily, one of the flight surgeons was on duty in the emergency room. After conducting a thorough exam, the doctor confirmed my suspicions. Both ears were very red. He gave us Amoxicillan for the infection, to be given three times per day for ten days. He also gave us Tylenol and Pedialyte and we were on our way.

I had done this many times before with little John. He had many ear infections from six months of age to two years of age. It looked to me like Danny was simply following in his brother's footsteps.

When I got home I gave Danny the medicine as prescribed and rocked him to sleep with a bottle of Pedialyte. It was around 3:00 p.m. John was expected home at 5:00 p.m. I sat with little John for a while and read him a story. He asked about Danny and if he was going to be all right. I assured him that Danny had the same thing he had had when he was a baby and that the medicine would surely do the trick. Around 4:00 p.m. I started preparing dinner, checking periodically on Danny. He was sleeping soundly and I was grateful for the medicine that I knew would help him get better.

Danny finally woke at 4:30 p.m. He was still warm and quite lethargic. I had stripped him down to his T-shirt and diaper and washed his face with a cool rag to help the fever down. When John came home, after being greeted by the dog and little John, he made his way over to Danny, who was sitting on my lap. It was obvious Danny wasn't feeling well. Immediately, John wanted to know what was wrong. I went through the entire scenario with confidence and eased my husband's worries with a simple response: "He'll be fine. Don't worry. He's got the medicine in him. Little John went through it and now it is Danny's turn."

I remember when little John was six months old and woke us in the middle of the night with 103-degree temperature. Both John and I panicked and in a flash were at the emergency room seeking help. We were given the Amoxicillan, Tylenol, and Pedialyte, just like this time. I remember very clearly not getting much sleep that evening. I hovered over the crib, watching the little guy breathe for hours. After a day of the medicines, little John seemed back to his old self. I expected much of the same with Danny.

I knew not to try to feed Danny too much for dinner that evening. Besides the Amoxicillan, Tylenol, and Pedialyte, I tried a little fruit. He ate a few bites and then cried a little. His eyes were droopy and I knew the best thing for him was sleep. Again, I rocked him as he sucked on a bottle of Pedialyte.

After the rest of us ate dinner, it was soon bath time for little John, and then a bedtime story. It was around 8:00 p.m. when I checked Danny again. He was sleeping soundly. I was happy that I was able to get all of the medicines in him as prescribed, and once again I was convinced that he would surely recover just like his brother.

The next morning, after getting John off to work at 6:00 a.m., I peaked in on Danny. He was still sleeping, which I took as a good sign. Around 7:00 a.m. little John awoke. We ate breakfast together and I explained to him that we had to be extra quiet this morning since Danny wasn't feeling well and was still sleeping. Around 8:00 a.m. I went in to check Danny. He was still soundly sleeping but I noticed his breathing was more rapid than usual. I placed my hand on his back and listened for a while. It sounded strange. I then placed my hand on his forehead and he felt a little cooler, which I thought was good. I decided to let him sleep a little longer before I woke him for another dose of medicine. I no sooner left Danny's room when the phone rang. It was the flight surgeon from the emergency room. He asked how Danny was doing. I told him Danny seemed to be cooler this morning but I explained my concern about the way he was breathing. The flight surgeon explained that Danny's ears were both infected and that the medicines needed time to work. However, since there was no longer a holiday and the Aviation Family Practice Clinic was now open, he suggested I take Danny to the clinic to have his urine and blood checked. I was beginning to realize that this was in fact a little different from little John's episodes. I don't ever remember little John panting while sleeping. And believe me, if he panted I would have noticed.

We were able to get a three o'clock appointment that afternoon at the Aviation Family Practice Clinic. As expected, Danny was not very interested in breakfast. However, I did manage to get all of the medicine down and he was still taking his bottle on a regular basis. The flight surgeon on duty examined Danny only to find both ears infected. He assured me that the medicine needed time to work and that as long as Danny was getting the full dose and plenty of fluids he would do just fine. As a precaution he did take a urine and a blood sample. Both came back negative.

Danny slept for a long time that day. Although the breathing went back to normal, I was quickly losing my confidence. This was very different from little John and I was beginning to worry. By the time John came home from work, I was deeply troubled by what was happening with our youngest son. I followed all of the doctor's instructions and still it looked like he wasn't responding. It had been more than twenty-four hours since I took him to the emergency room. After little John had had one or two doses of the medicine, he would start to come back to life. Danny had had five doses of the medicine and didn't look any better than before I gave him the medicine.

After dinner John and I talked about what the doctors said and did for Danny. It sounded right and it sounded like nothing was left out. The only thing left for us to do was wait for the medicine to start working. This time John was the one with the confidence. "He'll be okay, Mom. He's a tough little guy, like his brother. Let's give it some time like the doctor said."

It took a long time for me to get to sleep that evening. I remember whispering a little prayer before finally dozing off. The next morning I was up at 6:00 a.m. getting John off to work. Little John was up at 7:00 a.m., ready to eat as usual. This time I didn't say anything to little John about being quiet. I was determined to see a change in Danny. Around 8:00 a.m. I marched into Danny's room, pulled up the shade, and said with a cheery voice, "Good morning, Danny boy! How's my handsome guy today?" Danny did not look good. He was still a little warm. I picked him up and he immediately cuddled close to my neck. I said, "Come on, Danny boy. We're going to have a better day today. Mommy made you some cereal for breakfast and you've got to take your medicine again so you can get better."

I dressed Danny as if we were going somewhere, all while I was talking to him. He moaned a little as if to say, "Leave me alone. I don't feel good." I then sat him in his highchair. He started to cry. He wasn't comfortable in his chair and I didn't know why. I wiped his tears away and assured him it would be all right. I put the tray in place and tried to feed him some cereal. He began to vomit. I cleaned off the tray, wiped his face, and proceeded to give him his medicine. I tried the Amoxicillan twice and then the Tylenol. He wouldn't take the full dose and the little he did take in his mouth caused him to vomit it all back up.

Danny kept slouching and arching his back. I thought it was his way of saying he wanted out of the chair. I picked him up, cleaned him off, and sat him in my lap. I then tried to give the medicines but he wouldn't take them. I paced the floors back and forth with him in my arms. I tried to comfort him but every time I rubbed his back he arched and cried more. By this time I was scared.

Little John had no idea what was going on and was preoccupied with the idea that he might miss *Sesame Street*. As I paced the floors wondering what I should do next for Danny, little John tugged at my shirt. "I want to watch *Sesame Street*. I want to watch *Sesame Street*."

I ran to the TV, switched on the channel, and instructed little John to be very quiet while I called the doctor. I spoke to the receptionist at the Aviation Family Practice Clinic. She gave me an appointment with one of the flight surgeons for 3:30 that afternoon.

"It's 9:30. I do not want to wait that long. My son has a fever."

"I'm sorry, ma'am. That's the earliest appointment I have."

"Is the flight surgeon in now?" I asked in desperation.

"Yes, ma'am," she replied. "But he is with patients."

"Please tell the flight surgeon I am coming in *now*."

With that I hung up the phone. While putting on Danny's coat I yelled for little John to get ready. I gave little John his favorite toy truck before removing him from his spot in front of his favorite TV show. While driving to Madigan Army Medical Center, I could see through the rearview mirror that little John was holding Danny's hand. Neither little John nor I had a clue what was happening to Danny, but I think we both knew it wasn't good.

As usual, parking at the hospital was horrendous. There were over 50,000 soldiers stationed at Ft. Lewis, not including the retirees. I believe they all had appointments that day. Once we found a parking spot, I got out the stroller and, as fast as I could, headed toward the clinic. I found myself face to face with the receptionist who couldn't or wouldn't give me an earlier appointment.

"My name is Denise Mercado. I called a little while ago about my

5

son, Danny."

"Do you have an appointment?" she said sternly.

"No. You tried to give me a 3:30 appointment but I didn't think I should wait that long to see the doctor."

"Well, the flight surgeons are with patients now. I'll talk to them as soon as they are through."

Danny was in my arms crying, yet the receptionist did not move to help us. I guess she saw lots of crying, irritable children. But this was my kid and this was very different. I was scared and worried for Danny and I was not going to sit in a waiting room and wait. As I looked down the corridor, I recognized the doctor's name on one of the doors, I kept my eye on that door as I paced with Danny in my arms. He was still moaning and arching his back. Little John was still concerned with *Sesame Street*, but I was able to redirect his attention to several of the children's books in the waiting room. After about ten minutes that seemed like hours of pacing, the door finally opened. The doctor and his patient walked down the corridor toward the receptionist. I blocked the doorway and looked directly at the doctor. "Please see Danny next," I begged. "He has a fever and keeps arching his back and moaning."

The doctor glanced at the receptionist and then back at me. He immediately motioned to his office. I called for little John and quickly moved down the corridor to his office. I placed Danny on the examining table and removed his coat. He was still moaning. As soon as I got the coat off, Danny starting arching his back. The doctor approached the table with his stethoscope. He listened to Danny's heartbeat then touched his back. Again Danny arched. The doctor looked at me and said he'd be right back.

He left the room for just a second, but it was long enough for me to gather little John in my arms and ask him to settle down. How could I possibly expect this little three-year-old to sit still? Yet it was so very important to me that little John listened and did as he was told, an almost impossible task for a three-year-old. I was so frightened with what was happening. I was desperately trying to make sense of it all.

The doctor returned with another physician, who again examined Danny. They whispered something to each other and then the first doctor explained to me that they wanted to do a special test on Danny. With that, the other doctor took Danny in his arms and proceeded out of the examining room down the hall. I grabbed little John and walked behind Danny with the other doctor. As we walked very quickly, the first doctor explained the test they wanted to do was a spinal test. *Spinal test,* I thought. *Arching his back. Is there a connection here?* All the while little John was asking, "Where are we going? Where are we going? Where are we going?"

Once in the treatment room, Danny was placed on a huge table. Several nurses came in to assist both doctors. The first doctor continued to explain that the procedure was to rule out spinal meningitis. I was asked to wait outside the treatment room. The door to the treatment room closed and I was no longer able to see Danny.

What the hell is going on here? I looked over at little John. Once again he was preoccupied with several of the magazines in the waiting room and the little toy truck I remembered to snatch up for him before leaving home. With tears in my eyes, I reached for my purse and pulled out my rosary. Ever since Catholic school, I have always carried a rosary. The nuns told us we'd never know when we'd need one.

It seemed like forever as I paced the floor and prayed, but finally the door opened. Both doctors approached me very closely. I felt like they were very close to my face. One had his arm on my shoulder and the other held my hand.

"Mrs. Mercado, your son has spinal meningitis."

My back fell against the wall. They held me and once again got very close.

"Mrs. Mercado, we have to tell you that some children die from this."

I dropped my head in my hands and began to cry like never before. I couldn't control the tears. I was losing my breath and my hands started shaking.

"Mrs. Mercado, we have to take Danny down to the pediatric ward. Are you okay? Can you make it?"

"Yes, yes, we'll make it."

The first doctor took Danny in his arms this time. The other doctor took the stroller and diaper bag and he reached for little John, but I immediately gathered little John in my arms and started following down the long Madigan corridors. Little John saw my tears and asked what was wrong. All I could answer was that Danny did not feel good.

I did not know how to explain it, because I didn't really understand it myself.

In the pediatric ward treatment room there were more nurses and doctors. One of the doctors asked for John's work number. I asked him to please tell John to be careful coming to the hospital, since he was on his motorcycle and I didn't think we needed two Mercados in the hospital at the same time.

When John arrived at the hospital they were still working on Danny in the treatment room. John and I looked at each other and embraced like never before. We knew something horrible was happening to our son, but we still didn't have a clear picture of what we were facing.

The doctors finally came out of the treatment room and explained to us that Danny was going to be transferred to the ICU. They again explained that Danny had spinal meningitis, but beyond that they could say no more. Several other tests were being done and they assured us they would let us know the results as soon as they were available.

Again we followed Danny down the long corridors, but this time he was not carried. Our little six-month-old son lay on a bed ten times too big for his little body, with lots of equipment piled all around him. Several doctors and nurses escorted him. They all looked very concerned and very professional in all they did for Danny. They did not allow us to go beyond the ICU doors. We waited for them to get Danny situated in his bed and then one of the doctors sat with little John as John and I looked in on Danny.

As I walked in Danny's ICU room, I saw my little son's naked body lying on a very large bed. Where his diaper once was laid a small piece of material. I walked very slowly toward his bed, glancing through tears at all the equipment surrounding this little guy. Danny had tubes in his nose, an IV in his foot, and EEG monitor receivers on his chest. I kissed him ever so gently on his forehead and rubbed my lips down his face on one side and then the other. "I love you, Danny boy. Mommy's here. Daddy's here. We love you." He just moaned.

I wondered why he didn't have a diaper on, so I looked under the piece of material and saw that he also had a catheter. John then came over to Danny and he too kissed him and touched his head. As John spoke so softly to our son, I could see tears fall on Danny's face.

We knew we had to make plans for little John, so we left Danny with a nurse close by. Our minds quickly raced, seeking a plan that would suffice. By this time three pediatricians and two pediatric neurosurgeons were called into ICU. The flight surgeon assured us Danny was in good hands. He also volunteered to stay with Danny while we made arrangements for little John.

John and I were numb and said very little as we drove home. Little John asked about Danny but all we could answer was the same lame response: "Danny doesn't feel good." We could not comprehend what was happening.

Once home, we started calling family. Being the typical military family, none of our extended family lived close by—not even in the same state or on the same side of the country for that matter. All of our family was in New York and we were stationed in Ft. Lewis, Washington on the other side of the country. We spoke with my parents and Mom immediately volunteered to come and stay with little John. Then we spoke with Sister Mary Olivia and Sister Dorothy, better known as "Mom" and "Aunt Dorothy." Sister Olivia was the administrator of the Catholic boys' home where John spent all his growing years from age five to eighteen until college and the army. From early on, Sister Olivia and John "adopted" each other, resulting in her role as "Mom" and later on "Grandma" to our children. Sister Dorothy was Sister Olivia's partner in crime, so to speak. They were always together working on a number of different projects. Sister Dorothy was also adopted by our family as "Aunt Dorothy." I knew that once Mom and Aunt Dorothy knew about Danny's condition, prayers would be said, God would be called upon to watch over our son, and somehow our prayers would be answered and this nightmare would be over. We also called Father Joe, the priest who married us and grew up with John. He too would be praying for our son and would say morning mass for Danny.

John then called his unit. It was then I had a very strange realization. John was not supposed to be home. His unit was in the field on maneuvers the week Danny got sick and was not expected home for two more days. Hours prior to John's unit leaving, the battalion commander specifically requested Sergeant Mercado as the crew chief for his downed aircraft. Another crew chief was already assigned and John was packed for the field when the change was made. Had John gone to the field with his unit, he would not have been home when Danny was admitted to the hospital. Getting a message to him would have taken quite some time. I couldn't help but wonder what God was up to.

After speaking with my Mom, she made immediate plans to fly from New York to Tacoma, Washington the very next day. In the meantime, rather than leave little John with a stranger, John and I decided that John would stay with our oldest while I went back to the ICU to be with Danny. I sat by Danny's side, whispering the Our Father and Hail Mary in his ear while stroking his head, and waited desperately for him to get better. One of the pediatricians noticed my rosary and asked if I wanted to see a priest. My thoughts went immediately to the sacrament of last rites. "Is Danny dying?" I asked. The doctor chuckled and said the priest would be for me, not Danny. Well, in that case I most certainly wanted and needed to see a priest. In my desperate attempt to find an answer to *why* this was happening, I immediately remembered all the wrongs I committed as a teenager. Certainly that had to be the reason all this was happening.

The pediatrician returned to say that a priest could not be located in the hospital but asked if I would consider speaking with a Baptist minister. I reluctantly agreed. I had never spoken with a Protestant minister before. I didn't think it was the right thing to do. But in my desperation I was willing to put aside my prejudice in search of comfort and relief.

I remember sitting across from the Baptist minister and looking him over. He carried a small bible and wore a dove lapel pin on his white medical coat. He had dark hair and dark framed glasses and seemed very sincere in wanting to comfort and console. He smiled as he introduced himself and stated he was aware of my son as a patient of the ICU. I could feel the tears welling up and I immediately lowered my head so he would not see my eyes. Ever so gently, he reached over, touched my hand, and lowered his head in prayer. When I looked up, I couldn't help notice the bald spot in the center of his head, which reminded me of St. Anthony. I chuckled and asked, "Are you sure you're not Catholic?"

"No, ma'am," he said firmly. "I've been Baptist all my life."

We smiled at each other, easing the tension. Then with tears in my eyes I shared my desire to confess my sins.

"But you guys don't do confession, do you?" I asked.

"Sure we do," he said with confidence. "But we confess our sins directly to God." He then leaned closer toward me and asked, "Why do you feel the need to confess now?"

Immediately I remembered all the sneaky things I did as a teenager. I remembered feeling like I was getting away with a lot. I was taught there were always consequences, good or bad, for our actions. But as life went on in my teenage years, I was doing a lot of wrong things with very few obvious consequences because a lot of what I was doing was in secret, without my parents ever knowing. But God knew what I was up to. I believed what I was facing was the biggest consequence of all. I believed all I did wrong in my teenage years was added up to equal this major consequence. I really was sorry for all the stupid, selfish things I did as a teenager, but I never really took the time to say I was sorry to my parents, to myself, and more importantly to God.

I never responded to the minister's question. I just cried. After a short prayer I went back to Danny's room. I checked in with one of the pediatricians to see if there were any changes with Danny. There were no changes; however, he did mention the results of the spinal test showed Danny had Haemophilus Influenzae Meningitis.

I again whispered an Our Father and Hail Mary in Danny's ear, stroked his head, kissed his cheek, and sat by his bed with my rosary in hand, wondering when this nightmare would be over and we could go home.

Before I knew it, morning had come. White coats were everywhere. Pediatricians, neurosurgeons, and nurses all came in to check on Danny. He was no worse than the day before but he was still no better. I left Danny's side around 9:00 a.m. to call John. Arrangements were made for one of John's friends to watch little John so John would be able to come back to the hospital in the evening. Upon returning to the ICU, the doctors and nurses were moving Danny's bed toward the door.

"Where are you going?" I asked.

"We're going to x-ray to do a CAT scan."

As I followed the team of white coats pushing our son down the long corridors toward the x-ray department, I found myself getting a crash course in medical procedures. One of the doctors explained that the CAT scan would provide them with more information about the brain. I was confused as to why we were now discussing the brain. After all, Danny had *spinal* meningitis. How did we get from the spine to the brain? After arriving in the x-ray department, the doctor began to sketch a stick figure of a man on a piece of paper. He went on to explain that the fluid around the brain that cushions the brain is the same fluid in our spine. He further explained there are tiny hair-like membranes around the brain called meninges. Sometimes a virus gets in the fluid and attaches itself to the meninges, causing an inflammation.

It was starting to come back to me. I remember learning in biology class that an inflammation of any kind almost always ends in "itis." Meningitis is an inflammation of the meninges. The doctor continued, explaining that sometimes an inflammation of the meninges can cause brain damage. The purpose of the CAT scan was to determine if this was occurring and at what rate.

By this time Danny was ready for the test to be run. Danny was secured to a long narrow table that moved through a machine shaped like a spinning doughnut hole. No one was in the room with Danny. All the doctors, nurses, and technicians stood in a tiny room with a glass window where a large computer was running. On the screen I could see Danny's brain. There was an eerie silence in the room as the doctors viewed the computer screen. Several scans were taken.

It was 10:00 a.m. when we arrived back at the ICU. I spoke with every doctor and nurse that came into our room about Danny's condition and what was seen on the CAT scans.

"The CAT scan looks good. Your son is still very sick, but he is stable," stated one of the doctors.

There were an awful lot of people attending to Danny, but I wasn't sure what medications were being given.

"Danny has haemophilus influenzae meningitis," said the doctor. "Normally with most meningitis, we can prescribe an antibiotic. But with this type of meningitis, there is no antibiotic that can be given."

"So what do we do?" I asked.

"We simply have no choice but to let it run its course. We have him on an IV. We are administering Tylenol and monitoring his vitals regularly. I'm afraid that's all we can do right now."

I was stunned. *This really is a nightmare. How can we let this thing run through this little baby's body without fighting it in any way?*

Shortly after the doctor left the room, I approached one of the other physicians on duty and asked the same question about medication. The response was the same. We had no choice but to let this thing run its course, but I was assured that everyone was doing everything possible for our son.

I returned to Danny's side again in tears. He looked miserable. There was no smiling or response to me at all—just moaning. Even with his eyes closed, I could see his brow tensed in pain.

"Mommy's here, Danny boy. Mommy loves you very much."

The time on the clock in Danny's room read 11:15 a.m. I knew mass was said every day at the hospital chapel at 11:30 a.m. I really wanted to be there. I kissed Danny and started walking toward the door of his room. Just then one of the doctors came in to examine Danny. I watched him look into Danny's eyes with his flashlight. He repeated the process several times before turning and asking me to leave so he could examine further. I told him I was headed to the chapel for mass. He said that was a good idea and assured me he would be with Danny. As I walked down the hallway to the ICU doors, I could see through the glass window of Danny's room all the nurses and doctors surrounding our son.

I don't remember exactly how I got to the hospital chapel. I don't even remember the priest or any part of the mass. But I do remember the people. There were those in wheelchairs, bathrobes, walkers, and crutches. I sat in the back of the chapel with uncontrollable tears and a numbness throughout my body that would not leave. I didn't make it through the entire mass. I couldn't go to communion. I felt dirty inside remembering my past. I left the chapel and started walking toward the ICU. My body felt very heavy. I remember stopping several times to lean on the wall. People were moving about very fast, while I seemed to be going in slow motion. Just then the minister who visited me the night before tapped me on my shoulder.

"Denise," he said with concern in his voice. "How are you?"

"I don't know. I'm scared."

He immediately put his arm around me and asked if I was going back to the ICU. I nodded yes. He asked if he could walk with me since he was headed in the same direction. We started down the corridor ever so slowly. I wanted to move faster but I just couldn't get my legs to move correctly. I stopped at the end of the corridor and looked into the minister's eyes. "Danny can't die," I cried. "He can't die." With that I felt my body collapsing. The minister put his arm around me and held me up. No words were ever said by this man; there was just a strong arm to lean on and a soft handkerchief to wipe away my tears.

As I entered Danny's room again, there was a nurse by his side, writing on a clipboard. I no sooner sat in the chair by Danny's bed when one of the doctors came into the room and explained they wanted to do another CAT scan. When I inquired as to why this was needed, the doctor explained Danny had a grand mal seizure. I immediately looked at the clock in the room. I was only gone for thirty minutes. "I don't understand, doctor. When did this happen?" He went on to explain that when he examined Danny's eyes, he noticed the pupils were not responding. That is why he asked me to leave. I guess he knew what was about to happen.

"What is a grand mal seizure?" I asked. Before I could get a response, Danny was once again being moved to x-ray for his second CAT scan. John arrived as Danny's bed moved toward the ICU doors. We immediately took each other's hand and followed the crowd. John assured me little John was taken care of and immediately asked for an update on Danny. I told him all I knew. Danny was again secured to the CAT-scan table. The CAT scan this time showed a shadow on the left side of the brain. The terminology we were now being exposed to included the term *cerebral infarction*.

Within hours John and I were approached by Danny's team of doctors. It seemed that Danny's brain was swelling and he required equipment that Madigan Army Medical Center did not have to measure intracranial pressure. The recommendation was to airlift Danny to Children's Hospital in Seattle. However, Danny's condition was critical and the doctors were not sure Danny would survive the transport. This was the first of many gruesome decisions for us. John and I both agreed, if Danny was going to die, he would die trying. We therefore signed all the necessary forms to get him airlifted to the facility that would best meet his needs.

As we watched the scurry of doctors and nurses in Danny's ICU room, I noticed the hospital priest standing in the corner of Danny's room. I knew he was a priest because I recognized the scapular around his neck. He held a bible and rosary in his hand. His hands were folded in prayer. His eyes were closed so not to be distracted by all that was going on in the room. His lips were moving and I knew prayers were being offered for our son.

I don't know how John and I made the trip to Seattle from Ft. Lewis that day. As we got into our car we could see the helicopter lift off with our son. We didn't know if Danny would be alive when we arrived at Children's Hospital. It was a long forty-five-minute drive from Ft. Lewis to Seattle. John and I didn't say much to each other during the trip. However, my guilt got the best of me. I looked at John with tears in my eyes and told him I was sorry for what was happening to our son. He gently reached for my hand. With tears in his eyes he said, "What are you sorry for? This isn't your fault." All I could do was cry. There really wasn't much anyone could say to convince me this was not my fault.

Upon arrival at Children's Hospital, we immediately went to the pediatric ICU. We were relieved to know that Danny was being prepared for surgery. He had made it. The army doctor who traveled to Children's Hospital with Danny assured us our son was getting the best care. "The neurosurgeon has just arrived," he said. "He's one of the best in his field and has done this procedure many times before. As a matter of fact, there is another child in the unit with the same monitor." I immediately asked if this other child had meningitis too. The doctor hesitated and then replied, "No, he was hit." Before I could comprehend his words, the neurosurgeon was introduced to us. He explained the procedure and the intracranial monitor that would be placed under the scalp to monitor pressure. The entire procedure took approximately a half hour. During this time, we filled out a lot of hospital forms and drank a lot of hot tea and coffee.

Danny made it through the procedure and was placed in the critical ICU, where he received twenty-four-hour nursing care. He had his own nurse, who played music for him and watched him very closely.

It was hard to see Danny in this condition. It was just as hard leaving him. Our son lay in a large bed with a special monitor coming out of his head. He was attached to a respirator and a heart monitor. There were two IVs—one with valium and one with morpheme. A catheter was also used. Although he lay without a stitch of clothing, there were so many wires that he appeared fully dressed.

The silence in the car on the way home was devastating. What could we say to each other? Sure, we both wanted to believe Danny would pull through, but the facts made us doubt he'd ever leave the hospital.

We arrived home in time to meet my Mom and sister. Sleeping that night was not easy. I woke in the middle of the night only to find John gone. I went to the hall, thinking he might have headed to the kitchen for a bite to eat. On my way down the hall I heard sobbing coming from Danny's bedroom. I opened the door wide enough to see my husband on his knees by Danny's crib. He said no words but simply cried from deep within. I knew how he felt and I also knew he had to go through it.

The following day, we all headed to the hospital. My mom got to see her second grandson for the first time. It was nothing like we planned. Danny's life from this point on was nothing like we planned.

The doctors at this point were concerned with Danny's right side. Since the majority of the damage was on the left side of the brain, they feared paralysis on the right side of the body.

It was during our first visit with Danny that day we met Father Stanley, the hospital priest. Every day and sometimes two or three times a day, Father Stanley would come to pray with us over Danny. Two days after the doctors explained to us their fear of paralysis, John and I witnessed Danny moving his right leg. Sure it was only a wiggle, but it was all we needed to know that Danny would make it through this horrible ordeal.

Full of joy and excitement, John and I headed to the hospital cafeteria. It was there we met another Dad named Scott. Scott's son, Corey, was also in the ICU and was the other little boy with the special intracranial monitor. I immediately remembered the words of the doctor. Scott went on to explain how he and his wife were divorced and custody of the children was given to the wife. It was the wife's boyfriend who supposedly hit Corey. Corey was eighteen months old. During Danny's six-day hospital stay at Children's Hospital, Father Stanley gave last rites to Corey several times. We don't know if Corey made it. He was still in critical condition when Danny left the ICU.

After four days in the critical ICU, Danny was moved to the pediatric ICU ward. Slowly Danny was weaned from the respirator and IV medications. Reflexes and vitals were watched closely. By the sixth day, Danny was on the regular ward and paperwork was being completed for his return to Madigan Army Medical Center. Once at Madigan, I began to realize the severity of not only the illness Danny was fighting but also the side effects. We were told by Danny's pediatricians that the meningitis, along with the stroke and grand mal seizure, caused severe brain damage. They further stated that Danny would have difficulty doing the things children normally do, such as walking, talking, and functioning in society. Therapy was considered mandatory; however, no promises were made.

Never before had I been faced with a horror such as this: fear of the unknown, not knowing what to expect or who to turn to for answers. I visited Danny every day. I sat by his crib. I changed his diapers. I watched the nursing staff tube-feed our son through his nose. His sucking reflex was very weak. I felt so helpless. There had to be something I could do for Danny.

During one of my many trips to the vending machine, I noticed a sign: *Medical Library*. I needed to be educated in the things that happened to Danny and find out what my next steps would be. Every day for the next two weeks, I spent two hours a day in the medical library reading, taking notes, and learning. I studied meningitis, seizure activity, convulsive medications, hydrocephalus, and therapy models. This new knowledge tore at my heart.

I learned of the seven types of meningitis. Only one out of ten children survive haemophilus influenzae meningitis. Meningitis is a common cause of blindness, deafness, and **mental retardation.** The words were bouncing off the page, hitting me right in the face. If blindness was something we were facing, then I knew I needed to learn Braille; if deafness, then I needed to learn sign language. But what do you do for mental retardation? This was definitely out of the question.

The most disturbing yet interesting subject I researched was therapy. Several professionals had their own theories, each named for themselves. I learned of the Bobath therapy, the Rude therapy, and the Doman/Delacata therapy. Naturally, each felt his or her way was the best. Now it was my job to decide which method would be best for Danny.

During rounds one day, Danny's doctor talked with us about therapy. Good Samaritan Hospital Therapy Unit in Puyallup, Washington was highly recommended. Danny was scheduled for an evaluation immediately following discharge.

For the first time in my life I knew what it was like to be on an emotional roller coaster. One day I'd be up, full of hope and encouragement. And the next day I'd crash and hit bottom, wallowing in my own muck. I sat beside Danny's crib, staring out his window at the hospital chapel doors. It was a Saturday afternoon and a wedding had just taken place. I watched the smiles of all the family and friends. My eyes focused on the beautiful bride. She radiated with joy and happiness. The family and friends threw rice as a symbol of good luck. The bride and groom then left in a beautiful limo. I remembered my wedding day and the same joy I had felt. Never did I imagine my future would be filled with such despair. *Is this really what life is all about? What is the purpose of all this pain?* I felt so alone and wondered if there was anyone out there who knew what I was feeling.

My question was answered every time I looked past Danny's room and caught a glimpse of Paul. Paul was a near-drowning victim who, after one year of hospitalization, lay lifeless and alone in his hospital room. Paul had no visitors except the nurses, doctors, and orderlies. Where was Paul's mother? Why didn't she visit her child? Did she give up? In so many ways Danny looked like Paul. I couldn't give up. Danny depended on me. I couldn't let him down. I needed to learn more. Once again I found myself at the library, searching for information on therapy. As a last resort I flipped through the index file cards under *brain damage*. There was the book I was looking for: *What to Do about Your Brain Injured Child* by Glenn Doman. There was that name again. *Could it be the same person affiliated with the Doman/Delacata therapy?* Immediately I began reading. Morning, noon, and before bedtime I would read a little more. The book told the story of brain-damaged children who were predicted by the medical profession to never walk, talk, or function normally in society. These children did the impossible with the help of this therapy. The Doman/Delacata therapy method was a full-time program filled with intense stimulation. I found several books on this therapy method and read them all. I even found books written by the parents of hurt children who used this method and saw success in their children. Each book told of the hard work this therapy demanded. I was not afraid of hard work, especially if it would help my son.

The day finally came for Danny's discharge from the hospital. It had been a long month and now we were able to go home. John and I bought Danny a little navy blue suit with a red velvet vest. One of his pediatricians made the outfit, complete with a red-and-white carnation for Danny's lapel.

At home I dressed Danny in his night clothes and then we rocked in our favorite rocker. It was good to have Danny home. But no matter how hard I tried, Danny was different. He wasn't the same child I had known. He was sad and there were no signs of joy, laughter—not even a smile. The many tests given to Danny during his hospital stay concluded not only severe brain damage, but the question of sight was never answered. His eyes stared to the left at all times, except when you moved his head. He did not track lights or bright objects. However, the test did show the optic nerve and pathways leading from the eyes to the brain were clear of damage. Why Danny's eyes did not respond to light was a mystery. Everything was a mystery at this point. Danny also lost head control. He did, however, have normal hearing. He was healthy as far as heart, lungs, and kidneys were concerned. It was just his brain that suffered all the damage.

Danny's first few days home were like having a newborn again. I was awakened every two hours by the cries of a baby I could not help. I paced the floors. I rocked. I sang. I hugged. No matter what I did, it didn't help. It was almost as if Danny did not know me. After our first long week home it was finally time for Danny's first therapy appointment. I couldn't wait to get busy learning new techniques. I was determined to work hard. Danny was going to walk and talk and do all the things little boys do. I was going to see to that.

On our first visit to Good Samaritan Hospital Therapy Unit, Danny was assigned a therapist and the evaluation process began. The evaluation enabled the therapist to set goals for Danny. One of the main goals set was working on head control. A schedule was set for Danny's therapy time: Tuesdays and Thursdays from 1:00 to 2:00 p.m.

"Why can't I come every day?" I asked.

"Right now we are understaffed," explained the therapist. "There are an awful lot of children here. Besides, Danny's been through quite an ordeal. It is best if we take it slow."

Her answer did not sit well with me. All the books I read stated differently. The earlier we get started, the better the chance for the child. The more stimulation, the more results. I explained this to the therapist and told her about my research into the Doman/Delacata therapy. "We do not do that type of therapy here," she stated firmly. "We don't even recommend it to our families. Neither does the American Medical Association."

I couldn't help but ask why. She continued, "It causes too much stress on the family unit, especially siblings." I couldn't believe my ears. This therapy was considered stressful because it required six hours of therapy six days per week. I didn't see the stress. I saw the hard work. Living with a child who suffered brain damage—who does not respond to you in any way—now, that's stress!

I continued my research on this special type of therapy. I also kept the schedule made for Danny at Good Samaritan Hospital. I did everything I could to learn what the therapist was doing with Danny, but it wasn't much.

Good Samaritan Therapy Unit served many children. They had an excellent support group of parents that met monthly. Unfortunately our first meeting was our last. During this time I was looking for answers—for ways to get my son back. I refused to accept this disaster. This support group, like so many others, consisted of families who had come to accept their children's fate. It was far too early in this journey for acceptance.

After reading several books on the Doman/Delacata therapy, I wrote a letter to the California office concerning our son and the possibility of an appointment. I immediately received an application. The process required a letter from Danny's therapist, a copy of the latest CAT scan, and a letter from me stating my observations of Danny. I gathered all the necessary papers and mailed the package. As I patiently waited for an answer, I continued to research, all the time keeping my appointments at Good Samaritan Therapy Unit.

I met several moms with hurt children at the therapy unit. What amazed me was the number of children in attendance as a result of meningitis. Tricia, age two, battled meningitis at three weeks of age. Her mom, Kathy became a good friend. It was through Kathy that I met Benjamin. He was eight months old and like Danny battled meningitis at six months of age. Becky was a year old and battled the same devastating disease at eight months of age. What had caused this in all these healthy, beautiful children? I thought I knew why this was happening in my life, but was it really possible that all of us had rebellious and secretive teenage years?

Every day I combed through the mail, looking for a letter from the Doman/Delacata office concerning an appointment for Danny's first evaluation. Instead I received a phone call from Dr. Doman. "Mrs. Mercado, I am afraid I have bad news." My heart sank. *Now what?* "Danny is not a good candidate for our therapy. I believe he has hydrocephalus." He continued, "I've examined the information you sent us. The CAT scan showed severe swelling of the ventricles in the brain."

"I know, doctor, but I was told this was because there was so much damage to the brain that the fluid from the ventricles were filling in the empty spaces."

"That is only one possibility," he explained. "The development of hydrocephalus is another. The evaluation from the therapist stating irritability in Danny when moved in different positions is another indicator that hydrocephalus be taken into consideration."

"What do I do now?" I asked. "How do I find out if Danny has hydrocephalus?"

Dr. Doman offered a simply solution. "A comparison of a new CAT scan to this one would determine whether or not Danny has hydrocephalus."

"Thanks so much, Dr. Doman. I'll get in touch with Danny's doctors immediately. If Danny does in fact have hydrocephalus and it is corrected with shunt surgery, will Danny be considered a good candidate for your therapy?"

"Absolutely."

Okay, I had my work cut out for me. I immediately dialed Danny's pediatrician and explained my conversation with Dr. Doman. The name "Doman" did not sit well with any of the doctors at Madigan Army Medical Center. They were all very much aware of the Doman/Delacata therapy program and the fact that it was not approved by the American Medical Association.

"How can this Dr. Doman make a neurological diagnosis when he is not a neurologist?" asked one of the doctors.

"To be honest, doctor, I am not interested in his credentials. I sent him a copy of Danny's last CAT scan along with an evaluation letter from Danny's therapist. From this, he has reason to believe hydrocephalus is a possibility for Danny. I've come across hydrocephalus while researching the type of meningitis Danny had. I want to know if Danny has hydrocephalus. According to Dr. Doman, another CAT scan is all that is needed. Will you do it for us? If not, I need to make other arrangements."

"Let me speak with the neurologist and the CAT-scan people and I'll get back to you."

I picked up Danny and sat in our favorite rocker, where we waited patiently for a phone call. Could this Dr. Doman, who had never laid eyes on Danny, be right? If he was right, why in the hell didn't any of our doctors pick up on this? I remembered my research on hydrocephalus identified it as another brain-damaging disease. *Hasn't Danny been through enough?* Just then the phone rang. It was Danny's pediatrician. "I spoke with the neurologist and we've reviewed Danny's chart." This didn't sound good. He continued, "We do not agree with Dr. Doman and we feel, since we have to sedate Danny for the CAT scan, that we should make sure this test is necessary before we put Danny through this again."

"Doctor, I truly feel it is necessary. I need peace of mind about this."

"Mrs. Mercado, we have been charting Danny's head growth. If he had hydrocephalus, his head would be growing."

"What about the swelling of the ventricles?" Now I felt like I knew what I was talking about. "Is there the slightest possibility Dr. Doman is right? If there is, then let's do one more CAT scan. I just want to be sure."

After a moment of silence, the doctor responded, "Okay, I'll set up an appointment and get back with you."

Danny and I put a lot of mileage on our favorite rocker that day while waiting for the phone to ring. Our CAT-scan appointment was finally made for March 5, 1982, along with a follow-up appointment with the pediatric neurologist on March 8. It was at the follow-up appointment with the neurologist that the latest CAT scan was revealed to me and diagnosis was given. Dr. Doman was right. Danny had hydrocephalus. The neurologist explained that Danny would be admitted to the hospital first thing in the morning. "We'll run some tests and first thing Wednesday morning; he will be scheduled for shunt surgery." His next words were piercing. "This surgery is not an emergency. But it is urgent."

I stared at Danny's CAT scan as tears flowed down my face. *My God, where is his brain?* The second CAT scan taken during Danny's hospital stay showed the ventricles were indeed swollen and the shadow on the left and right front hemispheres was quite visible. In this latest CAT scan there was a solid mass of darkness with a tiny rim of gray matter along the skull. I couldn't believe my eyes. How much more could my baby take?

Once again we were packing a bag for Danny: his favorite blanket, his favorite stuffed animal, the cross in his room, a music box, and a rosary. At the hospital there was more paperwork to complete and a new corner of the pediatric ward to make comfortable for our son. Tuesday afternoon was spent running the necessary preoperative tests. Before we knew it, Wednesday was here. Danny was wheeled into surgery at 7:00 a.m. Before he entered the operating room, I held him in my arms and whispered in his ear, through tears, a Hail Mary and a plea: "Hang in there, Danny. Please hang in there." And he did. He made it through surgery like a champ. While Danny was in recovery, the neurosurgeon came to give me a report.

"How's he doing, doc?" I asked.

"He's doing great."

"Was the pressure high?"

"Let's just say your son had a severe headache."

Again uncontrollable tears flowed as I marveled at the strength of this little boy. Not once did I consider God in all of this. After all, I was still convinced all of this was happening because of my sins. It took many years before I realized God was in control and was holding Danny in the palm of his hand.

I walked back to the pediatric ward with a friend who stood by my side through all of this. John missed all the action. He was sent to Ft. Eustis, Virginia for special helicopter crew-chief training one week before Danny's surgery. We spoke so often on the phone. I dreaded seeing our phone bill. However, I thanked God that we had a way to communicate with each other. Back on the ward, Danny was visited periodically by both the neurosurgeon and neurologist. "Mrs. Mercado, I hope you realize this will not solve all of Danny's problems," said the neurologist.

"I realize that. But at least we are headed in the right direction."

I went home early that day and slept my first night of peaceful sleep. I was able to recognize God in the wonderful friends and neighbors who supported us through all of this. I had to leave little John so often and didn't want to leave him at a daycare center. So many people opened their hearts and families to little John so I was able to spend time with Danny. John and I were very sensitive to little John and his place in our family. We included him in all the family activities, including visits to see his brother.

The next morning, like so many mornings, I was back by Danny's side at the pediatric ward. Danny was starting to perk up a bit. I claimed a rocker for us and again we rocked for hours. I even took him for a walk down the pediatric ward to his old room. Paul was no longer at Madigan. He had been transferred to an institution several weeks earlier. Danny's old room was occupied by another little boy in a cast from the waist down. I remember looking at this child's face and seeing Danny. They didn't look alike. This little boy had blonde hair and a fair complexion, but I recognized the lifeless look on his face. My curiosity got the best of me, so I asked one of the orderlies about the story behind this little boy's sad face. I should have known. Meningitis was the culprit. Danny's nightmare started with an ear infection. This little boy's nightmare started with a hip infection, which explained the cast.

As Danny and I headed back to our room, I felt a warm hand on my shoulder. It was Father Jim from our parish. He walked with us to Danny's room and then prayed with us by Danny's bedside. He excused himself rather suddenly to see another patient—another Danny—across the hall. After his visit he introduced me to Della, Danny's mom. After the priest left, Della and I talked about our sons. Della's son was deprived of oxygen during the birth process resulting in brain damage. He was also born with a damaged heart. Her son, Danny, was being hospitalized for a heart attack at age eight. "I love my son," Della said with tears in her eyes. "When he leaves me, a part of me will leave that no one will ever be able to replace." Della took her son home on Friday. I took my son home the following Monday. After getting both little John and Danny tucked in bed, I sat down with a hot cup of tea and the newspaper. It was during this relaxing time that I read of Della's son in the obituaries. The next morning I called Della. "We knew when we took him home on Friday that we took him home to die," she said through tears. I went to the funeral mass the next day. I sat in the crying room at the back of the church with my Danny in my arms. Before the procession to the altar, the priest blessed the body of Della's son. "I bless the body of little Danny in the name of the Father, and the Son, and the Holy Spirit, Amen." I knew then why I was in the crying room. I held my Danny close and begged God that I'd never hear those words for my son. Little did I know that years later my prayer would change.

Once Danny recovered from shunt surgery, it was time to implement the Doman/Delacata therapy. We were once again discouraged by our team of doctors regarding this therapy. Ironically enough, they offered no other choices except the little therapy offered at Good Samaritan. We believed it best for Danny to pursue this unapproved therapy source. We traveled to Seattle for an evaluation with Dr. Doman. We then received an intense program of activities with specific instructions. Our guest bedroom became Danny's therapy room. John built a therapy table with a slide to accommodate some of the activities. The walk-in closet was turned into a black room with a special light. In this room we presented Danny with fluorescent colored objects and encouraged him to follow the objects with his eyes. The most important activity in this program was the "patterning" therapy. Patterning involved three adults working with Danny at one time, using the therapy table and slide. Danny was placed on his stomach on the therapy table. One adult held his head while the other adults held Danny's arm and leg, one on each side. In unison the three adults would move Danny's body in a crawling motion. A ten-minute timer was set. This activity was performed six times per day, six days per week.

Before any of this could be done, we needed to find volunteers. I called the president of the Catholic Women of the Chapel at Ft. Lewis and explained my situation. At the next meeting I presented our need for volunteers. A form was passed around the room and over twenty people signed up. The president suggested I make the same presentation to the Protestant women of the chapel. The list of volunteers grew to fifty-two. I then developed a charting system, scheduling three volunteers for each session. The women who came to our home to help our son were military spouses; some officers' wives, some enlisted wives. They were rosary-carrying Catholics and bible-carrying Protestants and everything in between. Most importantly, they were faithful to the cause.

Danny did well with the therapy. We had several follow-up evaluations. Progress was not nearly as fast as I wanted it to be. However, Danny tolerated the activities well and showed improvement in muscle tone. We were grateful and willing to press on.

In 1983, eight months after we began the Doman/Delacata therapy program, John was selected to attend Officer Candidate School (OCS) at Ft. Benning, Georgia. John had originally applied for OCS prior to Danny's illness. His packet was not accepted due to orders to report to Germany. This was very disappointing to us, especially John. The OCS requirements for admission had an age limit and years-in-service limit. At the time the age limit was thirty-two. John was twenty-nine. The years-in-service limit was no more than ten years of active duty. John had eight years of active duty. John was told he could reapply for OCS admission six months after arriving in Germany. However, the Germany tour was to be three years long. That would put John over the OCS limits.

When Danny was in the Madigan ICU, doctors explained to us that if Danny were to survive this ordeal, we would most likely be stationed near army medical facilities that could accommodate Danny's needs. We explained to the doctors that John had orders for Germany. The doctors immediately processed the necessary paperwork to void the orders so we could stay at Ft. Lewis during Danny's illness. Danny's illness opened the door for John's admission to OCS. During the later part of Danny's hospital stay, I pushed John to resubmit the OCS packet. He refused to consider the option. He felt we all needed to concentrate on Danny and was willing to forfeit his dream for what Danny needed. However, prior to Danny's discharge from the hospital we were visited by a social worker. We already had a list of supplies Danny was going to need at home. The social worker explained two funding sources that would help us with the supplies Danny needed. The first was Social Security Income (SSI) and the second was Crippled Children's Services. After completing and submitting a form of financial information, she informed us we made too much money to qualify. At the time, John was a Sergeant. It was at that point we agreed the OCS packet needed to be resubmitted.

Toward the end of 1983, John received orders to report to OCS for the January 1984 class. This was not a permanent change in assignment and therefore our family was not expected to move. However, our family had gone through so much in the last year that we really didn't want to be apart. After much persuasion, I convinced John that it would be better for our family to physically stay together than to begin living separate lives. I was also convinced that the Doman/Delacata therapy could be done anywhere. All that was needed was volunteers. If I could find fifty-two Christian women in the state of Washington, I was confident I could do the same in the Bible Belt.

We left Ft. Lewis pulling a U-Haul trailer filled with Danny's therapy table and other supplies. We rented a furnished apartment in Columbus, Georgia. John reported to OCS as scheduled and I began recruiting volunteers for Danny's therapy program. This wasn't as easy as I expected it to be. There were only six members of the Catholic Women of the Chapel on Ft. Benning. The Protestant group was just as small. With over 400 churches in Columbus, Georgia, it was hard to know where to start. I contacted the Catholic churches in the area but none of them had women's groups. I approached several Protestant churches, but they were more interested in our family becoming a member or were only willing to go as far as putting us on their prayer list.

I did as much of the Doman/Delacata therapy I could do alone. I also enrolled Danny in traditional therapy sessions. Once again he received only one hour per week of physical therapy. I didn't want to give up on the Doman/Delacata program, but I found myself having to prioritize things. The program was definitely not as important as our family. Somehow I was beginning to sense God's presence in this situation. One of the many women who came into our home to help us with the therapy program at Ft. Lewis gave me a card that I still have in my wallet today. It reads "Coincidence – When God does a miracle and remains anonymous." Was it really a coincidence that Danny's illness opened the door for John to go to OCS? Was it really a coincidence that we found fifty-two Christian women to help with our son's therapy? Was it really a coincidence that I was in the Bible Belt with no volunteers to be found? Having fifty-two Christian women in and out of my home not only helped my son with his therapy program, but also challenged me spiritually. I was now ready to find answers and face God with the big question: WHY? I thought I knew why this had happened to Danny. I took full responsibility and felt God was getting even with me for the wrongs I had done in the past. I knew that when I needed information about Danny's illness the knowledge could be found in a number of books in the medical library. I wanted knowledge about God, so I bought a bible and began reading. What I read was hard to understand at first. I knew I needed someone to help me understand. One afternoon, while Danny sat in his carrier seat with his floppy head tilted to one side, I opened the yellow pages to find a church in the Columbus area. Although I was raised Catholic, I did not choose a Catholic church. I wanted someone to explain to me what I was reading in the Bible. Therefore, I believed I needed a Protestant. I chose a non-denominational church: Victorious Living Chapel (VLC). I went to the service for the first time alone. After all, I was crossing the line and I didn't want to expose my children to this until I checked it out first. As coincidence would have it, the pastor's name was Danny and he too was an OCS graduate. I took my bible with me to the first service but found it very difficult to keep up. The pastor was all over the place—first in the Old Testament, then in the New. He never gave a page number—only the name of the book, chapter, and verse. I couldn't get fast enough from the table of contents to where he was reading. I finally leaned over to the woman sitting next to me and asked for a page number. She looked at me very strangely and helped me get to the proper place for the rest of the service. When the service was over I thanked her and introduced myself. She then told me I needed to go to the Christian bookstore and buy "tabs." I had no idea what she was talking about, but I did as she said. The name of each book of the Bible was listed on each of the index tabs. Each tab was secured to the first page of each book in the bible. This made it much easier to find where the books were; except now I had to learn whether the book he was announcing was in the Old Testament or the New Testament. Eventually I figured it out.

I was excited about our new church home. I remember sharing with John my discovery of VLC. "We are Catholic," he stated firmly. "We don't belong there." I explained to him that I was willing to do whatever was necessary to help Danny—even if it meant becoming Protestant for a while. Eventually John softened to the idea of going to the other side and joined us when his OCS schedule allowed. I was hungry to learn about God and why this had happened to our son, but I was also looking for a miracle. Many of the Catholic and Protestant women who came to our home in Ft. Lewis talked about the gift of healing and how miracles were happening all over the country. The "charismatic movement" was what they called it. Deep down I was looking for a miracle for Danny—a complete physical healing. A healing did in fact occur for us at VLC, but it was not a healing of Danny's body. The healing that occurred was my healing. I finally came to realize the role God played in life and how Danny's illness was not punishment for my sins. God truly loved me unconditionally and forgave me for all my sins. All I had to do was ask. And when I finally did, I was cleansed as white as snow. I discovered how God not only holds Danny in the palm of His hand, but we are all held in His hands and close to His heart. I continued, however, to struggle with the purpose for Danny's life if in fact a miracle of physical healing did not occur. Time eventually unfolded Danny's purpose.

I took little John and Danny to every service at VLC while John was at OCS. Every Wednesday evening, Sunday morning, and Sunday evening I attended service equipped with my bible and tabs. The Protestant schedule was hard to get used to. Protestants went to church so often throughout the week. Maybe that was why I couldn't find volunteers in the Bible Belt. They were too busy going to church to volunteer for anything else. I didn't mind being in service so often because I was learning so much. What I realized, though, was that what was being taught at VLC was no different than what I learned growing up in the Catholic Church. God loves us unconditionally. He will meet us where we are and take us where we need to be as long as we are willing to go with Him. The teaching at VLC, however, was simplified and of course I was finally open to really hear it. Eventually I became homesick. I thought often of mass and all I was taught in the Catholic Church. After several years away, John and I realized it was time to go home—back to our roots, back to the Catholic Church. We had a renewed love for Catholicism and a closer relationship with God because of our connection with our Protestant brothers and sisters at VLC. Danny was still a major concern in our lives, but somehow we felt better prepared to walk whatever walk God had prepared for us.

John graduated OCS as a second lieutenant in April 1984 with orders to report to Ft. Bliss, Texas for two months of training. We decided to leave the therapy table in storage while we traveled to Ft. Bliss.

Immediately following training at Ft. Bliss, John was assigned to Ft. Rucker, Alabama where he attended flight school. We were moving up the ladder. John's salary was increasing with each promotion; however, so was Danny's list of supplies. Through it all, our family learned to improvise. As my mother always says, "Necessity is the mother of invention." John built a number of items for Danny, such as Danny's bed to accommodate the height needed to care for him and the therapy table used during the Doman/Delacata therapy. However, there were other supplies that Danny needed that could not be made, such as diapers. Once Danny outgrew the extra-large Pampers, we could no longer take advantage of commissary prices. At one point we put Danny back in cloth diapers. But we could not send Danny to school in cloth diapers. The expense was inevitable and cut deeply into our budget. Because of Danny's intense needs, I was unable to work outside the home and contribute to the family budget. However, I became just as creative as my husband and learned to make my children's clothes to help stretch the budget. Despite our efforts, the stress level was mounting. Not only were financial matters at a critical point, but hope for Danny's recovery was fading. Volunteers were also hard to find at Ft. Rucker, where John attended flight school. As a result we were never able to continue the Doman/Delacata therapy. I learned a lot from this therapy and continued what I could. I also followed all the instructions from the many therapists who supported Danny. Still, Danny made little to no progress.

During our tour in Ft. Rucker, we were approached by a social worker from the local school system. At the time Danny was two and a half years old. It was time to consider school options for Danny. This was a very scary thought for us. My oldest son was in kindergarten at the time, where he experienced interaction with children his own age. Sometimes this interaction could be rough, especially with boys. We enjoyed little John's school stories and helped him strategize to get through a school day without losing his lunch or being bullied by a classmate. But now we were talking about school for Danny. I wondered, *How do I strategize with him?* At two and a half years old, Danny's abilities still did not register on the developmental chart. How would I teach him to protect himself? I shared my concerns with the social worker. She laughed. The regular classroom was never considered an option.

In Ozark, Alabama, ten minutes from our home, there was a school for special needs children. Vivian B. Adams School was started by a woman who had a grandson with disabilities. She began the school so that children like her grandson would have a special place to learn. Of course, I requested a tour before considering this option. What a beautiful facility. The school had a ceramic shop and an Olympic-sized swimming pool. Therapists, special education teachers, and nurses were available at all times for the students. "A safe, nurturing environment." That is what they called it, and it certainly looked that way to me. It relieved my fears. This was the bubble I was looking for, the protection I felt my son needed. Nothing else was offered. No other options were presented.

Upon flight school graduation, John received orders to Korea. After many long discussions, John insisted the family not go to Korea. It was a one-year unaccompanied tour. A year seemed like a very long time to be apart. John and I grew closer because of what had happened to Danny. We used each other as sounding boards and leaned on each other. When I was discouraged, he was there with encouragement, and vice versa. We didn't want to be apart, but John had been stationed in Korea before we were married in 1976. At the time, he was stationed close to the border between North and South Korea. This was the only part of Korea he knew, and it was not the kind of place he wanted to bring his family. This time, however, he was stationed in Seoul and it was ten years later. John left for Korea alone, but after a month of long-distance phone calls, we decided it would be cheaper if we joined him. Because this was an unaccompanied tour, the usual army provisions were not provided to our family. Although we were able to access the commissary, post exchange, and hospital, we were unable to get post housing and our oldest son was unable to attend the post schools. Little John was six years old and ready for first grade. I home-schooled little John for his first year of school in Korea. I also enrolled Danny in therapy services at the army hospital. Although it was a very different assignment for all of us, we enjoyed our tour in Korea. Danny was four years old at the time. He still did not have head control and was unable to sit independently. We modified a stroller for Danny with pillows and Velcro. Oh, the wonderful things you can do with Velcro!

Although my schedule was quite hectic with home-schooling and therapy sessions, our family did find time to take in the sites. During a tour of the Seoul zoo, Danny and I became part of the attractions. I was sitting on a park bench, holding Danny in my lap and feeding him very much like you would a small baby. I was so focused on feeding Danny that I did not realize two Korean women squatted five feet in front of us, staring at us and whispering back and forth in Korean. John noticed the women at the same time I did. He immediately came to our rescue and simply squatted between us and the women and stared at them as intently as they stared at us. This embarrassed them and they immediately walked away. Children with disabilities were a very rare thing in Korea. So were children with curly hair and green eyes, like our oldest son. As we walked and shopped throughout Seoul, people would stare at Danny and then at little John and talk about us as if we were attractions. We eventually got used to this and appreciated being back in the United States, where diversity was the norm.

We left Korea, however, with a very special souvenir. We had the opportunity to adopt a six-year-old girl. John and I had always wanted to adopt. We had talked about it a lot before Danny's illness. We were given the opportunity in Korea to fulfill a dream we thought would never come to pass, because of what happened to Danny. We extended our tour in Korea in order to finalize adoption papers. When we returned to the states our family had grown to include our daughter, Haelan Nicole. Haelan was a beautiful, bright little girl. She spoke no English when joining our family. However, she was eager to learn. Before long, little John and Haelan were chattering in both Korean and English. Once back in the States, little John and Haelan went to school for the first time. After a year of home-schooling, little John was ready to enter second grade. Haelan started first grade and continued for the next eleven years to excel and be on the honor role.

In 1987 Danny was five years old. After our tour in Korea our family was stationed at Ft. Benjamin Harrison, Indiana. Danny was enrolled in another special school in Indianapolis. This school, like the Vivian B. Adams School, was well equipped with all that Danny could possibly need. Because Ft. Harrison was a small military installation, all Danny's medical needs were met at Methodist Hospital in Indianapolis, Indiana. During a routine visit, a social worker introduced herself and offered to help. I explained our family's financial situation, but as always, were told we made too much money. I then explained we needed some help taking care of Danny in our home. The more therapists Danny had in his life, the more specialized instructions we received. Everything was a process, such as feeding Danny. This process was a long process that involved pillows and positioning first on my lap and then in a specialized chair. Nothing was easy and nothing was similar to the care I provided to my two older children. No matter how many times we asked for assistance, it seemed that financial eligibility was connected to receiving any support whatsoever.

Finally in September 1987, I called the social worker in tears. "I can't do this anymore," I cried. Up until this point I considered myself a plate spinner. I was dedicated to my family and committed to do whatever I had to do for my son, but I was like the clown in the circus that spun plates on long sticks. Although you rarely see the clown drop any plates during his act, I was dropping plates every day. There was a plate with my husband's name on it, two plates with each of my older children's names on them, and a very large plate with Danny's name on it. Of course, there was a very small plate with my name on it. I just left that one on the floor while I constantly picked up the rest and got them spinning on the appropriate sticks.

In response to my plea, the social worker immediately told me of a facility in New Albany, Indiana where Danny would live and receive intense special education services. We did not want Danny to live anywhere but with us, but we realized we could not continue on this journey alone. We needed help; we needed a break. The maximum amount of time an individual could live at the Silvercrest Developmental Center in New Albany, Indiana was eighteen months. This decision was very difficult for our family. John grew up in an orphanage in New York operated by the Sisters of Mercy. Although he appreciated the love and support he received throughout the years from the nuns, he vowed never to have any of his children live in an institutional setting. But here we were facing a decision to do just that. We hung on to the fact that it was only for eighteen months and promised ourselves that we would use the time to rest and get ready to tackle Danny's care once he returned.

Silvercrest Developmental Center was another beautiful facility. There was a swimming pool and whirlpool located on the lower floor. Classrooms were on another floor with teachers and therapists available to meet the students' needs. There also were several floors of dormitories where each student had his or her own room. A round-the-clock nursing staff was available to meet the students' needs. Everything Danny needed was there, except his family. It seemed that in order for Danny to have his needs met, he had to rely on others to become his family instead of relying on the family God gave him.

New Albany was a two-hour drive from our home at Ft. Harrison. Many mornings I put my two older children on the school bus and drove like a maniac to Silvercrest Developmental Center just to see Danny's face. I would peak into the classrooms to try to see if he was being treated right. There was never any indication of foul play. He received excellent care. There was a team of individuals who provided for Danny. The team consisted of therapists, special education teachers, nurses, and administrators. I was only one person, and although I was willing to learn and do whatever I could, I was afraid that I would not learn in time for Danny.

It was a long eighteen months, but finally Danny was coming home. Still, there was no educational progress. Although Danny was a happy child, his developmental level was at an all-time low. Danny still had no head control. He was unable to track objects with his eyes but had good hearing and would move his head to follow your voice. He did not reach for objects and did not have a grasp reflex. Splints were made for both his hands and feet to avoid contractures.

Upon Danny's discharge from Silvercrest Developmental Center, Danny was enrolled in another school for special needs children in Indianapolis where therapists and teachers continued to work with Danny.

In 1989 our family moved back to Ft. Benning, Georgia, where we were introduced to the public school system for children with special needs. Up until this point Danny's education was paid for by the public school system but was housed in separate school buildings with excellent accommodations, such as swimming pools, ceramic shops, and specialized professional support.

In Columbus, Georgia, Danny was assigned to a regular public school and was placed in a classroom for children with significant disabilities. Although the classroom accommodations and staff somewhat resembled our past experiences, the school was located in a very rundown part of town. Danny's bus ride was forty-five minutes each way. Danny was seizure prone and for the first time we were afraid for Danny's safety. John and I met with the exceptional children's director and requested that Danny be moved to a school closer to home. Soon after, Danny was reassigned to a new school.

During Danny's educational experiences I met with special education teachers and therapists who provided me with an overview of Danny's individualized education plan (IEP). At meetings that lasted no more than fifteen minutes I was given a brief review of the IEP and was asked to sign the document as Danny's legal guardian. This occurred on a regular basis throughout Danny's educational experience, until I learned what should have really been occurring for Danny.

At no time in this process did life stand still. In addition to John's new role as an officer and pilot, our two older children were busy with their lives at school and a number of extracurricular activities. Although I became much better at spinning plates, I did not spend a lot of time spinning Danny's plate. I had realized early on that Danny needed a team of specialized individuals to meet his needs. I believed the special education teachers, therapists, and administrators were the experts. They were trained in their field and knew what needed to occur for Danny. I did my part by sending Danny to school every day ready to learn and by following through with the recommendations of the special education teachers and therapists. Despite all our hard work, Danny made little to no educational progress. His abilities barely registered on the developmental charts.

Relying on the educational "experts" gave me the ability to focus solely on Danny's medical issues. The physical therapists were the first to notice hip dislocation. We immediately obtained an appointment with the specialists at Walter Reed Army Medical Center.

Our family was very fortunate to have Father Joe stationed in the DC/Baltimore area. John had met Father Joe while living at St. Mary's Boys Home. During the summer months, while studying at the seminary, Father Joe would work at St. Mary's. John and Father Joe became good friends and in 1978 Father Joe married John and I at St. Martha's Catholic Church in Uniondale, New York. Father Joe has been pastor of several churches in the DC/Baltimore area. This came in handy when we made our trips to Walter Reed Army Medical Center. Our entire

...ily would stay with Father Joe in the parish rectory. Our two older children would help Father Joe with whatever activities were going on at the church while John and I went to appointments for Danny at Walter Reed.

After several tests the specialists at Walter Reed confirmed hip dislocation in both hips and surgery was scheduled. I remember clearly Danny being wheeled to the operating room. John and I understood the surgery and its benefits and risks. To prepare for the surgery, John gave blood to be used solely for our son. Both John and Danny have the B+ blood type. Rather than risk taking blood from strangers, John wanted to do this for his son. We understood this was major surgery and several pints of blood would be needed. We made the arrangements so that John could be the blood donor for Danny. We understood the situation and planned with our heads, but there was no preparation possible for our hearts. As the gurney wheeled its way into the operating room, Danny laughed uncontrollably at the bumpy ride. Before entering the operating room, the gurney slowed down long enough for us to kiss our son. The gurney continued through the great big doors to the operating room. A nurse stood guard, making sure we did not go past the doors. We listened intently for Danny's laugh as uncontrollable tears rolled down both our faces. We looked at each other and embraced. Somehow we found our way to the hospital cafeteria, where we waited patiently for word on our son's situation.

After several hours we headed back to the operating-room area. After inquiring about our son's condition, we were told surgery went well. We were brought to the recovery area to see Danny. I will never forget his face. He looked baffled and confused, as if to say, "What the hell happened to me?" We were also told by the doctors that as Danny came out of the anesthesia, he displayed seizure activity. They had immediately given him high doses of seizure medication.

Danny was now in a body cast from the waist down. A hospital bed became part of our living room décor for the next six weeks. Once Danny got used to the cast situation, he went back to his happy self. Upon removal of the cast, we were told the surgery was successful, but the real test would be Danny's recovery over time. The physical therapists immediately began working with Danny's legs and hip areas.

Once again, however, it was time for another military move. Prior to leaving Ft. Benning, our chaplain asked if Danny had received his First Holy Communion. I tried to explain Danny's many limitations to the priest. The priest very calmly explained that Jesus's presence was enough. He then gave me samples of unconsecrated wafers to practice with Danny at home. Once Danny was used to the texture and process, we brought Danny to the priest's office at the Ft. Benning chapel. On October 23, 1991, after a small prayer and blessing, Danny received his First Holy Communion. He continued to receive communion at every mass he attended until he could no longer tolerate the texture of the Eucharist without choking or gagging. All throughout Danny's life we have included him in all aspects of life as much as possible. Even when I didn't think inclusion was possible (like receiving Holy Communion) someone was there to challenge my thinking.

In 1991 our family made its final military move to Ft. Bragg, North Carolina. Again Danny was assigned to a regular public school. This school was also located in a poor, rundown part of town forty-five minutes from our home. Despite the neighborhood and old school building, the classroom Danny was assigned to most resembled the quality offered at the Vivian B. Adams school and Silvercrest Developmental Center.

In the classroom was a waterbed donated by the Knights of Columbus where students would take their naps. The classroom had a long window where several bird cages were located. Children on prone standers were able to look and listen to the birds. The classroom was colorful and bright and provided an opportunity for children with significant disabilities to attain goals in their IEP. One of the goals Danny was working on for years was to track objects with his eyes horizontally and vertically. Upon recommendations from the physical therapists, John created a number of objects at home that involved blinking Christmas lights; large, colorful objects; and flashlights. Although we did not like where the neighborhood school was located or the long bus ride, the classroom was an oasis we believed would allow Danny an opportunity to reach some of his goals. Maybe the birds would help him master the tracking goal.

After almost two years in this classroom, the birds and all the other attempts to assist Danny in mastering this goal and others were fruitless. Danny was happy and would smile and laugh most of the time. He would cry and grimace when he needed to be changed or repositioned.

reaction to life was on the level of an infant.

In 1992 it was decided Danny needed a G-tube. Feeding Danny was always a long, cumbersome process. All of Danny's food needed to be pureed. He enjoyed eating all the things we ate, but because of the cerebral palsy, he was unable to eat a normal-sized portion. I worried about Danny's ability to eat a meal. I knew he needed proper nutrition to stay healthy. When we feed Danny he always started out enjoying his food. You could see how much he enjoyed the different flavors, textures, and smells of the food. However, he would get so tired trying to coordinate the muscles in his mouth that he sometimes fell asleep toward the end of the meal from mere exhaustion. As suggested by his occupational therapist, I tried feeding him more often during the day, but the process became more complicated. Because of poor muscle coordination, Danny spent a lot of his feeding time coughing and spitting and eventually tiring out. The doctor's recommendation for a G-tube put me once again in a research mode. By the time Danny was admitted to Walter Reed Army Medical Center for G-tube placement, I had discovered the Mikey G-tube. Shortly after admission, I presented my discovery to Danny's pediatric gastroenterologists. They explained in detail why the Mikey G-tube might not be possible for Danny.

During their explanation I learned more about the human anatomy. It seems that the esophagus has two flaps: one at the top to prevent food from going into the lungs and one at the bottom to keep food in the stomach. When the flap at the top does not work properly there is aspiration into the lungs. When the flap at the bottom of the esophagus does not work properly, there is reflux. Both doctors suspected Danny had one or both of these conditions and recommended a series of tests. They further explained that if reflux was an issue, a special operation would be performed. This procedure involved wrapping the muscle flap at the base of the esophagus to give it the strength and ability to function properly. If this procedure was necessary, a different kind of G-tube would be needed. This was major surgery and we worried about Danny's ability to make it through the process. During the first three days of Danny's hospitalization, a series of five different tests were conducted, including a barium swallow, a nuclear study that involved another horrible-tasting mixture, and a one-day study involving electrodes. During this last study I was instructed to press a button on a recording device whenever Danny ate, sneezed, or coughed. After all the studies were completed, the pediatric gastroenterologists came to Danny's hospital room to give us the results. All the tests were negative. Danny was not aspirating and he did not have reflux. I could see from the expression on the doctors' faces that these were not the results they expected. "Isn't this good news?" I asked. They agreed but stated they were perplexed with the results. They further explained that children with significant disabilities like Danny's almost always have reflux and aspiration. The only explanation they could offer was that, since Danny was not born with disabilities, his body had had time to mature enough before he encountered the meningitis and developed cerebral palsy. With this good news, the placement of the Mikey G-tube was scheduled. We continued to feed Danny by mouth but did not worry about the amount he was able to eat. The G-tube allowed us to provide nutritional supplements that provided Danny with the caloric intake required for his age and size.

Chapter 2

PIP Training Provides Knowledge

Although we were learning to recognize God in control of all that happened to Danny and our family, this was a very difficult process. Our family was being challenged on all levels. Physically and mentally we faced the challenge of caring for a child with severe disabilities. We learned to improvise and create whatever was needed. As our priorities became clearer, the love for our children and each other intensified. We made sacrifices we had no idea we were capable of making. Throughout the process we hung on to each other. We still had no outside support other than the educational system, and we were still being told we made too much money to qualify for help in the home.

By 1993 a tremendous amount of growth had taken place in our lives, but there was still plenty more to come. During all these years I was still spinning plates. I was tired and I needed a break. We knew we didn't want to send Danny away again, but I knew I was fast approaching a point of desperation. One day I received an application from Easter Seals North Carolina announcing the beginning of a new training program called Partners in Policymaking (PIP). This program was developed by the Governor's Council on Developmental Disabilities in Minnesota in 1987. This was a new program for North Carolina. Its purpose was to teach adults with disabilities and parents of children with disabilities the laws that protected the rights of people with disabilities. PIP also provided training on the legislative process, along with the skills necessary to influence policymakers.

The PIP training was held in Raleigh, North Carolina one weekend a month for six months. After discussing this possibility with John, I completed the application. I remember saying a prayer before dropping the application in the mailbox.

The announcement of the first North Carolina PIP class brought in hundreds of applications from across the state. After review of the applications, I received a phone call from the coordinator, congratulating me. I was one of the twenty-five participants of the first PIP class in North Carolina. This was truly an answer to a prayer—more so than I realized at the time of the call.

In order for me to attend these weekend classes, however, I needed to find someone to care for Danny. Easter Seals North Carolina, with the help of the PIP grant dollars, found a qualified staff to care for Danny on the weekends I attended the training. This was the first time support was being brought to our home instead of Danny being sent somewhere else.

I remember packing for the first PIP session. For the first time in eleven years I was getting time away by myself. Although we did follow John on all his military assignments, he spent a lot of his military career training in the field and on short overnight missions. This gave him the opportunity to take a deep breath and view our family challenges in a different light. John and I had many good conversations when he returned home from these short trips. Now it was my turn, although this would be different. The training I was about to receive would directly impact not only Danny's life but our entire family life.

The first session of PIP was held at a Raleigh hotel the weekend of June 12 and 13, 1993. The first session was an introduction to the PIP program and included an introduction of ourselves to each other. It was comforting to see so many other parents of children with disabilities from across the state and to meet adults with disabilities. This was my first encounter with adults with disabilities. This helped me envision Danny's future. The other parents involved became my best teachers. It was the experience of other parents that taught me strategies to successfully maneuver through the bureaucratic system.

The first PIP session also provided an introduction to the self-advocate and parent movements. We learned of the tenacity and persistence of adults with disabilities in their fight for the passage of the

Americans with Disabilities Act. Their fight continues to ensure this vital law remains in existence and is fully implemented. Prior to adults with disabilities taking a stand, parents of children with disabilities fought long and hard for their children's right to an education. Fifty plus years ago, parents were encouraged from all sources to institutionalize their children with mental retardation and other developmental disabilities. States guaranteed medical and educational services in the institution—not in the community. Those parents who refused to accept institutional life for their loved one faced the heartache of their children being denied public school education. Although families were obligated to pay taxes that supported the public schools, their children were denied access because they did not qualify. These children with mental retardation and other developmental disabilities were denied access because they were not able to function at the level comparable to the standard course of study. Even those children who did not have a cognitive disability, but had a physical disability that required the use of a wheelchair or other mobility device, were denied access to public education. There seemed to be criteria to meet before being accepted as a public school student. I certainly knew this to be true of the parochial school system. I attended Catholic school in New York for ten years before my family moved to Long Island, where I completed high school in the public school system. During my last year in Catholic elementary school, we spent time taking entrance exams and applying to Catholic high schools. We waited for acceptance letters to arrive in the mail. My only experience with the public school system in Long Island seemed very comparable to Catholic school educational standards. Although I did not have to apply and wait for acceptance to John F. Kennedy High School in Plainview, Long Island, the standard of education was high in this school and all students were expected to achieve excellence.

I graduated high school in 1974. The only student that came close to being identified as a student with a disability during my twelve years of education was a young girl named Teresa. She was born with only two fingers on her right hand. Teresa went to Catholic elementary school and high school with the rest of us. Her only disability was that she was left-handed. This was the extent of my experience with children with disabilities.

During the first PIP session, I learned that while I was preparing for high school graduation and was oblivious to the disability world, parents of children across the country were banging down the doors of their legislators, demanding the passage of the first special education law. I remember feeling overwhelmingly grateful to all the parents before me who pushed for this law, because now I was the parent of a child with a disability who desperately needed these supports.

Toward the end of the first PIP session, we were introduced to the current service delivery system in North Carolina. I knew nothing about this system. Whenever I tried to access services our family was always denied access due to income. However, that evening at dinner with several other PIP participants, I learned of the Community Alternative Program for Children and Adults with Mental Retardation and Developmental Disabilities (CAP MR/DD). I remember sitting at the dinner table with the other parents and listening to their conversation about CAP. I heard the acronym *CAP* several times before I interrupted and asked for clarification. The families simply stated it was a Medicaid waiver. I heard the word *Medicaid* and immediately gave the same reply I had heard for eleven years: "We don't qualify because of income." The conversation immediately stopped and all eyes turned toward me. "Income doesn't matter," said one of the parents. "It's a waiver," said another. I know my jaw hit the floor. I immediately teamed up with the parent sitting next to me and picked her brain on the particulars of this waiver.

It seems that the area program system we learned of earlier in the session was the lead agency for the CAP MR/DD waiver. Several of the area programs served more than one county. However, we lived in an area where the area program served only one county. I was told by this parent to go to the single portal specialist in our area program and request a CAP MR/DD "slot." The area program in my home county was called the Cumberland County Mental Health Center. I knew this agency existed but did not think it could help us. No one in our family had mental health issues. The title of the agency was deceiving. I did not know the mental health center served three populations: mental health, developmental disabilities, and substance abuse. The single portal specialist was part of the developmental disabilities section.

The parent continued to explain that the single portal specialist would send to our home a case manager who would do an assessment of our needs. She cautioned that the slots were few and far between and said if we wanted to receive services right away I needed to act needy. In other words, she cautioned, "Don't clean your house, leave dirty dishes in the sink, don't wear make up, and cry." Although I appreciated all the information this mom provided, I could not accept this role. I was desperate and needed help caring for my son. What did this have to do with the neatness of my home? I took pride in keeping a neat home. I would never invite anyone to my home with things not in their places.

At the end of each of the PIP sessions we were given homework assignments. In addition to what was assigned I added a personal assignment to make contact with the single portal specialist at our local area program.

Returning home from the PIP sessions was always a thrill. I couldn't wait to get home and share with John all that I learned. As he sat and listened wide-eyed, I would talk for hours about the new people I met and all the important information learned. From the very first PIP weekend, I began to realize a sense of anger within me as I learned of laws, rights, and services that were never shared with us throughout the eleven years we cried desperately for help.

Through the single portal specialist, an appointment was set for a case manager to come to our home to do an assessment. Amazingly enough, when the case manager called for an appointment, she said it was not necessary for Danny to be present at our meeting. I didn't catch on at first. I thought, *But how can you do an assessment without the child being there?* The truth of the matter was that the assessment was really for us and the advice given to me by the mom from PIP was very accurate. Unfortunately I did not realize this until it was too late.

At the time of the assessment we lived on Ft. Bragg in military housing. John was a captain and we lived in officers' quarters. The moment the case manager entered my home, her eyes drifted from one side of the house to the other. She was doing an assessment of our home. I made a pot of coffee and had a folder ready of medical statements from Danny's doctors. During small talk I prepared a cup of coffee for the case manager. We then sat at our dining room table. The case manager opened a folder and simply asked, "What is it that you need for Danny?" There was absolutely no review of the CAP MR/DD waiver—what it involved, how it could help Danny and our family. The case manager immediately began her presentation with a question, "What is it that you need for Danny?"

This was very odd to me. Before Danny was born, John and I purchased life insurance policies. When the life insurance representative came to our home, her presentation began with an overview of the company and what the company offered. She then asked questions specific to our family and offered advice on what to purchase. When we were first married we purchased encyclopedias from a door- to-door salesman. Again we were given an overview of the company and the product and then were given an opportunity to decide. The case manager representing the lead agency gave us no overview of the agency or the Medicaid waiver. She simply asked, "What is it that you need for Danny?" With a puzzled look on my face, I replied with, "What is it that you have and I'll let you know if we need it." She didn't like my response and mumbled something about person-centered planning. She insisted I answer her question. We went back and forth till finally I said, "Look, I need help taking care of Danny in my home and I need someone to relieve me so I can spend time with my other children and my husband." While I spoke she took notes. She then informed me that there was a waiting list. I immediately asked, "What are people waiting for?" She went on to explain that there are only so many slots available throughout the state. "Okay, so people are waiting for slots. But once they get a slot, what does that give them?" I asked. She continued explaining that people receive the support they need and that one person's needs may be different from another's. This made sense but there were still many holes in her explanation. After she wrote more things in her chart, the meeting seemed to be over. She said she would present Danny to the interagency committee and get back with me. How could she properly present Danny without meeting him? Something wasn't right here.

I was desperate for help and did not know how the system operated. I also did not feel comfortable telling the system that was to help me how it should operate. Fortunately my comfort level changed as years progressed.

My experience in purchasing life insurance is very comparable to what should have occurred when I was seeking help from the government system. When purchasing life insurance, we ask the insurance company to help us and our family in the event of our death. We know we need to provide for our families in the event of death and so we call upon an insurance company to help us meet this need. Because there is more than one insurance company to choose from, representatives each come prepared to tell us why their company is the better company and why we should purchase life insurance from them and not the competition. Unfortunately there is only one local lead agency selected by the state agency to provide Medicaid waiver services. This is a monopoly system. When you are a monopoly you don't have to be good and you don't have to be fair. You provide a service and the customer is never in charge, because you are a monopoly. If the customer does not like the way you do business, there is absolutely no other place for the customer to go. Once customers figure this out, they learn to study the monopoly to find ways to maneuver through the system to get what they need.

The analogy of purchasing life insurance includes the purchasing power of a customer. The local lead agency did not view families of children with developmental disabilities as customers with purchasing power. Families do not directly pay for Medicaid waiver services, but we do pay indirectly. All families pay taxes. Taxpayers' dollars support the local lead agencies. Only those individuals and families who have loved ones with disabilities will qualify and seek services through the local lead agency. The presence of the local lead agency and what it offers individuals with disabilities is to some degree an insurance policy for all taxpayers. If and when our loved ones ever need the services offered by the local lead agency, these services should be available to them. Unfortunately the average taxpayer is kept in the dark about the services available through the local lead agency, even after a disability has been identified.

The following week after my visit from the case manager, I called to find out the status of services for Danny. Again I was told there was a waiting list and was also informed that Danny received a score of twenty-nine for placement on the list. I asked if this meant he was twenty-ninth on the list and was told that a scoring system was used to determine where individuals are placed on the list. Based on my application and my home visit, Danny was scored at twenty-nine. This did not mean he was twenty-ninth on the list. His position on the list could vary depending on how many others scored higher. The highest score was sixty. This was very disturbing to me. Danny has significant disabilities. He has no head control, is unable to feed himself, is still in diapers at eleven years of age, and has vision problems. How could his score be so low? There seemed to be a very large gap between his score and the highest possible score. I asked for a copy of the scoring system. The system contained a number of questions. Each question, if answered positively, yielded a certain number of points. Those individuals with behavior issues received higher scores than those individuals who did not have any behavior issues. Danny did not have any behavior issues; therefore, he scored much lower. I immediately challenged this system. This was my first direct involvement with the local lead agency. What I learned from this experience is that not only is the local lead agency a monopoly, it is also a bureaucracy. Like all bureaucracies, this system operates in the slow lane—the very slow lane. Nothing is changed without lots of committees and meetings.

The scoring system the local lead agency developed did not take into consideration those individuals with significant physical and cognitive disabilities who required twenty-four-hour care. The change to the scoring system took over a year to materialize. In the meantime, when slots became available, families of children with significant disabilities, like Danny, were passed over because they all received low scores.

In addition to the local lead agency being a monopoly, there is the perception that the local lead agencies answer to the state agency. There are two state agencies involved in the North Carolina CAP MR/DD waiver – the Division of Medical Assistance (DMA) and the Division of Mental Health/Developmental Disabilities/Substance Abuse Services (DMH/DD/SAS). At the time I was seeking services for Danny, there was little to no accountability from the state agencies. The autonomy of the local lead agencies somewhat prevented state intervention. Although we presented the issues to the state agencies, there seemed to be little they could do about the situation except guide us and the local lead agency to mutual agreement. This got better as time went on, especially when I learned to recognize and access the entire chain of command to include the federal Center for Medicare & Medicaid Services (CMS) in Atlanta and Baltimore.

During the time we waited for services, I did my homework and continued to faithfully participate in the PIP sessions. The six PIP sessions for the class of 1993 included information on the following topics:

- History of the Independent and Parent Movements
- Overview of the Current Delivery System and Basic Values
- Values, Person-Centered Approach and Family Support
- The Supports Model: Supported Living, Supported Employment, and Inclusive Education
- Area MH/DD/SA Systems, County and Local Authorities, Boards, Commissions, Resources, and Issues
- State Legislative and Administrative Issues: The General Assembly, How to develop Legislation and have it introduced; The role of State Agencies and Commissions
- Leadership, Empowerment, How consumer and parent leaders effect change, How to be effective on Boards and Commissions

I remember listening intently to all the presenters. The three topics that highlighted my PIP experience were the Medicaid waiver, inclusive education, and the legislative process.

The legislative process was a common theme throughout the PIP sessions. It is an important process that we all need to learn. It was the legislative process that brought about the existence of the Medicaid waivers, led to the first special education law, and created the Americans with Disabilities Act along with other laws that protect the rights of people with disabilities. Although I agree the legislative process is important to get laws passed, what I was more interested in was experiencing what was written in the present laws.

The Medicaid waivers were discussed on the second day of our first PIP weekend session as part of the overview of the current delivery system. I had already heard about the waiver at dinner the night before with other PIP participants. The PIP presentation, however, provided the history of how this was made possible and who was responsible for its existence.

The story of the Medicaid waiver begins with a woman from Iowa named Julie Beckett. Julie is a formidable, tenacious woman who did what was necessary to ensure quality of life for her daughter Katie. I listened to Julie's story with amazement. I recognized the enormous love a mother has for her child. More importantly, I understood her fight, her grief, her frustration, and her loyalty to a cause.

Katie, like Danny, contracted a similar childhood illness at six months of age. For Katie, however, the illness was viral encephalitis. In the 2002 *Parent to Parent of Vermont* spring newsletter, Katie tells her story. "…After a grand mal seizure, which sent me into a coma, the encephalitis attacked my central nervous system and caused nerve damage to various parts of my body. Most significantly affected was my ability to breathe. I was placed on a ventilator and later a tracheotomy was performed. I required multiple medical procedures even after I awoke from the coma. I was totally paralyzed and could not even handle my own secretions. This paralysis resolved itself in the first few years but I did not breathe at all on my own until I was almost two years old. At this time the medical community and the insurance companies believed only medical professionals could perform the care that I needed. However, after three years in a pediatric intensive care unit and my parents' active participation in my day-to-day routine, it became clear that I needed to come home. But the government was not so easily convinced. Rules and regulations prohibited my family from safely taking me home. The government had to create a new standard so I could come home. The home and community-based waiver program, often called the Katie Beckett Waiver program, was the new standard. It allowed kids who were forced to be institutionalized or hospitalized, many on assistive technology, to be treated at home by keeping them eligible for Medicaid by waiving the income deemed to them by their parents, since that income could not or would not cover the cost of their care at home and would be waived if they remained in an institutional setting."

Throughout the Becketts' fight to bring their daughter home, the argument seemed simple. The Beckett's could care for their daughter in their home at a much lower cost than putting her in an institution or nursing home, and they could provide her a better quality of life. Finally after a long battle, the Medicaid waiver was signed into law, giving states the right to waive income criteria for families of children with significant disabilities and focus solely on the disability for eligibility rather than income.

No one learns of the Medicaid waiver without hearing the Katie Beckett story. This story was also shared in the March/April 2004 *TASH Connections* publication. TASH is a national non-profit organization focused on supporting individuals with significant disabilities. An article in this publication entitled "The Danger of a Literal Interpretation" by Nancy Thaler states, "Katie and her Mom are active participants in this public policy dialogue and tell the story best, but in a nutshell, this one mother and her child illustrated to the President of the United States the insanity of a federal policy that would pay for a child to live in an institution away from her mother, but would pay nothing whatsoever—even though it would cost less in federal and state dollars and would be better for Katie—to enable that child to remain with her mother and family in her own home."

The North Carolina 1994 CAP MR/DD manual states the following: "The program is authorized by a Medicaid Home and Community Based Services Waiver granted by the Health Care Financing Administration (HCFA) under Section 1915(c) of the Social Security Act." The manual further states the CAP MR/DD waiver started in 1983 in four areas of the state.

In addition to being able to waive the income requirement, states can also waive the statewide requirement. The North Carolina 1994 CAP MR/DD manual states the following: "The Social Security Act requires Medicaid services to be provided on a statewide basis. This requirement is waived to allow an area MH/DD/SAS program to choose whether it wants to offer CAP MR/DD."

I do not know when CAP MR/DD became a North Carolina statewide waiver, but I do know a family from Cumberland County who received CAP MR/DD services for their daughter in 1989. This means that when we arrived in North Carolina in 1991, the CAP MR/DD waiver was available in Cumberland County. There may have been a waiting list, but we were never told of the option and were never part of the list until I haphazardly learned of these services at dinner with other PIP participants. Although my son was a student in the severe/profound class in one of the Cumberland County schools and was a patient of the family practice clinic at Womack Army Medical Center, we were left in the dark about services that would help us in our home. I find it hard to believe the school system and the medical profession were also unaware of the Medicaid waiver. *Collaboration* was the "in" word in the 1980s and 1990s. Interagency councils were formed throughout the state to promote collaboration. So how is it we were left in the dark? And were we the only family unaware of these services?

Another haunting question had to do with cost. If in fact it is more cost-effective to provide services and support to children with significant disabilities in their homes with their families, then why is the waiver such a secret? If the waiver began in North Carolina in 1983, when did it begin in Indiana? Was it available in 1987 when I called the social worker in tears begging for help? If so, why was I told only of a residential facility two hours from my home? As I dug further for answers to my questions I became very angry. I also began to realize the battle before me was huge. In addition to accessing the Medicaid waiver, another important battle to bear was the educational system and its lack of compliance with the special education law.

Inclusive education was presented during the third PIP session in August 1993. One of the presenters was at the time associated with the United Cerebral Palsy Association. With great charisma the presenter spoke of inclusive education for *all* children. I remember being very angry at this man after his presentation. My PIP roommate was a mom from the coastal part of North Carolina. Her son had autism. The two of us talked all night about the presenter and how unrealistic and unfair his comments were. Certainly it would have made more sense to say, "Inclusive Education is for *most* children." But he didn't say *most*. The presenter said *all* and when he said it he meant it—like he knew it to be possible regardless of disability.

The first thing I needed to do before I could go any further on this inclusion thing was to read the special education law. I had never done this before; I had never had a need to. The only option offered for Danny's education was a separate classroom sometimes in a separate school. It made sense to me. So why change it? I felt compelled to pursue inclusion, because no matter what we did in education, Danny made little to no progress. Maybe we were missing something. I wanted no stone unturned.

Through the early intervention program on Ft. Bragg I met a young educator who had recently graduated from the University of Mississippi. I shared with her my concerns for inclusive education for Danny. After a long conversation about her positive experiences with inclusive education, she gave me several textbooks addressing inclusion from her graduate courses. The books clearly addressed the reality of the law and gave examples across the country of inclusive settings for children with a wide range of disabilities.

My goal for studying the special education law was to learn what was available to my son. I was perplexed by the inclusion concept and wondered how to implement this concept for a child with significant disabilities, like Danny.

As I read and studied it became evident that a simple response to the inclusion question uncovered an attitude that determined the quality of education provided to children with disabilities—particularly those with significant disabilities.

Throughout my reading I learned that if inclusion is embraced by education administrators, then children with disabilities are offered opportunities similar to those without disabilities. For example, they attend a school closer to home, giving them an opportunity to make friends in their neighborhoods. They are also educated alongside students without disabilities, giving them an opportunity to develop language and appropriate social interactions. Further reading uncovered the reverse interaction for students with disabilities when education administrators are not open to inclusion in their schools. When this happens, students with disabilities experience some level of segregation limiting the quality of education provided.

Up until this point, Danny experienced segregation throughout his education experience; although, we didn't look at it in that perspective. All of what I was learning was making sense; however, I struggled, not knowing how to implement inclusion for someone like Danny and whether or not it was truly the right thing to do. Certainly I wanted Danny to attend a school closer to home. I wanted him to have a quality education—to be given the opportunity to reach his full potential. Quite frankly, I had never thought about friends for Danny. I was so focused on recovery that I did not understand the importance of friends. I also feared the interaction of non-disabled children with Danny. I didn't want Danny to be laughed at or made fun of because of his differences and I was concerned with other children being too physically rough with him. Segregated classrooms and schools provided the bubble and protection I thought Danny needed, and they allowed him an opportunity to focus solely on recovery. But through the PIP presentation and now these textbooks, I was being challenged to look at things a little differently. If an inclusive education was a possibility for Danny, then why didn't any of the educators suggest this option?

Continued research and study revealed that regulations for the special education law (PL94-142) passed in November 1975 were published in 1977 (Federal Register, August 23, 1977). These regulations gave clarification and interpretation for an important part of the law known as the "least restrictive environment," or LRE. The LRE is the opposite of segregation and allows students with disabilities to enroll in their neighborhood schools and receive the services and support they need, as outlined in the individual education plan (IEP).

Throughout my research I read about strategies used to integrate students with severe disabilities. However, reading about inclusion was not enough. At the time I was learning about school inclusion, Danny was attending a school forty-five minutes from home in a rundown part of town. I certainly wanted him closer to home. I was struggling with *how* to make this happen for Danny and with the assurance that it was, in fact, the right thing to do.

Before we knew it, graduation for the first North Carolina PIP class was here. It was November 1993 and our six weekends of training were complete. I learned so much during these six important sessions. Hope was renewed. But I also recognized the enormous amount of work to be done.

I graduated PIP in 1993 with three burning questions. First – Is inclusive education the right thing to do for someone with significant disabilities like Danny? If so, how do you do inclusion for someone like Danny without taking educational opportunities away from other students? Second   How do I access the Medicaid waiver services for my son and family? How do I get off the waiting list? Third – How do I share all that I've learned in the PIP sessions with other families who were not selected for this training? How do I build a coalition of families across my home county to address needs that may require legislative intervention?

There was no choice but to address all three areas simultaneously. Life never happens one issue at a time. In addition to these disability issues, I had the rest of my family to consider. Many times I was forced to recognize my limitations and prioritize the issues so I could effectively address each area. I was always good at multitasking, but now more than ever I was being challenged to know my true limitations, set realistic priorities, and address each issue effectively and without waiver. Although I felt an overwhelming responsibility to each issue, I knew it was more important to be successful than to just go through the motions.

Over and over I could hear the words of Helen Reddy's song, "I Am Woman" (hear me roar). I expanded her words with, "I am woman; hear me scream, yell, bitch, rant, and rave." Like the Blues Brothers, I was on a mission from God. I took seriously my commitment to my son and family and understood firsthand the grief and frustration of other families. I felt a tremendous responsibility to families because of my selection to the PIP sessions. Carefully I planned ways for success in each of the three areas, trying desperately at the same time to meet the needs of my family. After all, these were just three more plates to spin.

Chapter 3

Time to Take Action

After PIP graduation I stepped back and looked at the areas in my life that needed to be addressed. I also thought about what I wanted to do with all the knowledge I obtained through the PIP program.

During this contemplation, John was approaching military retirement. This was not part of our plan. He was a company commander and maintenance test pilot for the Chinook helicopter. Life seemed to be going well for John. He had eighteen years in the military. He loved the military. He would jokingly say that the military was an extension of living with the nuns. Our original plan was to retire after twenty-five years of military service. However, President Clinton came into office and military downsizing began. It looked as though John had everything going for him. There were only a handful of commissioned officer maintenance test pilots for the Chinook helicopter in the US Army and John was one of them. However, John was a captain with eighteen years of service. His rate of pay was comparable to that of a major. When the promotion list for major was released, John's name (along with the names of most of the officers in his year group) was not on the list. Ready or not, military retirement would occur in two years. In preparation for retirement, John attended night school to complete his master's degree in computer information management. The transition to civilian life would not be an easy one for John. Although he spent many hours trying to convince me he was okay with the move to civilian life, he could never fake happiness. I knew he was dreading the transition. I worried more and more as the twenty-year mark got closer.

John II and Haelan were fourteen and thirteen years of age and in junior high school in 1993. With little to no warning, in three years we would be fully entrenched in the treacherous teenage years.

Since the time John II was in kindergarten I knew school would be a challenge. I remember the first parent-teacher conference John and I attended for our first son. We walked into the classroom and met this young attractive teacher. I put out my hand to introduce myself. When I said my name her face fell and her response was, "Oh, Mrs. Mercado!" Every teacher, every year has said the same thing about John II. "He is a very polite young man, never disrespectful. But he just doesn't seem to like to do his work." John II needed a reason to pay attention. It was important for him to like the subject matter or at minimum the way it was being taught. I remember a conversation I had with him during his senior year of high school regarding English class. He said, "English is stupid. Why do I have to take this?" After several different ways of approaching the topic, I finally barked, "Because it is a requirement for graduation." John II barely made that requirement, but he made it.

Haelan and John II were extreme opposites. Haelan was always studious and would go the extra mile in everything she was asked to do. From the time she entered first grade, she was on the honor roll. During conferences I would sign an IEP for Danny and walk across the hall and sign a GEP (gifted education plan) for Haelan and then go to the principal's office to sign John II out of detention. Haelan spent hours reading and researching topics. She loved to write stories and poems. She had dreams of being a journalist. I didn't worry one bit about Haelan's education. There was no doubt in our minds she was headed for college.

In addition to school activities, John II and Haelan had lots of extracurricular activities. At different times throughout his school years, John II was on the YMCA swim team, the Ft. Bragg hockey team, and the school soccer team. Haelan was on the school softball and soccer teams and took piano lessons after school. We certainly lived a fast-paced life, but it was typical of the activity that takes place in a family with growing children. In addition to the normal craziness of life, with all its worries and schedules, we had Danny's issues to consider.

When I graduated from PIP in 1993, Danny was eleven years old.

We were still waiting for help in the home. Danny was enrolled in a special education program in Cumberland County in a school forty-five minutes from our home in a rundown part of town. I was counting on the knowledge I learned at the PIP sessions to help me maneuver through the bureaucracy to obtain services in our home and in school. I also believed I had an obligation to other families of children with disabilities in my home county to share the information learned from the PIP sessions. As a result I began volunteering in different community organizations and eventually found myself serving as a board member for The Arc of Cumberland County.

The Arc is a national disability organization that began in the 1950s. It was created by parents of children with mental retardation and other developmental disabilities. Every state has an Arc presence. The original acronym for the organization was The Association of Retarded Citizens (ARC). In the 1970s it was decided the name of the organization would no longer be an acronym. During my time as a board member of The Arc of Cumberland County, I met many parents of children with disabilities. I began sharing with each of them all I learned from the PIP sessions. My phone would ring continuously with moms seeking help and support. One day in passing John said, "You should start a center." It always amazed me that when you are in the middle of craziness and life has you spinning in fifty different directions, someone can look in and conclude you have what it takes to take on one more thing. I remember clearly the day John said this to me. It was dinnertime. I was cooking with the phone cocked on my shoulder, talking with another mom about her child and their situation. John II and Haelan were doing homework, watching TV, and fighting with each other all at the same time. In between breaths of conversation, I would excuse myself to play referee. Danny was sitting in his chair, his head cocked to one side. He was exhausted after a physical therapy session. The dog was barking at the children outside and chasing John II as he instigated Haelan with whatever he could find to annoy her. The house was chaotic. John walked in and kissed me hello. His mere presence brought order to the two older children. I finally got off the phone and began explaining what this other mom was going through. "You are not going to believe this…" In the middle of my explanation and setting the table and preparing Danny's pureed food, John very calmly said, "You should start a center." I stopped dead in my tracks long enough to hear my jaw hit the ground. That evening John repeated the same ridiculous statement. We talked for hours about the idea. The more we talked, the more I realized it wasn't such a bad idea after all.

One of the things that surfaced almost immediately for me was a lack of confidence in my ability due to my lack of education. My parents were the first generation in their families to graduate high school. It was only natural for them to want and expect greater things for their children. We were all encouraged to go to college, but I didn't want to go. All I wanted in life was to be a wife and a mother. In high school I won awards for the fastest typing and shorthand skills. I wanted to go to work as a secretary and make money and then get married and have kids. My mother was adamant about college. She said, "Secretaries are a dime a dozen. You've got too much potential." The compromise was to go to the community college and be a medical secretary. To ensure that I would register for college, my mother escorted me on registration day. It was humiliating experience to be the only seventeen-year-old on college registration day with her mother. But I got through it. College wasn't all that bad. After all, I met John there. I had a great time during that first year of college. I didn't attend too many classes, but I met great friends, including my husband. After a year of college I dropped out and broke the news to my family. I was off to find a job. Within a short period of time I was working in Manhattan as a secretary for Macy's department store and then Bristol Myers. I also moved out of my parent's home, not once but twice. The first time was with a friend and the second time was on my own. This process was very disappointing to my parents. Of course, it included more than not going to college. There were boys, sex, drugs, partying, staying out late, not making curfew, etc. I knew all along what my parents preached to me about education was true. What I struggled with was direction. I had no direction for my life. I had no plans outside of being a wife and mother. I wanted that more than anything in the world. I knew after seeing how dedicated my mother was in her role that being a wife and mother would take every bit of my life, so I wanted to spend my time before I became a wife and mother having fun and being free.

John's idea for a center included me as the director. I remember saying to him that I wasn't qualified because I didn't have a degree. "So get one," he said. Again my jaw hit the floor. Getting a degree sounded like the best solution, but where would I find the time to pursue this and what would I major in? Once I found the direction and realized it was important enough to pursue, I had to make the commitment and make the time to fulfill the goal. It took me two years to finally move forward and pursue my degree.

In the meantime, the idea of a center was beginning to take form. In July, 1994, a meeting was set with the Cumberland County Mental Health Center. I attended the meeting with three other parents. At the meeting we presented a proposal for the Cumberland County Special Needs Education Center (SNEC). John developed an excellent presentation package utilizing his newfound computer skills. The purpose of SNEC was "to train and educate parents and other individuals of Cumberland County to become effective advocates for children and adults with special needs." Our proposal included a number of statistics. Over 5,000 children with disabilities were educated in the Cumberland County school system. Over 1,000 children with disabilities were educated in the Ft. Bragg school system. Almost 200 adults with disabilities were identified in sheltered workshops and day programs throughout the county. The proposal also identified three requirements of families of children/adults with disabilities: Support, education, and resource and referral. A support-group survey was conducted with six nonprofit organizations. The survey confirmed the need for additional support to families. The proposal was signed by thirteen parents of children/adults with disabilities. Funding for SNEC was addressed in the proposal through two recommended solutions. The first was exploring the ability of the Cumberland County Mental Health Center to allocate funds for the proposed SNEC. The second was applying for grant funds under the umbrella of the Cumberland County Mental Health Center.

The director and assistant director of the Cumberland County Mental Health Center were very impressed with our proposal. However, everything has a process, especially in a bureaucracy. The Cumberland County Mental Health Center is the local lead agency/area program for the state. The center is a state agency whose operation is similar to a nonprofit agency. There is a board of directors that approves all funding activities. In order to prepare for the presentation to the board, a one-page abstract was developed that clearly outlined the need for SNEC, its purpose, and the results expected from the center. This abstract was sent to an extensive list of individuals, soliciting letters of support. The following individuals replied with letters of support for SNEC: Governor James B. Hunt, Jr.; Mayor J.L. Dawkins; Senator Lura Tally; Representative Eva M. Clayton; the Cumberland County school superintendent; the director of the Department of Social Services; the director of the early intervention program, Womack Army Medical Center; the exceptional family member coordinator of the U.S. Army Community Services; the Tourette Syndrome Association; the parent-to-parent support group for Ft. Bragg and Pope Air Force Families; United Cerebral Palsy; Easter Seal Society of North Carolina; the director of the exceptional children's programs, Ft. Bragg Schools; the director of Head Start; The Arc of Cumberland County; Eastern North Carolina School for the Deaf; the director of the Exceptional Children's Assistance Center (North Carolina parent training center); the director of Community Partnerships. These letters were instrumental in securing startup funding from the Cumberland County Mental Health Center. They were also used to secure funding through other grant sources.

The vision for a center was beginning to be realized. However, as I met professionals in the disability field, my lack of education was more prevalent. This void heaped feelings of incompetence upon me as I dealt with a lack of self-esteem. Although I did all the work of the director efficiently as a professional, the lack of education prevented me from moving forward. I knew I needed to stop kidding myself and head back to school.

Chapter 4

Headed to Mediation

When first arriving at Ft. Bragg, Danny was placed in a school across town. After learning about the Least Restrictive Environment provision in the law and how it related to the neighborhood school, I approached the exceptional children's director of the Ft. Bragg Schools about Danny attending his neighborhood school on Ft. Bragg. I was told this was completely out of the question. Ft. Bragg schools did not have a program for Danny. They contracted with the Cumberland County schools to provide one program for all the county children with significant disabilities, and that program was located forty-five minutes from our home in yet another rundown part of town. As I listened to the exceptional children's director speak, I wondered if she had ever read the special education law. What I realized throughout the years is that it was not lack of knowledge that prevented this bureaucracy from implementing the law. It wasn't even a lack of funding that prevented implementation. A lack of willingness to have basic beliefs about education challenged was the reason PL94-142 was never fully implemented across this country. I was challenged when I heard the PIP presentation about inclusion. I had a choice to accept the challenge or remain firm in my beliefs. When your child is not directly involved there is no need to accept the challenge. But that was not the case for me. I wanted the best for Danny. I had no choice but to accept the challenge to move away from the perceived bubble of protection in the segregated schools to understanding that the best protection is provided through integration and interaction with people of all different abilities. Most of the professionals we meet in the school system and other bureaucracies that are in place to "help" us are individuals who have not experienced the heartache and struggle of raising a child with a disability. It is important to recognize that their perspectives and agendas are very different. I certainly learned a lot from these professionals but would have saved myself a lot of grief had I not been so naïve in thinking they knew what was best for my son.

Monitoring and accountability are key factors to ensure this federal law is properly implemented. But, again, if the federal monitors and auditors have not accepted the challenge of full implementation, it is foolish to depend on them. The special education law exists today because families across the country came together and convinced legislators that it was wrong to deny children the right to education. Yes, our children have mental retardation. That means our children are slow to learn—not that they cannot learn. They learn at a different rate and sometimes in a different way, but they learn. Furthermore, all families are taxpayers. How can you expect families to pay taxes for public schools and then tell them their children cannot attend the public school because they cannot pass an admission test? This sounds like a British colony dilemma: taxation without representation or participation! These were the arguments presented by the families. The congressional legislators understood their constituents and put into law education for all children regardless of disability. However, monitoring and accountability of the full implementation of this law has been lax from the beginning. As a result, monitoring and accountability rests solely on the shoulders of parents of children with disabilities. This is very unfair since it gives us one more plate to spin.

During our four-year stay with the Ft. Bragg school system, it took three major battles that ended in the mediation process to obtain what was specifically outlined in the special education law. The first battle was to get Danny to his neighborhood school. Besides reading and studying the federal law, I learned of an organization called STOMP (Specialized Training of Military Parents). What a great name! This organization is based out of Ft. Lewis, Washington, where Danny was born, and consists of all military parents of children with disabilities. The Ft. Bragg school system is part of the Department of Defense, not the Department of Education. Therefore, the rules were a little different. I received a lot of support from STOMP and spoke with many other parents across the country at Ft. Campbell, Ft. Rucker, and Ft. Lewis. I did my homework and moved through the process of first requesting that Danny be educated by the Ft. Bragg school system. After receiving a denial letter from the Ft. Bragg exceptional children's director, I then requested mediation. I learned from STOMP that an outside Department of Defense mediator would be assigned to our case. Shortly after requesting mediation, I received a letter stating the date, time, and location of the mediation. The letter also identified the mediator as the exceptional children's director of Camp Lejeune. I looked at my husband and said, "Oh my God. The marines are coming!" I continued to do my homework and prepared for the day when I would sit across from the entire Ft. Bragg school system, defending my position that Danny belonged in his neighborhood school.

As I prepared so diligently for mediation, I remembered something my Aunt Cathy said to me while we waited in the ICU waiting room when Danny was first diagnosed with meningitis. As I cried and listened to her voice over the phone, she told me the story of "Footprints" and that when we walk in the sand there are always two sets of footprints. One belongs to us and one belongs to God. But sometimes we look down and find only one set of footprints. That doesn't mean God has abandoned us. It means He is carrying us.

I was so nervous about going through mediation. When I walked in that room I could feel my knees shake and when I talked I knew my voice trembled. But I was convinced it was the right thing to do for Danny. I was physically alone that day. These things always happen in the middle of the day, making it very difficult for John to participate. But as I remembered what my Aunt Cathy taught me, I realized I was far from alone. I've learned throughout the years that there is never an "I" in what I do. God always makes it "We." And so "We" went to mediation that day.

I sat on one side of a very long table and on the other side was the Ft. Bragg exceptional children's director, the Cumberland County exceptional children's director, the occupational therapist, the speech language pathologist, and the physical therapist from both the Ft. Bragg school system and the Cumberland County school system. At the head of the table sat the exceptional children's director from Camp Lejeune. I did a double-take when I first met her. She was about my age and had a bubbly, sweet smile. This is not what I had expected. The word *marine* has thrown me off. I'd expected a bulldog type that would barely give a grin. She was nothing like I expected. However, it didn't take long for me to realize she was a true marine, although not literally. The Department of Defense employees on both Ft. Bragg and Camp Leujune are not active-duty soldiers and marines. They are civilians, but she had something about her that separated her from what we were experiencing at Ft. Bragg. She had a beautiful face and a sweet smile, but most importantly, she had conviction and the spirit of a piranha. Later I learned her father was a retired marine. That explained it. I also learned she was very innovative in providing support to children with disabilities and she did all she could to live by what was written in the law.

After she clearly outlined the rules for mediation, each side was asked to present their case. She listened and took notes. She also presented facts about the law. Since it is a fact that a child should attend the school he would normally attend if he did not have a disability, and since it is also a fact that the next step was due process, a mediation agreement was developed. Danny would be brought back to the Ft. Bragg School system and would attend Bowley Elementary School. In making this decision, Ft. Bragg further decided to bring all Ft. Bragg children back to their home schools by not renewing its contract with the Cumberland County schools. VICTORY! But there were a lot more battles to come.

While preparing for mediation, I learned about Extended School Year (ESY). It seems that the law allows school systems to provide services through the summer months for students with disabilities who qualify, ensuring there will be no regression of skills learned during the regular school year. Extended School Year can be in the form of occupational therapy, physical therapy, or speech language pathology services, or it can include academic services as well. The way you qualify is through discussions of strengths and needs during the IEP process with the entire IEP team. Extended School Year is part of the IEP document. It was my experience that ESY was always marked off with a "no" and was never discussed with the team.

At one of Danny's IEP meetings I asked that we discuss the possibility of Extended School Year for Danny. ESY was discussed but the answer was no. There were lots of reasons, such as a kid should be given the time to be a kid and therefore summer is very important. Another response was to wait to see if Danny showed any regression before they would consider Extended School Year. This didn't make much sense at all. Once again, I sent my letter requesting Extended School Year. I received a formal letter of denial and then in writing requested mediation. This time mediation was much different. First of all, John was able to be there. Up until this point, John received all his disability education secondhand (from me). I was very worried about John being at the meeting. I most definitely wanted his support, but I wasn't confident I had provided him with enough information to understand the entire process. As we sat on one side of the table with the entire Ft. Bragg school system on the other side and the Camp Lejeune exceptional children's director at the helm, John sat very quietly listening to the arguments back and forth. Most of our arguments centered around whether Danny qualified for ESY. After several hours of debate, John cleared his throat and said, "I'd like to ask a question." I thought I would die. I thought, *My God, why are you interrupting me?* John said, "I've been listening to what everyone is saying but I don't know why we are having this discussion. Danny's IEP was written last May for the entire year. The date at the top of his IEP says May 31, 1994 through May 31, 1995." John had the IEP in his hand and clearly pointed out the section in the upper right hand corner that stated, "Date Beginning and Duration of Special Education Services and Related Services." The dates for services clearly read May 31, 1994 through May 31, 1995. He further stated, "These dates include the summer, so why are we discussing it?" There was dead silence. I sat back in my chair and couldn't help but chuckle. There was the answer as clear as could be. We were so busy digging in the law for qualifications of Extended School Year when in fact the answer was already decided. I was so proud of John. As I looked his way to thank him, my eyes drifted to the expression on all the faces connected to the suits and ties on the other side of the table. Their mouths were hanging wide open. After collecting themselves, they stated it was never the intent that summer would be included. John then took over the discussion by asking questions directly to the mediator. "Is the IEP a valid document?" he asked. "Are the items in the IEP to be followed during the dates listed on the IEP? If it says occupational therapy is to occur one time per week but the teacher decides to not let the therapist work with the student in a particular week because she feels the student needs a break, would that teacher be out of compliance with the IEP?" John paused long enough after each question to get a nod of confirmation from the mediator and then without any hesitation continued with more questions. "If the IEP team met and decided services were needed for a child from May 31, 1994 to May 31, 1995, then shouldn't services be provided throughout that entire time period? What are the consequences for being out of compliance with an IEP?" As the questions were being asked, the other side of the table fidgeted in their chairs. The result of this meeting was a mediation agreement that stated Danny would receive continued services for the dates outlined in his IEP. As an even more ideal result, ESY became a regular occurrence for Danny throughout his school years. Unfortunately, after our mediation session, the Ft. Bragg school system met with the Department of Defense to try to get clarification on this issue. The Department of Defense verified the decision, however, and instructed the school system to change the dates on all IEPs to reflect the school year only and not the entire calendar year. Whether or not this was the right thing to do was a battle we chose not to pursue. But it shows another important characteristic of the bureaucracy. When backed into a corner they will comply. However, they will do all they can to regroup and change the rules so that it becomes difficult for others to access the benefit of a service. The goal is to remain on top of the game. The one in control wins. Bureaucracies want to be in control and do not like being challenged.

Students with disabilities almost always need continued education and reinforcement in order to make progress. This enforcement can of course come in many different ways and settings. But to say you would wait to see if the student regresses before you determine he needs support is a gamble most parents are not willing to take.

The next battle with the Ft. Bragg school system was a little more complicated. I was learning all I could on inclusion and now it was time to implement it. I still was not convinced it was possible for Danny. I read all the books I could find on the subject. I remember clearly the PIP presenter's words, "Inclusion is for *all* students." But I needed to see inclusion for someone like Danny before I could pursue it further.

I again called STOMP and learned that many inclusive opportunities were happening in the Camp Leujune school system. I wasn't surprised, especially after meeting the exceptional children's director at our last two mediation sessions. I called the exceptional children's director at Camp Leujune and asked for a tour of the inclusive settings.

I spent the day in Camp Leujune and visited three classroom settings. The first setting was a preschool setting. We entered a very large room with many children and play stations everywhere. There was a sand box, a coloring center, and a climbing section with tunnels and brightly colored climbing boxes. I made a fast sweep of the room and then looked at the director and then back again at the children. Certainly we were in the wrong room. Just then the director leaned over and whispered, "We have ten children with disabilities in this class." I was stunned. Where are they? Who are they? Again I looked back at the children, but this time I studied each child, trying to find those with disabilities. It was like the story books John II and Haelan had, the *Where's Waldo?* series. As the books told a story, on each page there were lots of pictures of people and things, and Waldo was not noticeable in the picture. You had to really look for Waldo and the challenge was to find him in every picture. I was looking for ten Waldos in a classroom of more than thirty students. After very close observation I found a little girl with two hearing aids. I also recognized a prone stander in the corner of the room and eventually found the little boy who belonged to it. He was laying on a mat with another child, who was reading a story to him. They seemed to both enjoy the experience of each other. I then saw another child with leg splints, better known as AFOs. Another child with glasses had the facial characteristics of down syndrome. I never found all ten children with disabilities in this classroom, but what I did see was beautiful interaction between thirty-five children who seemed to accept each other for their unique abilities. The adults in this classroom supervised and monitored all activities and encouraged interaction between all the children. Although this was a beautiful experience, I could not relate this to Danny, because no one in this classroom had the extensive limitations Danny experienced.

The second classroom we visited was a third-grade classroom. We met this class in the hallway as they were coming back from the school cafeteria. This classroom had two students who were deaf and used sign language. As a result the entire classroom learned sign language. The teaching method for this classroom was a team teaching approach and was headed by a special-ed and regular-ed teacher. As we approached the students, the special education director asked one of the students what she was doing. The girl was using sign language with one of the deaf students, but her movements were very pronounced and dramatized—extreme movement. In response to the director's question, the girl said, "He won't listen to me, so I'm shouting in sign language." We both laughed at the innocent logic of the answer provided. The girl was instructed to get back in line. Again, what a beautiful experience to see children accept each other for who they are, regardless of ability or difference in learning and communicating. The books I read and the special education law were starting to come to life as I walked through this school and saw the interaction of *all* students. Although this looked good and felt good, it was not something I could relate to Danny's situation, since his disabilities seemed so much more involved than those of anyone I had met so far.

The third classroom, however, was the clincher. This was a kindergarten class. We first met this class in the school cafeteria. Again there was a regular and special-ed team approach. A little girl in the class had all the same disabilities as Danny and was very involved. She sat in her wheelchair at the end of the table with a one-on-one aide close behind. The student with disabilities sat with her peers on either side. She did not eat at the table with her peers. I was told by the director that she had already been fed at the nurse's station via G-tube. I watched as the students interacted with her. When lunch was over the students fought with each other to push the wheelchair. Finally one of the teachers had to intervene and select one student to complete the task. We followed the students back to their classroom. This was a very large classroom. In a corner of the room there was a screened divider. The little girl was brought to the section of this room and behind the screened divider diaper changing occurred. While this was being done, the teachers instructed the students to get ready for reading and music time. They each scrambled for their beanbag chairs. By this time the little girl was ready to join the group. She was placed in a Tumble Form chair next to her peers. I stayed in the classroom as the story was being read and I watched the students, especially those around this little girl. At one

68

point the little girl grimaced and looked like she was going to cry. Almost immediately another little girl sitting next to her gently touched her hand, whispered something to her, and then they both focused on the rest of the story.

After the story it was time for music. The students were instructed to put their beanbags in the storage area. The one-on-one aide lifted the student out of the Tumble Form chair. One of the first students to put his beanbag chair away came to do the same with the little girl's Tumble Form chair. The students were instructed to get a partner. Two girls joined hands with the girl with the disabilities. The aide held the girl under her arms so that she could stand. There was no standing ability. Her feet barely touched the floor, but she was going to dance with the rest of her peers. As the music began, the two little girls held her hands and there was jumping and swaying and laughing and giggling. I stood in a corner of this room sobbing. What a beautiful sight. This little girl didn't need a special classroom or a special school to keep her safe. She was safe among her peers because they were being taught respect for each other.

I gained as much control of myself as I could and thanked the director for her wonderful hospitality. Once in my car, I cried from deep within. *My God,* I thought. *What have we missed!* How fortunate this little girl was to have friends who cared for her; but most importantly, how brave her mother was to allow this interaction to occur. None of this could have happened for this child without the vision, direction, and support of that special education director. My two-hour drive back to Ft. Bragg was full of ways to get our new Ft. Bragg special education director to make this possible for Danny.

Shortly after the two mediation sessions with the Ft. Bragg school system, the special education director was removed from her position. Unfortunately I've learned throughout the years that a bureaucracy never fires employees who are proven to be incompetent in their positions. Instead they move them to a new position and sometimes create a position for them so they can continue on through retirement. Unfortunately these individuals are not put in janitorial positions until they reach retirement. Therefore, they continue to interact with students and parents. God only knows how much more damage they will do before they reach retirement.

The new Ft. Bragg special education director was a woman born and raised in the Bronx, New York. Although she had no military background, her upbringing in the Bronx was all she needed to take on this challenge. While meeting with the new director in her office, I explained what I saw at Camp Lejeune. My conclusion to her was, "If the marines can do it, certainly the army can!" We had a good laugh and then to my surprise she offered to put together a team of both special education and regular education teachers to tour the Camp Lejeune schools and see for themselves the inclusive opportunities offered. Shortly after their tour of Camp Lejeune, the special education director called an IEP meeting for Danny. It was decided at that meeting that Danny would be assigned to a fourth-grade class for mainstreaming purposes. His homeroom would still be in the severe/profound class, but he would participate in music, art, and PE with the regular fourth-grade class.

Danny's special education teacher resisted this change. She was old-school and had taught the severe/profound class for close to thirty years. She felt it was better for these students' health and safety to be separated rather than included. *Not too long ago I would have agreed completely with her approach,* I thought. However, this is not what the law says and it is not what I saw happening in Camp Lejeune. Despite this teacher's vocal apprehension to this new approach, the special education director moved forward with the plans to have Danny mainstreamed.

About three months into the program, I visited the school during PE class. Although the goal was to have Danny included with the fourth-grade class, PE for the special education students was at the same time as the fourth-grade students but Danny was not with the fourth-grade students during this class. The fourth-grade students were on one side of the gym while Danny was participating in wheelchair activities with the students from the severe/profound class on the other side of the gym. I immediately left the school and walked to the neighboring building to the office of the special education director. I explained what I had seen. Together we went back to the school. By the time we arrived all the students were back in their prospective classes. As it turned out, the special education teacher was so concerned about the health and safety of her students that she did all she could to sabotage inclusion of any kind. Once this was realized, it was decided by the IEP team that Danny would be removed from the severe/profound class into a multi-handicapped class. The difference in the classes had everything to do with the teacher. The teacher in the multi-handicapped class accepted Danny and agreed with the challenge to include him with the fourth-grade class.

Danny was given a one-on-one aide who understood she was to promote integration and interaction with the other students. Danny was finally making friends. These students who probably had no prior experience with kids with disabilities opened their arms to Danny and accepted him as part of their class. He enjoyed PE, art, and music with his new friends. In an effort to show other families that this was possible, I contacted the Ft. Bragg *Paraglide* newspaper. An article was done on Danny and the success of inclusion with his new fourth-grade friends.

Six months into this arrangement, the special education director invited herself to Danny's IEP meeting, at which time she challenged the team to think about adding science to Danny's inclusion classes. I remember looking at her and asking, "How are we going to do academics?" She began explaining how the fourth-grade science curriculum was a hands-on curriculum that involved lots of lab work. Despite the fact that Danny would not be able to complete any of the lab work or other curriculum requirements, the vision was that Danny's prone stander could be positioned against the lab table and he would participate and interact with the students as they completed their lab work. I was quite skeptical about this idea but figured we had nothing to lose. If it didn't work at least we could maintain PE, art, and music. It seemed to be worth a try.

I observed during one of Danny's science classes and was absolutely amazed at what I saw. The teacher announced there would be a lab to complete and gave thorough instructions. After the students understood what was expected of them, they were instructed to partner with another student and find a place at the lab table. A cute little blonde-haired girl approached Danny and asked if he would like to be her partner. Without any hesitation, Danny moved his head and eyes toward her direction and followed her around the room as she made a space for them at the lab table. The aide positioned Danny on his prone stander next to the girl. She was sitting on Danny's left side. This was Danny's weak side and he did not like to turn his head or eyes in this direction. But not today! Danny's eyes were fixed on this cute girl and everything she did. For years Danny's IEP consisted of a goal that addressed eye movement from left to right. Throughout the years we tried every possible object to get Danny to respond. We used bright lights, blinking Christmas lights, and large colorful objects. Even the birds in his first classroom in Cumberland County didn't provide the response I saw today. As I watched this interaction, I asked the aide, who was standing behind the lab table, if this was a new thing that was happening. She replied, "No, he's been doing that for a while now. Several different children interact with Danny, but he seems to prefer the blonde-headed girls." I know my mouth was wide open. When I shared this observation with John, he chuckled and said, "That's my boy!" I later found out that the aide understood Danny's needs according to his IEP and encouraged student interaction on the side he did not like to go to. Not only did Danny learn to move his head in the direction of his peers, but his eyes were now searching and following his friends.

I wish Danny could have spent the rest of his educational time with the Ft. Bragg school system. We finally had leadership that cared and was willing to do whatever it took to follow the law. Not only did Danny benefit from inclusion under this administration, but many other students were moved into the mainstream of school life because of the vision and leadership of this special education director. Unfortunately John was fast approaching military retirement.

Chapter 5

No More Waiting

In addition to dealing with school issues, I was determined to obtain services in our home to alleviate the stress and allow me to spend time with my husband and my other children. We were still on the waiting list for a CAP MR/DD slot and Danny still had a low score for receiving services. We were ineligible for Medicaid because of John's income. The CAP MR/DD waiver was the only opportunity we had to receive help in our home, because it waives the income criteria of the family and looks solely at the income and disability of the child. It was CAP MR/DD or nothing.

By this time I was a member of The Arc of North Carolina. I first learned about this organization through PIP. One of the presenters during the PIP session was the executive director of The Arc of North Carolina. It was evident that this man was savvy when it came to the legislative process. He spent most of his professional career with legislators in the general assembly, advocating for increased funds for children and adults with disabilities on the waiting list.

The SNEC was also moving forward in its mission to identify parents of children with disabilities in Cumberland County. The SNEC goal was to keep families informed on what should be happening in the school system and throughout their child's involvement in community life. Throughout the waiting process for CAP services and the interaction with the mental health center staff regarding SNEC, I was learning the dynamics of the blame game. In approaching the mental health center staff about the CAP MR/DD waiting list, they would blame the division for not giving them enough slots. The division would blame the legislators because they didn't provide enough state dollars to match the federal dollars provided for waiver funding. The legislators didn't take any responsibility either. They blamed their constituents who by the way are you and me. Round and round and round we go as we wait endlessly for services. While we wait, we pray that we will not fall into bankruptcy and that our family will have the stamina to sustain however long it takes to get relief. I learned also that the squeaky wheel gets the grease. I would mark my calendar weekly to call the Cumberland County Mental Health Center to see if there were any more slots and to find out where Danny was on the list. I also made calls and wrote letters to the Division of Mental Health/Developmental Disabilities/Substance Abuse (DMH) staff to ask when more slots would be coming down to Cumberland County. I also called and wrote letters to my state representatives begging them to fund more slots. Every week for months I called and wrote letters and pursued a slot for Danny. Finally, while working at the SNEC, I received a call from the executive director of The Arc of North Carolina announcing that slots were being distributed across the state and that four slots were headed to Cumberland County. I immediately called the mental health center for confirmation. An interagency meeting was held to determine which four people on the waiting list would be the winners of the slots. This was an insane process but I was desperate and willing to do whatever it took to get relief for my family.

Every morning, in order to get three children ready for school, I'd start my day at 4:30 a.m. John II and Haelan's routine were typical routines. However, no matter how structured the routine is, some children, like our oldest son, need a lot of motivating to get started in the morning. Danny's routine was far from normal, although it was normal for him. It included feeding, which was a long process of spitting and coughing. When feeding Danny it was important to pay attention to the process to ensure he would not choke on his food. Most of my school mornings were spent feeding Danny and barking orders to the other children. Finally school buses arrived and there was peace—at least for a little while. Although the morning was full of activity, the afternoon was even more active. Danny was always in my lap as I helped our older children with homework and he sat in his Tumble Form chair in the kitchen as I prepared dinner. I always fed Danny dinner first because there was so much spitting and coughing involved. After he ate he would sit in his chair at the dining room table with the rest of us. It was the best arrangement we could have for family time. After dinner it was time for homework review, then bath time for all the children and lunches to be made for the next day. By the end of the day I would crash from exhaustion. It wasn't just physical exhaustion. I was worried about how long our family would be able to hold out with this kind of routine. We improvised the best we could for equipment to help Danny in our home. But it wasn't enough. More importantly, our finances were in bad shape. By this point we were using credit cards to purchase Danny's diapers. There were also no babysitters for Danny. Outside of school, Danny was with me or his Dad. If I didn't get to run the errands that needed to be done while Danny was in school, I had to wait for John to come home.

My case manager at this point was the same woman who had come to my house to do the assessment. Since I was desperate for help in my home and for some financial relief in purchasing supplies, I was not going to trust this case manager would present our case well enough to win a slot. I called the CAP MR/DD supervisor at the Cumberland County Mental Health Center to confirm when the interagency meeting would be held. Since the Cumberland County Mental Health Center is a public agency with an open meeting policy, I invited myself to the meeting and brought Danny with me. However, when I arrived at the meeting place they would not let me bring Danny into the meeting. Since the decision-makers never see the person with the disability, they felt it would be unfair to all the other families waiting if Danny was presented at the meeting. I had never made a presentation in front of a group before and I was scared. One of the case managers said she would be happy to sit with Danny outside the meeting room. I did not have Danny's stroller with me. I took him from his car seat and carried him in. Danny lay on a mat under the supervision of a case manager while I went into this meeting room to present my case.

When the door opened to this room, I felt a sick feeling in the pit of my stomach. Presenting my case was humiliating. I was begging for help. I was desperate and I needed these decision-makers to understand our need. I carried with me a small index card with notes on what to say. I sat next to the assistant director at the head of the table. I don't remember the words I said, but I remember shaking and feeling tears well up, although I tried desperately to hold them back. My son was twelve years old and we had taken care of him completely on our own except for the eighteen months he lived in an institution in Indiana. I did not ever want to be in a position to have to choose another institution for him. It was critical that this group understood my concerns and awarded him the slot.

After my begging session was over, one of the case manager supervisors stood up and said that the decision of awarding a slot was not up to them. She further stated that we would have to qualify for CAP MR/DD and that was determined by the Department of Social Services (DSS). She continued by saying that we would have to bring our financial information to the DSS for approval. I spit out for her what I had learned and read so many times about the waiver. "The waiver waives income criteria for the family and focuses solely on the consumer's income and disability." She spoke with conviction and insisted that the DSS was the determining factor. As a result the assistant director thanked me for coming. He stated that my case manager would be in touch with me and I was escorted out of the room.

After securing Danny in his car seat, I sat in my car for a long five minutes and cried uncontrollably. I looked at Danny and said, "My God, what are we going to do?" I decided I needed to talk with the director of the mental health center. Since this was at a time before cell phones, I drove as fast as I could home. After settling Danny down I grabbed the phone and called the director's office. There was a board meeting that day and he was unable to come to the phone. I was crying hysterically and would not get off the phone. "You get me someone to talk to now, damn it. I have just been through one of the worst meetings of my life with your staff and I want to speak with someone NOW." The developmental disabilities director excused herself from the board meeting and came to the phone. Through tears I explained the humiliating experience and the remark from one of the CAP MR/DD supervisors. "How is it that I learn one thing from the state and another from your staff? What is the truth?" Her first response was to calm me down and then she wanted time to speak with the supervisor. She promised to get back with me first thing the next morning. I explained to her that if I did not hear from her by the time my children left for school, I will be at the director's office. She assured me she would contact me in the morning.

Exactly at 8:30 a.m. the next morning the phone rang. It was the development disabilities (DD) director. She asked how I was doing. I explained I would be doing better if I wasn't experiencing the run around from her staff. She assured me that she would get an answer for me regarding the slot and the correct procedure to follow before the end of the day. I had no choice but to wait. Finally at 4:00 that afternoon the DD director called to explain that Danny was awarded one of the four slots. She further explained that my case manager had been instructed on the correct process to follow and would be in touch with me the next day to begin the process. Unfortunately the process did include a visit to the Department of Social Services (DSS). I was instructed by the case manager to bring all our financial information to the DSS office. It seems that the process involved making sure our family did not qualify for Medicaid. I explained to the case manager that a simple look at my husband's military pay voucher would suffice, but that was not sufficient. I was clearly instructed to bring life insurance policies on everyone in the family, the most recent bank statements for all savings and checking accounts, pay vouchers for all who worked in the family, titles to cars if we owned them, along with titles to any land owned by the family. This was another humiliating process. In order for us to receive help from an outside source, we had to be willing to give up our privacy. For twelve years our family was turned down for services because of my husband's income. Now that we had been approved for a service, all our private financial information (which wasn't much at the time) was exposed to complete strangers. Many forms were completed by the DSS staff. We were then told we should receive a letter in the mail from Raleigh in about two weeks. "Two weeks!" I gasped. "Why do we have to wait two weeks?" The DSS staff explained that this was the timeframe Raleigh needed to review the documents and determine that our family did not qualify for Medicaid. "What happens after we receive the letter?" I asked. She then explained that paperwork would be completed with only Danny's financial information. This would then be sent to Raleigh for review. "How long will that take?" I asked. "It usually takes a week for Raleigh to review and return the documents back to us," she answered. Three more weeks of nonsense! For twelve years we were turned down for support as soon as my husband's rank was revealed. Now we had to go through a ridiculous three-week process. We were learning the waiting game. The bureaucracy moves in its own time and never on your time. No matter what you face in life, no matter how long you've endured the unthinkable, the bureaucracy, like an evil god, moves in its own time and in its own way.

Finally, after three weeks of waiting, we were approved for the slot. The next step was deciding services appropriate to meet Danny's needs.

Chapter 6

No Exemptions

With military retirement fast approaching, we spoke with our case manager to see how we would transfer Danny's services to the Charlotte or Raleigh area, where the job market was conducive to John's computer skills and education. We were given false information by the case manager and were told if we moved out of the county we would have to begin the process of accessing services all over again in the new county. Our family had waited too long for help. We did not want to lose the slot. As a result we purchased our first home in Fayetteville and John began job hunting in the Fayetteville area. After many low-paying jobs and short-term contracts, John finally landed a long-term computer contract position with a company providing computer support to the Womack Army Medical Center (WAMC) on Ft. Bragg. During his job search, John experienced many stress-related health problems. In a way it reminded me of the movie, *The Shawshank Redemption*. John had forty years of institutional life behind him—first at St. Mary's Boys Home and then in the U.S. Army. He was now out in the civilian world and he seemed lost. The transition took a toll on his health. But there was no turning back. We spent many hours talking through this transition. Working at WAMC was a blessing for John. Although he served in a contract position, being around the camouflage uniforms gave him a sense of home.

Making the transition to civilian life also included a transition for our children from the Department of Defense school system to the

North Carolina Department of Public Instruction school system. In the middle of this transition, our two older children were beginning to transition into adulthood. I still signed a gifted education plan (GEP) for Haelan in the Cumberland County school system and continued to bail John II out of detention. Some things never change!

Somewhere along the line, however, Haelan made a sharp turn in life that shocked all of us. She was always the perfect student and had great friends. However, around sixteen years of age she began developing friendships with students who had no ambition in life, no direction, and no moral standards. During a sleepover for her sixteenth birthday, I realized something was terribly wrong. The girls who came to the sleepover had their hair colored black and wore several earrings, tattoos, and very dark make up. I tried to talk with Haelan about what I saw. Haelan really didn't look like she belonged to this group of girls. As I talked with Haelan about my concerns, her response was something I remembered telling my mom about many years earlier. "Just because they're my friends doesn't mean I am going to turn out like them." From this point on it went downhill not only for John II, which we sort of expected, but now for Haelan too.

Every week I called my parents and gave them an update on the children. It was always a great report, however, lately my conversations with my parents were full of tears. It was very overwhelming for this to be happening on top of John looking for a job and all the challenges Danny brought to life. After one of my tearful conversations with my parents, I received the following letter from my Dad, which I still carry today in my day planner.

March 4, 1997

Dear Denise,

I am sorry to hear about the headaches the teenagers are causing. Believe me, it is not easy and there are no simple solutions. I speak from experience and also as a former teenager (a long-long-long time ago).

First, as a teenager your parents know nothing. They are out of it, etc. Home is the pits and everything out there is paradise. Peer pressure is tremendous. They are told what to do and when to do it, at home and at school. "No one understands me," they think. "I want to do my own thing."

Denise, it has never changed. We rebelled in my era, you rebelled in your era, and our children and grandchildren are presently rebelling.

As a father of teenagers you do what your heart says is right because that is a parent's responsibility. You try not to let it disrupt your life and most importantly do not let it come between you and your spouse.

Let them know you will always be there for them. Make them aware that your confidence has to be earned. Interject your opinion, or if need be, lay the law down because that is your responsibility.

A home has to have rules or guidelines and each child in that home should be held accountable for his or her actions. It sounds easy, but understand that these teens do not see things clearly. They want their freedom. They want the liberties their peers have. "Joe has no curfew." "Mary goes away every weekend." Etc.

You have to stick by your convictions. They will only understand when they are in your shoes.

Up to this point you have done a commendable job. All the curve balls thrown your way have not deterred you from being a responsible parent. Do not change course now. Do not give in. They do not see the potential consequences.

Even though you have your differences of opinions, do not let them get you to the point that you throw them out. Trust me, you will probably regret it.

If, for example, they elect not to continue their education, make them aware of the added responsibilities they face. They will have to contribute toward the expenses of running a home, etc.

Forcing them into higher education is a bad move (in my opinion). Make them realize they are cheating themselves. In today's job market a high school diploma just does not make it.

I could go on and on. I just want to let you know that I as a father am extremely proud of your accomplishments as a wife, mother, and human being.

Do not let up. They will test you to no end. Your love and understanding will prevail. In due time they will realize your intentions. Until then roll with the punches and keep the faith.

Know that you are in our prayers always and that things will calm down. Parenthood never will be an easy task. It is very unrewarding, but we do not look for rewards—only that our children become good, upstanding citizens and decent human beings. Unfortunately there are no guarantees. Our only consolation is we did the best we could. Do not second-guess yourself. There is no sure solution and no right or wrong. It is trial and error, and a lot of praying.

You and John have done whatever is best for your children. Remember that God blesses us with children but they are only loaned to us. One way or another, sooner or later they will fly the coop. We only hope and pray they are prepared for the cruel world out there.

As I said before, let them know you are there for them. I speak from experience, as we have made some blunders along the way. But that is all part of the process.

Our prayers are with you, and maybe a change of scenery will be good for them. We again offer our home, as this is their home away from home. There are lots of activities for young people and Bennington College is within walking distance. Maybe a week in a different environment might open their eyes. Give it some thought and pass it by them. Keep your chin up, babe. You have your mother's spunk.

Mom sends her love and I love you all dearly.

Dad

With lots of prayer and persistence we got through the teenage years with our two older children. We were amazed at the turn life took and how our expectations were unrealistic for each of our children. Our son John II followed in his Dad's footsteps and joined the United States Army and became a United States Army diver. After a short stay in this field, he decided to switch gears and study to become an army medic. On September 8, 2006, John and I attended the Ft. Bragg Special Forces graduation ceremony. Our son, John II received his Green Beret and a special Leadership Award in the Special Forces Medical Sergeants Course. It was hard to believe this was the child who had barely made it out of high school. Throughout school John II would excel if he understood the purpose and enjoyed the topic. Shortly after completing diving school the Iraq war began. John II called us on a Thursday morning to tell us he was headed for a visit to Atlanta to see his high school sweetheart. He also announced he would be speaking with her Dad about marrying his daughter. The next day I received a call from John II. "How did your conversation with Christie's Dad go?" "GREAT," he said with excitement. "So when's the wedding?" I asked. "TONIGHT!" he explained. I couldn't help but drop the phone. Thanks to frequent-flier miles, John and I were able to fly to Atlanta that afternoon to see our son, in his army green dress uniform, marry his high school sweetheart.

Unfortunately life did not turn out as we expected for our daughter, Haelan. At seventeen she announced she was tired of high school and decided to quit. At eighteen she married a twenty-one-year-old Ft. Bragg soldier. By nineteen she was divorced with a baby and had a serious drug problem that she has yet to overcome.

When you give birth to a child they call it labor for a reason. When the child finally enters the world it is wet and slimy and hard to hold onto. Very carefully newborns are held and cuddled and protected. But there are no guarantees that the child you bring into the world will be healthy. Physical birth is not the only birth process in an individual's life. The labor a parent goes through in raising a teenager is similar to the labor pains experienced during the physical birth process. Getting a baby to make their physical entrance into this world is no less labor-intensive than the birth of an adult from childhood. You raise a child with love and a foundation rooted firmly in God and country. You nurture children as you do your own body when you carry them inside. But in order for them to make their entrance into adulthood, the labor pains begin in the teenage years. Dad is right; there are no guarantees. Teenagers are like newborns. They are hard to hold on to. As a result you learn to cuddle and protect in a very different way. My daughter is at the top of my prayer list every day. At every mass I light a candle for her and pray that she will turn and face God and submit to what is right. Like the prodigal son, she made choices and decisions that led her to a pigpen of slop. My prayer is that she will not only recognize her existence, but decide to make a change.

Chapter 7

A Coup Is Formed

After battling the Ft. Bragg school system for inclusive education and the area program for Medicaid waiver services, I began to sense a direction for my life. I thought my calling was to go to law school. I felt a tremendous urge to sue the hell out of all the bureaucrats who refused to follow the law and as a result hurt children with disabilities and their families. To satisfy this urge I took a copy of my resume and college transcript from 1975 to the Campbell University office on Ft. Bragg. The advisor looked at my resume and my transcript and chuckled as he said, "It looks like two different people." He then asked what I wanted to do in life. I told him I wanted to go to law school and specialize in disability law. He looked back at the resume and the transcript and said, "I suggest you start over."

In January 1995 at the age of thirty-eight, I began classes at the Ft. Bragg extension of Campbell University. To prepare for law school I chose government as my major. Surprisingly enough, I loved school. I was back to being the studious, responsible student I was when I first entered school. It was not easy going back to school at thirty-eight. But I was dedicated to see this through. After four long years of night school, I graduated cum laude. John proudly tells people, "My wife went to college and graduated cum laude. I went to college and graduated kumbaya."

In order to get through college I knew I needed to focus on my education. As a result I left the SNEC in the hands of another parent. Before the summer of 1997 I received a call from the new SNEC director. The SNEC was growing and it needed more funding to meet the needs of the families of children with disabilities identified by the center. The Arc of Cumberland County was a small chapter of the state affiliate. The director of The Arc of Cumberland County was a part-time staff member and not a parent of a child with a disability. The Arc of Cumberland County was also located on the second floor of an inaccessible building and had been for the past six years. On several occasions the director of The Arc of Cumberland County and the new director of SNEC met to discuss a possible merge between the two organizations. Most of the parents on The Arc board were older parents who were satisfied with what The Arc offered their adult children. The Arc provided an annual dance for adults with disabilities and supported adults in the sheltered workshop and day programs throughout the county. The families from SNEC were young families who were beginning to understand that the laws offered more for their children than warehousing in sheltered workshops and day programs. They wanted more for their children than an annual dance. The two boards continued to clash, meeting after meeting. Finally the SNEC director called to say, "Denise, we need to take over The Arc."

Through the SNEC director I met another parent who grew up in Fayetteville and was also a parent of a child with significant disabilities. Mary's was also one of the first families in Cumberland County to receive CAP MR/DD services in 1989.

This was the plan: The SNEC families would take over The Arc of Cumberland County. The SNEC director would become the program director for The Arc of Cumberland County. Mary would become the president of the new Arc board and I would become the new executive director. By this time I was wracking up a large student loan bill. A part-time job would help offset some of these costs. I also understood the plight of the SNEC families. After much discussion, the three of us agreed to embark on a coup to take over The Arc of Cumberland County. We studied The Arc's bylaws and Robert's rules of order. We carefully planned, arranged, and coordinated an event that took place in the meeting room of our local library. In order for SNEC families to participate in the coup, they had to become Arc members. One of the SNEC moms stood across the street from the library with a picket sign that read, "SNEC families register here." Forty SNEC families received phone calls about the merge prior to the meeting, with instructions to first go to the parent holding to sign, pay fifteen dollars for Arc membership, and then walk across the street as newfound Arc members ready to vote in favor of change.

Also attending the meeting were several of The Arc of North Carolina staff along with the president of The Arc of North Carolina board. To ensure we were conducting ourselves according to the bylaws, we met on several occasions with a local attorney who provided instructions and guidance before and during the meeting.

Since the SNEC director was a paid staff member, we thought it best she take a back seat to the meeting events. Mary and I read carefully planned bullets that ousted the present Arc board and put into position the new Arc of Cumberland County board, consisting of parents of children with disabilities who wanted a change from the annual Arc dance and warehouse placement at sheltered workshops and day programs. Voting was unanimous on each bullet point read. That evening Mary was introduced to the newest Arc members as the new president of The Arc of Cumberland County. The next day the executive director of The Arc of Cumberland County resigned. We obtained the keys to the inaccessible office on the second floor and began moving all Arc documents to the SNEC office. Shortly after, the new Arc of Cumberland County board met to develop an ad to hire the new executive director. After an interview process, I was selected as the executive director of The Arc of Cumberland County.

The entire county had watched with amazement as three mothers orchestrated a coup on behalf of all families of children with disabilities in the county. We were finally in a position to make a change throughout the county. However, this time we were not alone. We took the state affiliate with us in every battle and drew from them support and knowledge as we developed battle plans to make change in a number of areas.

One of the areas of interest to the new Arc of Cumberland County families was education of children with disabilities. There was still a separate school for children with disabilities in Cumberland County, located in the worst part of town. Children who were fortunate enough to be educated in the regular school building were not part of the school activities. Instead they were located in segregated wings or sometimes huts behind the school building. Almost none of the children with disabilities attended their neighborhood schools.

Shortly after purchasing our home in Fayetteville, I met with the principal of the middle school. I introduced myself as a new family to the area and explained that our son, Danny, would be enrolled in her school. She welcomed and commended me for taking the time to meet her. I then explained that Danny had special needs and would need accommodations.

"Danny uses a wheelchair and is presently being educated with a fourth-grade class during PE, art, music and science with a one-on-one aide."

"Oh," she gasped. "If he uses a wheelchair, he won't go here. He'd go to Walker Spivy School."

"No, ma'am. We bought our home in your school district. He will go here."

"We can't accommodate him here. That school is set up for kids like your son. We are not."

"Ma'am, my son is going to this school. I would be happy to begin meeting with your staff to help with implementing whatever accommodations are needed."

"I will have to talk to the exceptional children's director about this," she barked.

"Yes, ma'am."

I left the office knowing full well this would be a major battle. Shortly after, I began communicating with the exceptional children's director from hell.

Chapter 8

Special Education Injustice Exposed

While I challenged our neighborhood school to comply with the Individuals with Disabilities Education Act (IDEA) The Arc of Cumberland County board of directors decided to review the 1992 Cumberland County exceptional children's audit conducted by the North Carolina Department of Public Instruction (DPI). The Arc of Cumberland County then approached school administrators regarding the results and was told things had improved with a few exceptions. To see if the comments of the school administrators were correct, The Arc of Cumberland County conducted a survey of seventy-five families of children with disabilities educated in the Cumberland County exceptional children's program. There was a definite correlation between North Carolina issues reported in the DPI audit and the results of The Arc's survey. According to the parents surveyed, things had not changed, as the school administrators would have liked us to believe. The Arc of Cumberland County decided to hold a public meeting. A large meeting room was secured at the local arts council. TV, newspaper, and radio media were invited along with school administrators and school board members. The Arc of Cumberland County families were all invited to the event. Once again our state affiliate was witness to the presentation. Over forty-five people attended the meeting. During the presentation, we shared the DPI audit results and the family survey results, pointing out how the audit deficiencies were still issues experienced by children with disabilities in our county schools. The 1997/1998 Cumberland

County audit results were as follows:

Records Reviewed	92
Records in Compliance	32
Records Out of Compliance	60

Highlights of Monitoring Report: It was reported that children with disabilities arrive late or leave earlier than non-disabled students. During interviews, several parents reported that Extended School Year (ESY) was not discussed at all and in two records ESY was not considered according to documentation. Twelve records indicated that the three-year evaluation was not done in a timely manner. Twelve records showed no evidence that the parents had been involved. Fifty-two classes exceeded the pupil/teacher ratio standard. Forty-five students were expelled from thirteen to twenty-seven days with no team meeting. Thirty individuals, either teachers or related service providers, had an expired license or no license.

The Arc of Cumberland County's concern with the education of children with disabilities received radio, TV, and newspaper coverage. In addition we took this issue one step further and asked the following questions: What kind of follow-up was provided in regard to the audit findings? Were corrective action plans developed? If so, by whom? Who monitors the corrective action plans? What good is a law if it is not being enforced? If the monitoring and accountability part of the law is lacking in any way, the implementation of the law will be flawed.

These questions led us to a presentation to The Arc of North Carolina board of directors with a request that The Arc of North Carolina review the DPI audit results for all 118 North Carolina school districts. As a result of the request, the state Arc board of directors assigned the education committee and support staff to the project of reviewing and compiling audit results for all 118 North Carolina school systems. The Arc of North Carolina education committee review results were published in a report entitled *The North Carolina Department of Public Instruction Exceptional Children's Program Audit System by System: SO THIS IS WHAT WE GET AFTER 25 YEARS OF "PROGRESS"?*

The report was presented to The Arc of North Carolina board of directors and membership at the 1998 annual convention.

The following was part of the report's introduction.

"During the summer of 1997, The Arc of Cumberland County reviewed the 1992 Cumberland County Exceptional Children's audit by the North Carolina Department of Public Instructions (DPI). The Arc then approached school administrators regarding the results and was told that things had improved with a few exceptions. The Arc surveyed the families of 75 children in exceptional programs and presented the results to the Board of Education. The Arc of Cumberland County was invited to be present at the Exit Oral Report of the 1998 DPI audit. This audit not only confirmed the results of the 1997 parent survey, but also shows a recurrence of the non-compliance issues from the 1992 audit. The 93.8% rating received from DPI in 1997 did not appear to be in line with the results. Denise Mercado, executive director of The Arc of Cumberland County, brought this to the attention of The Arc of NC's Board of Directors. They in turn charged the Children's Issues/Education Committee with obtaining the audits of each school system and determining statewide trends of compliance/noncompliance issues."

The introduction continued.

"A review of the statewide summary reveals some disturbing trends. The most glaring concern occurs in the section covering the Individual Education Plan (IEP). With the IEP being the basis for a child to be successful we found it appalling that so many gross non-compliance issues would fall in this category. Compenents of the IEP were found to be non-compliant for such items as goals and objectives not being specific to the child's disability or not written in a manner that could produce clear measurable results. Some folders were found to have no IEPs and many placements were made without the required people or evaluations in place to make the decision. Clearly, LEAs (local education agencies) need more training in the development of IEPs. With the recent reauthorization of IDEA, intensive training would seem timely.

"Our committee seriously questioned whether the audit results in the area of Least Restrictive Environment are a true reflection of what is taking place for students with disabilities. Given the high number of self-contained classes, the existence of several segregated schools and the growing parental unrest regarding inclusion, it is difficult to believe that over 85% of the students are being served in the least restrictive environment. The same skepticism exists with students attending the neighborhood schools that they would attend if they were not disabled. Nearly 90% of the systems are reported to be in compliance in this area, something committee members, Arc staff and advocates know not to be the case.

"It also appears that many Administrative Placement Committees (APC) have been 'rubber stamping' the results of the School Based Committee (SBC). In most of the compliance issues involved, the same records appeared to have been non-compliant with both committees. With the reauthorization of IDEA, these committees will be eliminated and parents will have greater involvement in placement decisions.

"These and other concerns led the committee to pose a number of questions to the Department of Public Instruction.

"What DOES it really mean to be Compliant or Non-Compliant?

"What does it mean to be in compliance with LRE (least restrictive environment) when the system has 90+% of exceptional children in self-contained classes or self-contained school settings?

"How meaningful is each audit to DPI in knowing how an LEA is operating?

"What conclusions can our committee draw from the audits?

"How does the audit address the substantive entitlements provided by IDEA?

"The Arc of North Carolina and its chapters across the state have the ability to reach an extraordinary number of people concerned with the education of children with disabilities. We must educate the parents and caregivers as never before. Parents and others who know their rights and who know what their children are entitled to must not continue to let the school systems get by with the gross violations of IDEA compliance issues we have found in these reports.

"The committee surmised that there are a number of reasons parents may not be advocating for their children with disabilities. There are:

Those who don't know there is a system.

Those who don't know how to use the system.

Those who do not care to use the system.

Those who have used the system and are 'burned out' because of it.

Those who are trusting the system to do right by their child.

Those who know how to use the system.

"History shows that a statewide effort of working through local representatives to the North Carolina General Assembly to create incentives for compliance with audits is very necessary. How many of our schools that have 'met standards' or are 'exemplary' or are 'schools of distinction' have the violations we have seen from the most recent audits of exceptional children's programs? We feel that the standards to achieve the state's ABCs accountability incentives should also include the audit of Exceptional Children's records in any school before it is labeled as EXEMPLARY or SCHOOL OF DISTINCTION. The burden will therefore be on all teachers, not just those who teach students not exempted from the End of Grade and End of Course testing.

"The non-compliance issues monitored by the audit are for the most part the responsibility of the teachers and the SBC (School Based Committee) as it existed. School administrators must know that we need the very best teachers available. They must put in place standards and checks to make sure the personnel are writing and following through on the very best IEP for each child with a disability in North Carolina.

"Our work has just started...again."

The Arc report also included a follow up letter from the North Carolina exceptional children's director addressing the questions posed by The Arc committee. Below are excerpts from this letter.

"Appropriate staff and I have reviewed the recent letter in which you posed several questions with regard to the Exceptional Children Division's monitoring process. As you are aware, the Office of Special Education Programs requires that the State Education Agency Department of Public Instruction (DPI) monitor local education agencies to ensure compliance with federal and state laws and regulations. Our monitoring/audit process is designed to comply with this requirement. It has been reviewed and approved by OSEP (Office of Special Education Programs) on two occasions, during their compliance visit in 1991 and again in 1995. The on-going analysis of the results of our monitoring visits leads to continuous refinements and improvements to the process. We believe that we have a monitoring system that is one of the most effective in the country. We welcome your interest, and our responses to your specific questions follow.

"How does the audit process improve the substantive entitlements of IDEA?

"The audit process has resulted in improvement in special education programs in the individual school systems. First, we have seen significant improvement in IEPs. The present levels of performance, annual goals, and short term instructional objectives/benchmarks are vastly superior to those founding IEPs in the previous five year cycle. During their 1995 compliance visit, team members from OSEP (Office of Special Education Programs) remarked that they were seeing some of the best IEPs they had seen anywhere. This is a far cry from their findings in 1990, when such annual goals as 'Will improve reading' were common. We completed a training of trainers IEP staff development activity in April, 1998 during which staff provided intensive IEP training for three people in each of the LEAs (local education agencies), state operated programs, and charter schools. We are seeing justifications for least restrictive environment decisions that truly address the issues. However, we will continue to monitor IEPs closely during this school year.

"Protection of parent rights is another area where we have seen great improvement. It is rare that we find evaluations and placements completed without written parental permission. The attempts to involve the parent at appropriate times have also improved. School systems appear to make diligent efforts to invite parents, reschedule meetings at parent request, and schedule meetings at times that are convenient to parents. It is not unusual to find teachers at a 5 p.m. meeting that lasts for two to three hours, or at early morning meetings.

"The monitoring process investigates other areas much more closely than ever before. Examples are length of the school day, participation in extra-curricular activities, age appropriate settings, and access to physical education. The LEAs (local education agencies) do an excellent job in providing multidisciplinary evaluations that are used in establishing eligibility.

"On site interviews with parents, teachers and administrators are a relatively new component of the monitoring process which has provided us with invaluable information that we were unable to obtain before. It is through the interviews that we find out that sometimes the services in the IEP are not being delivered, or that signatures can appear rather mysteriously on committee documents, or that placements can sometimes be made without considering the effects on the student, or the requirement of the law. In some instances, interviews are the only way to substantiate that certain actions are occurring or not occurring, and when it results in non-compliance, we can cite it."

The director's letter continued with another question posed by The Arc.

"What does it mean to be "in compliance?" For example, the least restrictive environment is an area in which nearly all LEAs (local education agencies) are 'in compliance'. However, we (The Arc) know how many school systems have mostly self-contained classes, some have segregated schools and an overwhelming majority discourage inclusive practices. This goes beyond a continuum of services. By the letter of the law ('extent possible'), they are in compliance, but in practice – in particular best practice – many allow programs to drive placement."

The director's response to this question is as follows.

"The Division has no authority to overturn a decision that is made by a duly constituted committee of persons who are knowledgeable about the child. Decisions about appropriateness of services, including setting, are made by such committees. When there is a disagreement, the appropriate avenue of resolution is mediation or a contested case hearing (due process hearing). The monitors, along with their teams, have made some LRE (least restrictive environment) calls in the past year because the interviews have allowed us to ask direct questions of parents and school staff. As we continue using interviews we expect we will make additional citations. In our zeal to embrace inclusion, we sometimes forget, as practitioners, that inclusion is a methodological term, basically a philosophy, and is not included in law. Separate schools and self-contained classes are, however, a part of the continuum as defined in law.

"Monitoring deals with compliance with the law, not best practice. It is important to remember, however, that part of the Division's mission is the promotion of best practice. The Areas of Exceptionalities Section has done several on-site visits in the past two years to review programs and to make recommendations for the improvement, as well as the establishment, of programs, including looking at separate programs with an eye to making them less restrictive. These activities are different from monitoring, because the Division cannot mandate that any LEA (local education agency) implement any of the recommendations that are contained in the final report. 'Strongly recommend' or 'strongly encourage' do not have the force of law, and in times of limited resources – including building space, classrooms, and staff – school systems may have other priorities."

The Arc's questions continued.

"Considering the above questions, what conclusions do you want us to draw from the audit reports?"

The director's response as noted in the letter:

"Basically, LEAs (local education agencies) are in compliance with federal and state laws and regulations.

"The primary focus on accountability and high student achievement is the second area of contention for special educators. IDEA '97 (Individuals with Disabilities Education Act) requires the participation of students with disabilities in the statewide assessment program unless it is clearly inappropriate. At the same time, the pressure on teachers and principals to report student scores that will result in bonus monies for school staff may intensify the efforts to exclude students with disabilities who might not perform as well as non-disabled students.

"Thank you for your interest in children with disabilities."

This letter was signed by the North Carolina director of the exceptional children division.

The North Carolina Department of Public Instruction audits of 1993 through 1998 showed the following:

Length of School Day – **44.9% noncompliant**

Extended School Year – **52.5% noncompliant**

Persons Involved in Writing the IEP – **62.7% noncompliant**

Components of the IEP – **90.7% noncompliant**

IEP Timeliness – **61.9% noncompliant**

Parent Participation – **73.7% noncompliant**

Prior Written Notice/Consent – **56.4% noncompliant**

Content of Notice – **74.4% noncompliant**

As stated so honestly by The Arc of North Carolina in their report, **"Our work has just started – AGAIN!"**

The attitude toward people with disabilities, their parents, and their families begins with the school system. Families learn early on that in order for their child to receive an education and not just a babysitting service, a family must learn and study special education law.

Families must also learn to overcome intimidation tactics that begin with IEP meetings as you sit alone across from a team, outnumbered by professionals who many times bring their supervisors for support. Unfortunately the school system is only the beginning. The attitudes and tactics continue as the family accesses needed services from other bureaucracies.

Chapter 9

Self-Determination in North Carolina

Despite my new role as executive director of The Arc of Cumberland County, I was able to remain on schedule with college graduation. I began college for the second time in 1995 at thirty-eight years of age. I started over with my sights on law school. I took a full set of classes each semester, except for one summer. The summer of '97 was dedicated to The Arc of Cumberland County takeover. Once that was completed, I was back to a full set of classes. Finally in May 1999, I graduated from Campbell University. My husband insisted I walk for my diploma as payback for making him do the same years earlier. My parents flew in from New York for the occasion. They sat in the audience in tears. My mom cried, "I waited twenty-five years for this day." Well, better late than never. It was a proud day for all of us.

With 11,000 dollars in student loans, it was time to find a higher paying job. One day a letter came across my desk from the North Carolina Developmental Disabilities Council announcing the start of five self-determination projects in North Carolina. Each project would have a project director and a project manager. Shortly after, I received notice that one of the projects would be a joint effort between the Orange/Person/Chatham area program and Easter Seals North Carolina. Knowing Easter Seals was involved, I immediately wanted to be a part of this endeavor. I applied for the project manager position with Easter Seals. After a long interview process, I was selected as the project manager for one of the North Carolina self-determination projects.

Self-determination is an excellent concept that shifts control from the bureaucracy to the individual with the disability and his or her family. When I first learned of this concept I thought to myself, "This will never happen." I could not envision the bureaucracy letting go and allowing families to be in control of dollars that supported them. As it turned out, after almost three years of trying, the five self-determination projects in North Carolina failed and were dismantled. Everyone seemed to be struggling with how to implement the principles of self-determination. The focus for the projects was the North Carolina Medicaid waiver – CAP MR/DD. The principles that challenged all of us were:

Freedom – the exercise of the same rights as all citizens. People with disabilities with assistance (when necessary) will establish where they want to live, with whom they want to live, and how their time will be occupied. They do not have to trade their inalienable rights guaranteed under the Constitution for support or services.

Authority – the control over whatever sums of money are needed for one's own support, including the reprioritizing of these dollars when necessary. This is accomplished through the development of an individual budget that "moves" with the person.

Support – the organization of these resources as determined by the person with a disability. This means that individuals do not receive "supervision" and "staffing." Instead folks with disabilities may seek companionship for support and contract for any number of discrete tasks for which they need assistance.

Responsibility – the wise use of public dollars. Dollars are now being used as an investment in a person's life and not handled as resources to purchase services or slots. Responsibility includes the ordinary obligations of citizens and allows individuals to contribute to their communities in meaningful ways.

It was very easy for me as a parent of a child with a disability to understand these principles. As I realized much later on, my mistake was looking to the bureaucracy for permission to implement these principles.

As I fulfilled my role as project manager, I still had my sights on law school. I couldn't afford to leave my full-time job and pay for law school. I had already accumulated 11,000 dollars in student loans.

North Carolina Central University is the only university in North Carolina that offered an evening law school program. I attended the orientation and decided to apply. I began studying for the LSAT and enrolled in a Kaplan course to prepare further. The LSAT is a timed test. I could eventually figure out the answers to the questions, but I had great difficulty doing so within the timeframe allowed.

I took the LSAT at Fayetteville State University. I remember saying a prayer before entering the classroom. I had never learned to overcome the timer, which made the testing period very difficult. After paper and pencils were collected, I left the classroom. To my wonderful surprise, waiting on the other side of the classroom door was my husband. I fell into his arms and began to cry. Although his words were encouraging, I knew the last few brain cells left from four years of college nights were completely fried. I did not feel confident about my performance on this test. As I completed the admission process with North Carolina Central University, I wondered if this was truly what God wanted me to do. As it turned out, I was not accepted to the evening program but was encouraged to reapply for the day program. Due to personal finances, the day program was not an option.

Chapter 10

OCR – Waste of Time

By this time Danny was no longer in school. We took him out of school at age eighteen after filing a complaint with the Office of Civil Rights (OCR). Danny attended a high school in Cumberland County that was not his neighborhood school. But as we learned in the IEP world, although the IEP team makes decisions that are based on the child's educational needs, families are expected to negotiate and compromise in order to ensure the child's educational needs are met. In the spirit of compromise, we approved Danny's placement in an OHI (Other Health Impaired) classroom in a high school outside his neighborhood school. The IEP team agreed to provide a one-on-one aide and mainstreaming opportunities in this high school setting. This unfortunately was not offered in our neighborhood high school. After sending Danny to school one morning, I decided to go to the school to see how he was doing. Danny was not himself that morning and I thought he might have been fighting a cold. It was a cold, wintry morning. As a result Danny left for school bundled in a coat, hat, and gloves. When I arrived at the school Danny was sitting in his wheelchair with his coat, hat, and gloves still on. The teacher was busy with paperwork. I asked the teacher, "Was the bus late?" He said, "No, it arrived on time." That means the bus had arrived at school forty-five minutes earlier. I then asked, "Where is Veronica?" Veronica was Danny's one-on-one aide. The teacher then informed me that Veronica was out sick. I then asked who would be Danny's one-one-one aide today. The teacher said, "I guess I will. I am short-staffed today."

It was obvious to me on that particular day Danny was not going to get the attention he needed for educational goals. I don't know how many other days this same scenario occurred. I took Danny home and immediately called the exceptional children's director. Amazed that the question was necessary, I asked, "What is the contingency plan when the one-on-one aide is out sick?" Much to my surprise, there was no contingency plan. I asked the EC director, "When a regular teacher is out sick, are the students sent home or are they expected to educate themselves?" I explained that appropriate accommodations as determined by the IEP team include a one-on-one aide. Without this accommodation, Danny could not function in school. This too had been determined by the IEP team. Again I asked, "When this accommodation is not available to Danny, what is the plan?" As usual, I received a typical bureaucratic answer. "Mrs. Mercado, I will look into this and get back with you."

I didn't send Danny back to school until the one-on-one aide was back on duty. I continued, however, to press the issue with the EC director. He had no backup plan and was stalling to provide one. Shortly after the incident I filed a complaint with the Office of Civil Rights (OCR). It was my belief this situation violated my son's civil rights. The IEP had clearly defined an appropriate education for Danny, along with the support he needed to participate in education. School was in session. Danny was not sick but was ready to learn. The support he needed from the school, however, was unavailable and therefore he could not attend. OCR agreed with my logic; however, they offered no support in the complaint process except to schedule the meeting between our family and the school. I was very disappointed in this system. I learned through other families that this was another drastic flaw of the bureaucracy that continued to prevent children with disabilities from getting the education they needed. Once again I found myself sitting across the table from an array of school officials. This time, however, the school board attorney was present. After a two-hour process the contingency plan was developed and became an addendum to Danny's IEP.

As I endured many of these frustrating processes, a comforting thought was that I was setting a precedent for future students so that no other child with a disability would have to sit in a coat, hat, and gloves for forty-five minutes or longer because adults did not take into consideration backup plans to accommodate the students. As comforting as this thought seemed to be, it was far from reality. Several years later one of Danny's support staff members at home continues to battle the same injustice with her son. This child has little to no cognitive disabilities. He does, however, have a severe lung and heart condition that requires twenty-four-hour oxygen and a special heart- and lung-monitoring system. The IEP team decided he needed an RN one-on-one support staff. This accommodation is written into his IEP. However, whenever the RN is out sick or the RN's children are home sick, or the RN is on vacation, or the RN has to leave school early, this child is not allowed to attend school. The principal and assistant principal have stood guard at the school door and will not allow the student in the school building if the RN is absent. The mom has spoken with the EC director and the director of nursing. No contingency plan is in place. Both the EC director and director of nursing were on staff when I filed the OCR complaint on behalf of Danny. They were both aware of the results of the complaint and participated in the development of the contingency plan. But what we did for our son was not considered a precedent for other students, and so the madness continues. This student loses days of education every year because there is no contingency plan. This same student scored a thirty-five percent on his last spelling test. A lack of contingency plan has a tremendous impact on this child's education and his future. Yet funding continues to come down the pike on behalf of this student because this student is enrolled.

Chapter 11

No Fiscal Responsibility!

The North Carolina Medicaid waiver, CAP MR/DD, was not only the primary focus of the self-determination projects, but it became my primary focus in general as well.

Shortly after the fight to obtain the slot was over, I mistakenly received a bill for $10,960.70. This bill came from the supply agency that provided diapers, gloves, underpads, G-tubes, Ensure, and syringes for our son. A simple phone call to the supply agency resulted in apologies for sending the bill. However, it sparked curiosity of costs for the items being provided.

Prior to receiving CAP MR/DD funding, John and I provided the supplies Danny needed. It was a financial burden that almost pushed us into bankruptcy. We were able to improvise on some things. For example, we checked with Danny's doctor about using Carnation instant breakfast mix instead of Ensure. But when it came to diapers, there was no substituting. We used cloth diapers as much as we could at home, which was very difficult on an eleven-year-old. But in order for Danny to go to school, we had to use the disposable diapers. By this time Danny had outgrown the extra-large Pampers that were available in the army commissary. While reading an issue of *Exceptional Parent* magazine, I noticed an ad from HDIS (Home Delivery Incontinent Services) in Minneapolis. At a little over fifty dollars per case, the diapers from this company were the cheapest we had found anywhere. They were also the best quality. At one point my parents even chipped in to the "Danny Diaper Fund." We were so grateful when we finally received CAP MR/DD funding. However, the ten-thousand-dollar bill revealed a practice of the North Carolina Medicaid system that seemed unjust and unnecessary to taxpayers. The same case of diapers provided by the North Carolina agency was $98.22 per case. This was almost double what we were paying through HDIS. I immediately called the Cumberland County Mental Health Center and explained the discrepancy. Again the reply was, "We will check into this and get back with you." After a week of waiting I climbed the chain of command and sent my letter of concern to the CAP MR/DD coordinator at the state level. As it turned out, a contract could not be set up with the Minneapolis agency. Only North Carolina agencies could be part of the contract list. The question of letting the family be reimbursed for purchasing diapers at a cheaper cost was definitely out of the question. The bureaucracy could not fathom trusting families to do this. They squawked, saying it would not be fiscally responsible to put taxpayer dollars directly in the hands of families. So the tax dollars go into the hands of bureaucrats who do not do a good job of comparison shopping. As a result costs are high. This same dilemma was shared by many families of much younger children who were in the regular Pamper sizes. Once these families receive waiver funding, the diapers are supplied by North Carolina agencies at a cost double that of Wal-Mart or Food Lion. Families would beg their case managers to let them buy these items using CAP dollars. But the bureaucracy would not hear of it. Families could not continue to bear the financial burden of purchasing these items and were grateful, as we were, for waiver dollars. However, we all struggled with the excessive, unnecessary cost of items once on this program.

As I researched further into the cost of the supplies provided to our son, I noticed the rate for personal care services and respite. At the time Danny began receiving services, the rate for both personal care services and respite was $10.80 per hour. In a conversation with my home staff I learned that the provider agency was providing a wage of $5.50 per hour for these services. Being naïve to the business side of providing services, I sent a letter to the provider agency asking for an explanation as to why the wage was so low. Easter Seals North Carolina was our provider agency at the time. I trusted this organization explicitly. This was the agency that had saved my life. Easter Seals North Carolina was the lead agency for the Partners in Policymaking Program (PIP) in North Carolina. They provided competent support staff for Danny in my home so I could attend these monthly PIP classes. The response to my request for an explanation came in a three-page letter that specifically outlined payroll tax, worker's compensation insurance, and the training costs required for each direct care staff member. The costs seemed rather high, but this was prior to shifting control to families.

As the years went on there was a slight increase in the rate of personal care services and respite, but as families we were never made aware of an increase in wages to our staff as a result of the increase in the rate. Wages were considered confidential information. Employees were discouraged from sharing wage information with the family and were disciplined if they did. Again, this was before control shifted to families.

It wasn't until 2001 that we saw a decrease in the cost of diapers. Each year, beginning in 1994, Danny's cost summary averaged ninety-six dollars per case of diapers. Finally in 2000 the cost for the same case of diapers was $38.75. It had taken the bureaucracy six years to respond to a request to save money.

While fighting for cost efficiency with waiver dollars, The Arc of North Carolina was planning its 2001 convention. The Arc decided to hold its annual convention in Myrtle Beach, South Carolina in conjunction with the South Carolina Arc chapters. All The Arc of North Carolina members would be crossing state lines to attend the convention. Many adults with disabilities, in order to attend, had to travel with support staff. The state informed all individuals receiving waiver funding that they could not use waiver funding to travel out of state. A barrage of e-mails from families, adults with disabilities, and The Arc staff provided scenarios to help the bureaucracy understand that crossing state lines did not change the disability and that, more importantly, as Americans we should not be confined to any particular state. Finally in July 2001 the results of unified advocacy efforts produced a letter from the division of medical assistance stating the following:

"These guidelines are to be used when families/individuals are traveling out of state. These services are for family members/individuals who have been receiving services from direct care staff while in state and who are unable to travel without their assistance. These guidelines only apply to individuals who do not live in residential facilities.

"Provider Agencies employing staff who would be involved in this process must give written prior approval of this request for their staff to accompany families/individuals out of state. Provider Agencies must ensure staffing needs of all their clients can be met. Provider Agencies must continue to provide supervision and monitoring of care. If the Provider Agency can meet all these responsibilities and approve the request for staff to travel with a client the following Medicaid guidelines must be followed:

"Treatment plans must not be changed to increase services while out of state.

"Services can only be reimbursed to the extent they were provided within the state's boundaries and for the benefit of the individual.

"Respite, based on the definition, would not be an appropriate service since the care giver is present during the travel.

"If licensed professionals are involved, Medicaid cannot waive other state licensure laws. A North Carolina licensed professional may or may not be licensed to practice in another state.

"Medicaid will not be responsible for room, board or transportation cost.

"Provider Agencies must assume all liability for their staff while out of state."

Although this letter was a step in the right direction, it displayed the bureaucracy's lack of common sense and mistrust of people with disabilities and their families.

First, the guidelines, as indicated in the first paragraph, only apply to individuals who do not live in a residential facility. Aren't individuals living in residential facilities Americans? Why are they being confined to the state? Why are these individuals not allowed to travel freely throughout the United States like the rest of us?

Second, although the bureaucracy maintained control, it shifted responsibility to the provider agency.

Third, as noted in the following scenario, the restriction of respite makes no sense to families. The following e-mail was received from a family member.

"Denise, here's a scenario to consider. I drive to Myrtle Beach with my son's direct care staff on Thursday afternoon (no one is billed).

When we arrive, I go to the hotel lounge and the caregiver stays in the room with my son (we bill three hours respite). At 7:00 a.m. on Friday the caregiver gets my son up and works on training goals (billing takes place same as home). At the end of day we all go out to eat (no one is billed for this time). I play miniature golf after dinner while my son and his staff go to the arcade (we bill four hours of respite). Saturday morning we drive home (no billing). Shouldn't this work?"

I forwarded this e-mail to the assistant director of the Division of Medical Assistance. The response received was as follows: "The guidelines indicate that respite is not to be used while traveling out of state." The family's scenario was a perfect example of how to use respite while on vacation.

So far we had learned that the bureaucracy moves at a snails pace. When the bureaucracy finally moves, there is no guarantee it will move in the direction that makes sense or go as far as families need it to go.

To ensure the experiences we faced in the disability world were finally written down, John and I decided to spend quiet, relaxing vacations, giving me an opportunity to write this book. Many chapters of this book were written at a Sandals Resort in Montego Bay, Jamaica. As I wrote this book on my laptop, with papers flying in the warm Jamaica breeze, my husband sparked a conversation with a couple from Yorkshire, England. Much to our surprise, our encounter with the bureaucracy was no different from their battles on behalf of their thirty-five-year-old daughter with cerebral palsy. The husband talked about turning down job opportunities because he would lose services if he moved out of a certain area. The wife talked about writing letter after letter and an exhausting process to make even the smallest progress. This confirmed my premise that there is no utopia anywhere. The United States and England are two civilized countries. Yet the treatment experienced by families of children with disabilities is far from civilized.

Chapter 12

What Is This EPSDT Thing?

The little skirmishes we experienced with the bureaucracy thus far were no comparison to the battle we encountered with EPSDT. By this time the supplies Danny received on a regular basis were diapers, Ensure, blue pads, a suction machine, G-tubes, a pulse oximeter machine, a feeding pump, and an oxygen concentrator. He also received his wheelchair and bathing equipment as a one-time purchase. In addition to the equipment and regular supplies, Danny received personal care services, respite, and training services which over the years changed names from community inclusion, to supported living, and home and community supports.

In March, 2001 the state in their infamous wisdom raised the rates for services but did not raise the maximum amount available for CAP MR/DD recipients. The maximum annual dollar amount allowed for CAP recipients at the time was $68,000. Those recipients like my son with extensive needs were sitting at the $68,000 maximum level when the rates for services were raised. As a result the state sent case managers to families to inquire what services or supplies the family wanted to cut from their loved one's cost summary.

When my case manager asked the question her discomfort was obvious. Unlike many professionals higher on the chain who made decisions that impacted our son, our case manager met Danny and knew his needs were extensive. I refused to answer her question. Instead I asked for a meeting with her supervisor. At the Cumberland County

Mental Health Center (CCMH), I met with the CAP coordinator and the case manager. I asked for clarification as to the request made by the case manager. The CAP coordinator explained the increase in rates made it necessary for families to make this difficult decision. I then asked the CAP coordinator which she would cut if it were her son, "the oxygen or the feeding pump?" She was quick to respond that person-centered planning did not allow her to make that decision. Because of person-centered planning, the decision was to be made by the person or the person's family. I still refused to give a response to this ridiculous request. Before leaving the room, the CAP coordinator reminded me that my decision needed to be made quickly. The area programs were instructed to have the information to the state by April 1, leaving us less than one month to find a resolution.

This encounter taught me that although the bureaucracy moved at a snail's pace, they required all others, including families, to respond quickly. The bureaucracy requires months and sometimes years to formulate a decision but will never give people with disabilities and their families the same leeway. As families we constantly struggle with the length of time the bureaucracy takes to make decisions, because it is our children's lives and our families' lives that are put on hold.

After meeting with the Cumberland County CAP coordinator, I sat in my office staring at my son's cost summary. I started looking very carefully at each of the supply items, wondering how I was going to put these items back in my personal budget without going into further debt. I was unable to give up any of the services, because the services allowed me to work and pay off the enormous debt we had accumulated while waiting for waiver approval. What were my alternatives, I wondered. If we did not remove something from the budget to accommodate the increased rates and remain within the $68,000 maximum, we would lose CAP services altogether. If I lost this funding source, we would have no choice but to put Danny in a residential facility. It would be Indiana all over again and neither John nor I wanted that heartache. In tears, I realized the state was putting my son at "risk of institutionalization."

As I thought about the five state-run institutions in our state, I wondered if any of the parents of those children and adults were asked to cut services. When a child is placed in an institution in North Carolina, the state guarantees twenty-four-hour care along with medical and educational opportunities. What guarantees do we have? We are saving the state hundreds of thousands of dollars each year by keeping our children at home. Yet when the budget gets tight, the bureaucracy looks to us rather than the institutions.

The term *risk of institutionalization* immediately brought to mind the Olmstead ruling.

A letter dated January 14, 2000 sent from the director of CMS (Center for Medicare & Medicaid Services) and the director of OCR (Office of Civil Rights) best describes the Olmstead ruling and its challenge to all states. This letter was addressed to all Medicaid state directors. An excerpt from the letter is as follows.

"The Olmstead case was brought by two Georgia women whose disabilities include mental retardation and mental illness. At the time the suit was filed, both plaintiffs lived in State-run institutions, despite the fact that their treatment professionals had determined that they could be appropriately served in a community setting. The plaintiffs asserted that continued institutionalization was a violation of their right under the ADA (Americans with Disabilities Act) to live in the most integrated setting appropriate. The Olmstead decision interpreted Title II of the ADA and its implementing regulation, which oblige States to administer their services, programs, and activities 'in the most integrated setting appropriate to the needs of qualified individuals with disabilities.' (28CFR35.130(d)). In doing so, the Supreme Court answered the fundamental question whether it is discrimination to deny people with disabilities services in the most integrated setting appropriate. The Court stated directly that 'Unjustified isolation….is properly regarded as discrimination based on disability.' It observed that (a) 'institutional placement of persons who can handle and benefit from community settings perpetuates unwarranted assumptions that persons so isolated are incapable or unworthy of participating in community life,' and (b) 'confinement in an institution severely diminishes the everyday life activities of individuals, including family relations, social contacts, work options, economic independence, educational advancement, and cultural enrichment.'

"Under the Court's decision, States are required to provide community-based services for persons with disabilities who would otherwise be entitled to institutional services when: (a) the State's treatment professionals reasonably determine that such placement is appropriate; (b) the affected persons do not oppose such treatment; and (c) the placement can be reasonably accommodated, taking into account the resources available to the State and the needs of others who are receiving State-supported disability services. The Court cautioned, however, that nothing in the ADA (Americans with Disabilities Act) condones termination of institutional settings for persons unable to handle or benefit from community settings. Moreover, the State's responsibility, once it provides community-based treatment to qualified persons with disabilities, is not unlimited.

"Under the ADA, States are obliged to 'make reasonable modifications in policies, practices, or procedures when the modifications are necessary to avoid discrimination on the basis of disability, unless the public entity can demonstrate that making the modifications would fundamentally alter the nature of the service, program, or activity.' (28CFR35.130(b)(7)). The Supreme Court indicated that the test as to whether a modification entails 'fundamental alterations' of a program takes into account three factors: the cost of providing services to the individual in the most integrated setting appropriate; the resources available to the State; and how the provision of services affects the ability of the State to meet the needs of others with disabilities. Significantly, the Court suggests that a State could establish compliance with title II of the ADA if it demonstrates that it has (a) a comprehensive, effectively working plan for placing qualified persons with disabilities in less restrictive settings, and (b) a waiting list that moves at a reasonable pace not controlled by the State's endeavors to keep its institutions fully populated.

"Olmstead challenges States to **prevent** and correct inappropriate institutionalization and to review intake and admissions processes to assure that persons with disabilities are served in the most integrated setting appropriate."

The Olmstead ruling was an important ruling for Americans with disabilities. I remember reading and printing from the Internet volumes of information about this ruling. The revelation of *risk of institutionalization* reminded me of an Amici Curiae brief written by an attorney who represented three important disability organizations: ADAPT, National Council on Independent Living, and TASH. I dug through my files for this document. Once found, I noticed on the front cover the name, address, and phone number for the attorney. I immediately dialed the phone. After barely one ring the attorney answered. I was stunned to hear his voice and stammered to explain my situation. Before I got very far in my explanation, he interrupted and asked, "How old is your son?" It was March 2001, shortly before Danny's nineteenth birthday. The attorney replied rather emphatically, "This is not Olmstead. This is EPSDT." After a long pause I asked, "What the hell is that?" I couldn't help myself. I had never heard this before. I don't know why I was so surprised. After all, we were in the dark for eleven years before we ever learned of the waiver.

The attorney went on to explain the acronym EPSDT, – Early Periodic Screening, Diagnosis, and Treatment. He then instructed me to research the Social Security Act, section 1905. I took copious notes as he shed light on this issue. Before hanging up the phone I asked, "As I research this and find this pertains to my son, how do I get the state to move on this?" Because he was located in Pennsylvania he wasn't as readily available to us as we would have liked. "There is an outstanding Medicaid attorney right in your back yard," he shared. He went on to tell me about the National Health Law Program and offered to speak with their attorney about my issue and ask that they call me. I thanked the ADAPT attorney profusely. God was truly navigating my way. Immediately I began researching as instructed. I went to the Social Security website (www.ssa.gov). EPSDT is part of the Social Security Act, Title XIX, Section 1905(r). EPSDT provides medically necessary services and supports to children under the age of twenty-one who have a Medicaid card. Section 1905(r) gives reference to Section 1905(a). In Section 1905(a) a laundry list of services available to children under the age of twenty-one is provided. These services include occupational therapy, physical therapy, speech/language pathology, personal care services, home health care services, case management, preventive and rehabilitation services, etc.

At this point I was quite anxious to speak with the National Health Law Program attorney. Although I believed the ADAPT attorney would do as he said and call the National Health Law Program on my behalf, I wasn't willing to wait, especially after reading Section 1905(a). With only a first and last name to go on, I called information. Much to my surprise, the telephone number was readily available. After only two rings the National Health Law Program attorney answered the phone with cookie batter on her hands. She was right in the middle of baking cookies with her daughter but was very interested in talking with me further. She gave me her office number and asked that I call her in the morning.

After speaking at length with the National Health Law Program attorney the next day, she faxed me several letters from the Health Care Financing Administration (HCFA). HCFA is now known as CMS (Center for Medicare and Medicaid Services). One of the letters faxed was dated September 18, 1990. The letter was sent to all Title XIX state agencies and addressed the "monetary cap on services provided under the EPSDT program." The letter reads as follows and can be found in its entirety in Appendix A.

"After April 1, 1990, the effective date of Section 6403 of the Omnibus Budget Reconciliation Act of 1989, States must provide any medically necessary service to a child if the service is found to be needed as a result of EPSDT screening services.................**Overall monetary limits or caps may not be set which could prevent the provision of medically necessary services under EPSDT.**"

This letter seemed to provide the answer to my dilemma. Danny received a Medicaid card as a result of the Medicaid waiver. The Medicaid card provides him with all the benefits of Medicaid to include EPSDT. Screenings and assessments were done at the time of enrollment in the Medicaid waiver to determine services and medically necessary supplies and equipment. Danny was under twenty-one years of age at the time and therefore qualified for EPSDT services. His oxygen and feeding pump are most definitely medically necessary items. Therefore, according to this letter, Danny should be able to keep that equipment even if it meant going over the $68,000 waiver maximum.

I was running out of time. The National Health Law Program attorney faxed the letters to me on March 28, 2001. The deadline for letting the area program know what I wanted cut from Danny's cost summary was April 1, 2001. After researching further on the National Health Law Program's website (www.healthlaw.org), I found another letter sent to all state Medicaid directors from the director of CMS. The letter was dated January 10, 2001. Attachment #4B of this letter outlined the interplay between EPSDT and the home- and community-based waivers. It was time to throw a monkey wrench into this wheel and stop the clock.

Thank God for e-mail! As project manager for one of the North Carolina self-determination projects, I began developing an e-mail list of families throughout North Carolina, many of whom were being asked to cut services or supplies in order to meet the $68,000 limit. On March 30, 2001 I sent an e-mail to families, self-advocates, and other advocates throughout the state to include the CEOs of prominent nonprofit disability organizations. I also made an appointment with the director of the North Carolina Medical Assistance (DMA) agency. DMA is responsible for the North Carolina Medicaid Program and its director received all the newly discovered letters regarding EPSDT and the waiver.

After sending the e-mail, the CEO of Easter Seals North Carolina came to my office asking about EPSDT. She too was unfamiliar with the program. She in turn contacted her colleagues at The Arc of North Carolina and the United Cerebral Palsy Association. All of these organizations provided support and services to Medicaid-eligible children with disabilities for decades. These same CEOs had served over twenty years in the state of North Carolina and none of them knew the acronym EPSDT.

My appointment with the director of DMA was set for April 4, 2001. The wheel had stopped and the April 1 deadline was lifted for a time. To prepare for this meeting I continued to research and study.

Attachment #4B of the January 10, 2001 Olmstead Update #4 letter gave clear- cut direction to states regarding the interplay between EPSDT and the waiver. Excerpts from the letter are as follows.

"In this attachment, we clarify ways in which Medicaid HCBS (Home & Community Based Services) waivers and the Medicaid EPSDT services interact to ensure that children receive the full complement of services they may need...States must ensure that (1) all children, including the children made eligible for Medicaid through their enrollment in a HCBS waiver receive the EPSDT services they need, and (2) children receive all medically necessary Medicaid coverable services available under EPSDT...a child's enrollment in an HCBS waiver cannot be used to deny, delay, or limit access to medically necessary services that are required to be available to all Medicaid-eligible children under federal EPSDT rules...State Medicaid programs must make EPSDT services promptly available (for any individual who is under age 21 and who is eligible for Medicaid) whether or not that individual is receiving services under an approved HCBS waiver."

After an extensive study of the North Carolina Medicaid state plan, I was beginning to understand the dilemma. North Carolina used the term EPSDT throughout its state plan. This unfortunately is a document most families do not read and therefore they are unaware of its existence. North Carolina also hid the EPSDT benefits under a name called "Health Check." On the North Carolina Division of Medical Assistance website, I found a flier on the "Health Check Program." The flier provided the following information.

"North Carolina expanded the federal EPSDT program (which has been in existence since Medicaid began) to form the Health Check program in 1993. EPSDT serves as the standard for providing health-care to Medicaid recipients under the age of 21. The purpose of the Health Check program is to facilitate regular preventive medical care and the diagnosis and treatment of any health problem found during a screening."

The first problem for families is making the connection between EPSDT and Health Check. The second is understanding that these services are available to all Medicaid-eligible children with disabilities, even if the child became eligible through a Medicaid waiver. As I studied further I wondered how much knowledge case managers had on this subject. When a child with a disability joins a family either through birth or medical tragedy; the family needs guidance on how to access the bureaucracy. I certainly was getting no guidance from my case manager or her supervisor. They were still waiting for me to make my decision on cutting services or supplies.

The Health Check flier continued with an explanation on how Health Check coordinators across the state "determine which Medicaid-eligible children in their respective counties are receiving regular and periodic Health Check screenings, immunizations, and referrals for special healthcare problems." What happened to treatment? EPSDT stands for early periodic screening, diagnosis, and TREATMENT!

Further research revealed the CMS requirement for each state to provide an annual EPSDT participation report. The September 7, 2000 North Carolina report can be found in Appendix A. This report states there were 672,374 North Carolina children eligible for EPSDT between the ages of birth to age twenty. The number of children indicated as categorically needy was 663,862. The number of children listed as medically needy was 8,512. The number of children in the medically needy category who were referred for corrective treatment was twenty-one. There were **zero children** listed in all age groups and categories for enrollment in continuing care arrangements.

To further prepare for my meeting with the director of the North Carolina Division of Medical Assistance, I developed an outline that included how I learned of EPSDT. I wanted the director to know I learned of this vital service from an out- of-state attorney during a crisis situation. Danny was eighteen years of age and once again we learned we had been left in the dark. I also wanted to review with the director the Olmstead Update #4 letter from CMS that clearly outlines the interplay between EPSDT and the waiver.

In my naivety I believed I would have a one-on-one meeting with the director of the Division of Medical Assistance. Those around me, however, knew better. The CEO of Easter Seals offered to join me at the meeting. We arrived on time to find, to my surprise, the director, his assistant, and another DMA staff member. It would not be a one-on-one meeting as I had thought. I came with lots of newfound knowledge. I did my homework and asked the hard questions.

I began the meeting by sharing a picture of Danny and then outlining my experience in learning about EPSDT. I shared how Danny's CAP slot was in jeopardy because his needs required more than the $68,000 allowable and how the area program offered no other options except ICF/MR (Intermediate Care Facility for people with Mental Retardation) or one of the state-run institutions. I also shared my conversation with the ADAPT attorney in Pennsylvania and his referral to the National Health Law Program in Chapel Hill. I shared the letters from HCFA stating "no monetary limits for EPSDT recipients," and of course, the Olmstead Update #4 letter, with Attachment #4B.

The primary concern of DMA was whether or not EPSDT services can "wrap around" the waiver and therefore allow the waiver recipient to go over the allowable budget amount. Obviously the director hadn't read his mail. After all, the Olmstead Update #4 letter went to all state Medicaid directors. The DMA director is North Carolina's Medicaid director. This letter very clearly states, "States must ensure that (1) all children, including children made eligible for Medicaid through their enrollment in a HCBS waiver receive the EPSDT services they need, and (2) children receive all medically necessary Medicaid coverable services available under EPSDT." This update, in conjunction with the 1990 letter which states, "overall monetary limits or caps may not be set which could prevent the provision of medically necessary services under EPSDT" should have answered his concern about "wrap-around" services.

During our conversation, comments were made about the budget implications this would have on our state and the cost-effectiveness test. Because of budget concerns the director commented that "this is a bad time for Olmstead." The director then asked for time to develop the state's definition of medical necessity and time to get confirmation from HCFA regarding the use of EPSDT to wrap around the waiver. Not recognized at the time, this was a tremendous stall tactic on the part of the director. How can you have a Medicaid state plan with EPSDT written throughout the plan and not have a definition for *medical necessity*? Because I did not recognize the tactic, the best I could do was ask for a timeline. The director's response was "one month." The director also stated that we would see aggregate funding because of Olmstead but did not give a timeline. He also mentioned that we were still going to have to stay budget neutral.

Throughout the years there were several familiar catch phrases. "Budget neutral" was one of them. I was determined to research this further and find out its meaning as it relates to people with significant disabilities.

In the meantime, we continued our discussion with the director by posing several questions.

"What is the local agency that handles EPSDT?" The director's response was "There is none."

"Why are we not informed of EPSDT services by our CAP case managers?" The assistant director's response was that we were already receiving these services under the waiver. But of course, no one tells us it is EPSDT and we do not receive the full benefit of the EPSDT services because the waiver provides a budget limitation that all recipients must comply with. Once again they shared their concern with EPSDT wrapping around the waiver, and the cost issue.

The next question asked was, "How is North Carolina informing families about EPSDT?" The director made it very clear EPSDT services in our state are "enormously accessible." I suggested the Best Practice Conference and The Arc of North Carolina Convention as two possibilities for DMA to start publicizing this program. The director felt what they were doing was enough to reach everyone who needed to be reached. I challenged that and asked if he was confident he was reaching the middle class. There was silence.

EPSDT is a federal program for all Medicaid-eligible children under twenty-one. The waiver is the only way a middle-class family can get services. I shared with the director that I'd never seen anything from the schools on EPSDT or Health Check and said that Danny had been in special education in North Carolina since 1991. I also never received anything from any of Danny's doctors. "So how are you advertising this program?" There were comments on the thousands of brochures that go out and again an assurance that DMA was doing everything they could to reach the masses. I listened in utter disbelief. Not only were I and hundreds of other waiver recipients and their families across the state left in the dark about EPSDT, but so were the three CEOs of Easter Seals, United Cerebral Palsy, and The Arc of North Carolina.

I then shared with the director the advice given to me by the ADAPT attorney and the National Health Law Program. Their suggestion was to get a letter from Danny's doctor outlining the additional services needed above the $68,000 limit. The doctor's letter was also to indicate that these services be provided under EPSDT. Since I was able to confirm in my research everything the attorneys told me about this program, I decided to follow their advice and submit my doctor's letter to the director. The director accepted the letter but mentioned he could not do anything with the letter until he heard back from HCFA. And he again gave a one-month timeline. To ensure there was no breach of confidentiality, I shared a list of fifteen first names of children who also qualify for EPSDT, stating that this was the tip of a very large iceberg. I asked if the families should send their doctor's letters to his office. He emphatically stated no, because it would backlog the system. I had made a tragic mistake by first asking permission and then complying with his response. This director needed to be bombarded with doctor's letters from not only 15, but 150 and then 250 families. He received the Olmstead update letter in January 2001, outlining the interplay between EPSDT and the waiver. He did nothing to comply with this mandate. If he had questions, why didn't he present them to HCFA/CMS? Instead he authorized an increase in rates and further authorized the movement of case managers to consumer's homes to find out what families wanted cut from their loved ones' budgets. He focused solely on his state budget and gambled that families would accept the guilt given and be willing to cut services, supplies, or equipment.

When returning to my office I immediately summarized the meeting in an e-mail to over 150 consumers/families, advocates, and professionals across the state. I also continued my research and began sending e-mails directly to CMS staff both at the Atlanta regional office and the federal Baltimore office. As you can imagine, the barrage of e-mails on this subject were intense in number and content. The term *EPSDT* in North Carolina uncovered not only incompetence and corruption from North Carolina Medicaid officials but also CMS officials.

In an e-mail to one of North Carolina's many consultants, I wrote, "We have been threatened by our area program to lose our son's CAP slot because his needs require a cost summary above the allowable amount. During my research, I learned of the EPSDT program and have been told that this program must be available to children under the age of twenty-one who have needs based on medical necessity. The question is whether we can use this program to exceed the CAP allowable. It looks like I will be facing an appeals process within the next two weeks because my son needs approximately $700 more a month to live in the community. I have asked the area program what Danny's options would be if we lost CAP. The response was an ICF/MR (intermediate care facility for people with mental retardation) or one of the mental retardation centers at a cost of $120,000 per year. Can you help me with information on EPSDT and whether or not we can use this to exceed the CAP allowable budget?"

During my research I stumbled on the average cost of ICF/MR, or state institution care. The cost at the time was $120,000 per year. My son's budget was presently $68,000. With the additional costs his new budget would be far less than the $120,000 cost for institutional care. The proposed budget was far less than what the state would have to pay if we did not pitch in as a family and provide the difference in care.

The consultant forwarded my e-mail to a CMS staff member in Atlanta. The CMS staff response was received on April 6, 2001 and was copied to several other CMS staff members both in the Atlanta and Baltimore offices, along with North Carolina DMA staff. The CMS staff response received on April 6, 2001 was as follows:

"EPSDT reimburses for medically needed services and these services are limited only by medical necessity. The waiver services are limited by criteria set forth in the waiver. North Carolina operates this waiver using an individual cost cap. If it is determined that your son no longer meets waiver criteria (in this instance, his care would exceed the cost allowable through the waiver), Medicaid would continue to pay for needed medical services through EPSDT. It is possible that these services could be provided in an institution rather than in the community."

I was floored by the last sentence in this e-mail. How could a member of the CMS staff in a time of Olmstead make that remark to a family member? Was she trying to scare me into submission? Well it did not work. In addition I began to wonder why CMS allowed North Carolina to operate a waiver using an individual cost cap knowing full well EPSDT would also be limited. I continued studying everything I could on EPSDT. Through the power of e mail I shared what I learned with families and other advocates across the state. The word was getting out to everyone. I was connecting with hundreds of families and organizations. One day, in the middle of this battle, I received an e-mail from the President of the North Carolina Community Support Providers Council strongly encouraging me to keep up the good fight and "not to let the lies surrounding the non-compliance for the state persuade you to do anything other than to fight on!"

At the time these were encouraging words from a reliable, credible source. However, as the years went on I learned that many organizations, both nonprofit and for-profit, keep their distance from those fighting in the trenches, in order to keep their hands clean and ensure survivability. To some degree they are allies in that they will help you strategize to win a battle; however, they will not get in the thick of battle with you. Their fighting tactic is one of diplomacy. Their battlefield is a conference table. Their battle dress uniforms are suits and ties. These are very different tactics than those used by families and people with disabilities. More often than not these different tactics cause conflict between families, people with disabilities, and the organizations that supposedly represent them. Because the diplomacy tactic requires "relationship building" with the bureaucracy, it sometimes is very difficult to tell the difference between an allied organization and the bureaucracy.

As part of the Easter Seals North Carolina leadership team, on April 10, 2001 I received an e-mail from a fellow team member informing the team of the particulars of EPSDT. The EPSDT light was shining for the first time on an organization that for decades supported Medicaid-eligible children through therapy services and home-care services. The power of the bureaucracy to camouflage services despite a diplomatic relationship was evident in the way this prominent nonprofit organization was left in the dark.

During one of my many phone calls with CMS Baltimore staff, I asked for clarification as to what should be occurring for our kids on the waiver in North Carolina. The response was that EPSDT services needed to be used first and that no medically necessary services should be part of the waiver cost summary. What I was being told was the opposite of the reality faced by a countless number of North Carolina children receiving waiver services. *How can it be that CMS Baltimore and CMS Atlanta do not know what is occurring in our state?* North Carolina cannot implement a waiver without CMS Atlanta and CMS Baltimore approval. Part of the waiver application includes a sample copy of the plan of care and cost summary. The cost summary for this waiver includes three columns. The first is titled "Medicaid." The second is titled "CAP." The third is titled "other." The instructions for cost summary calculations are that the total dollar amounts of the Medicaid and CAP columns determine waiver costs.

On April 17, 2001 I received a phone call from CMS Atlanta staff informing me they would have a conversation with North Carolina to determine if EPSDT was being added to waiver costs. I told her it was and explained column one and column two being added together for all five thousand plus waiver recipients. At the time I thought it very puzzling that CMS did not know what North Carolina was doing. But the reality was they did not know because they did not pay attention when they approved the waiver.

"I'll check and get back with you" was once again the response. Before letting her off the phone, however, I managed to ask where families should send their child's doctor's letter. We still had not gotten an answer from DMA regarding this and families were anxious to send their letters. She assured me that she would get me a point of contact at the North Carolina DMA office. Unfortunately this never happened.

The following day I received a call from another CMS Atlanta staff member. She informed me that after speaking with the state, CMS Atlanta believed "the way they (North Carolina) are calculating the cost summary is okay." She further stated that the state has the option to disqualify an individual whose budget exceeds the nursing home average cost. There's the threat again! But more importantly, how did we get to nursing home costs? The CAP MR/DD waiver is for individuals who qualify for intermediate care facilities for persons with mental retardation (ICF/MR), not nursing homes. Not realizing this at the time of the conversation, I asked, "What is the cost of nursing home care." She could not answer the question because the CMS Atlanta staff was unable to "get up with the state's finance folks." She did, however, say that she believed the waiver maximum needed to be raised based on the conversations CMS Atlanta had with the state. I asked about EPSDT and the unlimited medically necessary services and supports that were to be available. She stated very clearly that she did not believe it was unlimited. Not only did I hear this straight from CMS Baltimore staff, but also read it in the letter dated September 18, 1990 from the CMS Regional Administrator to all Title XIX state agencies (See Appendix A). She replied that she did not think CMS Baltimore understood the situation. This was crazy! No one at the CMS Atlanta office seemed to understand what the CMS Baltimore office had to say about EPSDT and the waiver. Who was in charge here? CMS Atlanta is a regional office of CMS Baltimore. It was time for CMS Baltimore to get those under them in line with the facts.

Throughout this entire fiasco I was running out of support hours to take care of my son while I worked. I made it very clear to the CMS Atlanta and Baltimore staff that I would not quit my job to take care of my son and wind up on a welfare line simply because I could not get the

CMS Atlanta office to understand Medicaid policy regarding EPSDT. It was not my job to explain policy to CMS staff. However, their knowledge or lack thereof certainly impacted my life. This was an unnecessary emotional roller coaster ride that I desperately needed stopped.

Finally on April 25, 2001 a memo was sent from the director of the North Carolina Division of Medical Assistance to all area program directors. The subject of the memo was "Individual Cost Limit for the CAP MR/DD Waiver." Excerpts from the letter are as follows:

"Effective April 1, 2001 with the waiver renewal, the cost limit for an individual recipient funded by CAP MR/DD will be set at the average ICF-MR cost of $86,058 a year, or $7,171.50 per month. As written in the North Carolina waiver, the cost billed to Medicaid may not exceed this amount for an individual to remain funded under the CAP MR/DD waiver. This amount covers all CAP waiver funded services and regular Medicaid funded services that would be provided if the individual were in an ICF/MR. This includes medically necessary services...as justified in the individual's Plan of Care."

This was a partial victory. Those individuals needing more than the $68,000 limit were now able to obtain the medically necessary supports and services without jeopardizing their slots. However, we learned that medically necessary EPSDT services have no dollar limitation. So why was the Medicaid column still being added to the CAP column to determine waiver costs?

My continued investigation led me to a phone conversation with the budget section of DMA. I was told that the Medicaid rate for the state-run institutions was a daily figure that was "pretty close to cost." At the time, North Carolina had five state-run mental retardation (MR) centers. The rate for each individual living at the facilities was as follows:

Name of Facility	Daily Rate	Annual Rate
State MR Center A	$278	$101,470
State MR Center B	$282	$102,930
State MR Center C	$307	$112,055
State MR Center D	$308	$112,420
State MR Center E	$332	$121,180

The individual I spoke with at the budget section informed me that the daily rates were based on the overall cost of the facility and the number of clients served. He also stated there were new proposed increased daily rates because "costs have gone up." It would seem to me that if costs have gone up for the state-run facilities, the same would be true for families. However, my concern was the letter from the director of DMA stated the $86,058 waiver limit was the "average ICF-MR cost." Based on the numbers above, $86,058 was not the average of the five state-run ICF-MR facilities. How did North Carolina determine $86,058 as the average cost of ICF-MR care? How I prayed I wasn't the only one asking this question.

In the meantime, the North Carolina Council on Developmental Disabilities was developing a consumer friendly document on the CAP MR/DD waiver for consumers and families throughout the state. In its first draft it announced, "EPSDT services are included in the total calculation toward the total limit of $86,000. If the child requires more services than can be paid for under the CAP MR/DD waiver, they would need to discontinue participation in the CAP waiver, and be served either through regular Medicaid State Plan services if they are eligible for Medicaid without the waiver, or be served in an ICF-MR." My God, our state is committing all children with significant disabilities of middle class families to ICF-MR facilities! This was contrary to Olmstead, contrary to the Olmstead #4 letter, and contrary to the 1990 letter to all Title XIX state agencies.

A meeting was scheduled with a North Carolina Division of Mental Health/Developmental Disabilities/Substance Abuse (DMH) staff member and my area program developmental disabilities coordinator to develop a new cost summary for Danny using the $86,058 limit. Understanding the Medicaid budget deficit North Carolina faced, I developed an individual budget based on the principles of self-determination. I followed the fiscal intermediary line items and fee schedules established by Easter Seals North Carolina (ESNC) for the self-determination project. ESNC modeled its fiscal intermediary services according to the successful project implemented by Easter Seals New Jersey (ESNJ). At the time, ESNJ was providing fiscal intermediary services to over 300 individuals in the New Jersey Self-Determination Project.

In addition to the line items presently on Danny's CAP cost summary, I included six additional line items according to the self-determination individual budget model. The individual budget provides flexibility in dollars across line items and also allows the consumer or family to purchase items cost effectively. The concept of letting the family shop around for cheaper costs is permitted through the individual budget. Although this budget model indicated a savings in Medicaid dollars, we could not implement this in the present waiver. The rules of this waiver needed to be followed, resulting in an $86,058 budget to meet Danny's needs. By this time the cost of supplies had increased along with the rates for services.

On April 30, 2001 I met with the National Health Law Program attorneys to discuss the waiver and EPSDT. I shared Danny's new $86,058 cost summary along with the possible savings offered using a self-determination model. The main focus of our meeting, however, was EPSDT and the waiver. To prepare for this meeting questionnaires were distributed to seventy-three families across the state. Some of the questionnaires were filled out by families with children on SSI. These children were also Medicaid eligible. Their families had been told they could only receive eighty hours per month of personal care services because that was the maximum allowed in the state Medicaid plan. It did not matter if the personal care services were medically necessary. Eighty hours per month was all that was offered. These same families indicated on the questionnaire that they had never heard of EPSDT. For those families who knew of Health Check, they indicated the only thing they received under Health Check was doctor appointments and immunizations.

Questionnaires were also filled out by families of children under twenty-one who had significant budget issues under the present waiver. These families were doing without services or equipment in order to keep their waiver slots. The increase to $86,058 might help some of these families, but our next important step was to prove to the state that focusing on self-determination and individual budgets would not only more effectively meet the needs of people being served, but would also provide true cost effectiveness for a state facing a large deficit.

The National Health Law Program attorneys were very interested in pursuing a "multi-tiered strategy" that involved federal and state advocacy, media, and public education through media and other sources. The National Health Law Program attorneys stated they were interested in helping both this group of people and the state Medicaid agency to understand the interplay between EPSDT and the home- and community-based waivers.

Unfortunately there is always a cost to making change. Easter Seals North Carolina used a credible communication organization that gave us a quote of $1,500 to orchestrate the media campaign. Although the National Health Law Program immediately began working on the issues presented, they estimated $5,000 for support to their non-profit organization as they pursued the issues. Throughout this entire ordeal, we were nothing more than a group of parents. Although organizations supported us behind the scenes, no one came forward to help with funding. As a result, there was no media campaign. However, the National Health Law Program continued to address the issues.

On May 2, 2001 I received a letter from the Atlanta CMS associate regional administrator stating they determined that "North Carolina is administering the approved waiver program within federal guidelines. One of the requirements is for states to demonstrate cost neutrality..." The letter continued with the following: "The service needs identified in Danny's care plan, effective April 1, 2001, are covered through a combination of waiver and State Plan services. Should Danny require services that are determined medically necessary by the state and not available through the State Plan or the MR/DD waiver, EPSDT would cover these services. However, the costs of the EPSDT services (with the exception of physician and dental services) identified on the care plan, if needed, would be included in the waiver/ICF/MR cost comparison. **Within their purview, the state has chosen** to use the cost of the services in the care plan to compare against institutional costs."

Throughout the years I learned the power of state choice. Whether or not the choice the state makes is **within their purview** is certainly debatable. The issue presented over and over again had to do with the interplay between EPSDT and the waiver. There were several documents written by the CMS Baltimore staff that clearly stated it was not in the state's purview to make any changes to this interplay. However, this letter was copied to two members of the CMS Baltimore staff without any follow-up letter contradicting its content.

The EPSDT fight was becoming more and more frustrating. The dilemma of cutting services, equipment, or supplies was resolved with the increase in the maximum dollar limitation for the waiver. However, the EPSDT issue remained unsolved. In my opinion, EPSDT had a tremendous impact on children with significant disabilities from middle-class families. The only way a North Carolina middle-class family can receive Medicaid for its child with significant disabilities is through the waiver. If the medical needs of the child are more than the waiver can handle, the family will be burdened with unnecessary decisions.

Almost ready to throw in the towel on this EPSDT fight, I attended an Olmstead meeting hosted by the North Carolina Protection and Advocacy (P&A) agency. At the time the P&A in North Carolina was part of state government. As a result the North Carolina P&A was a very ineffective organization when it came to helping consumers and families battle injustices identified throughout the state bureaucracy. After all, how do you sue yourself?

One of the speakers at this meeting in late July 2001 was an attorney with the National Association of P&A Systems. Also present at this meeting were the directors of DMA and DMH along with several other DMA and DMH staff members. Unfortunately the attorney with the National Association of P&A was the last speaker. Hind sight is always 20/20. It is very possible this was part of the bureaucracy's plan. By this time, one by one, the directors of DMA and DMH along with several of their staff members quietly excused themselves from the meeting. With mostly parents, self-advocates, and nonprofit organization staff members in the audience, the attorney from the National Association of P&A went through the North Carolina Olmstead plan pointing out what she believed was missing from the plan. Much to our surprise, EPSDT was her main focus. She explained the importance of EPSDT for Medicaid-eligible children under the age of twenty-one and how it needed to be part of the North Carolina Olmstead plan because it "prevents unnecessary institutionalization." My inspiration for this fight was renewed. I continued to study and read everything I could on EPSDT. I also continued to ask questions.

All that I learned of the incompetence of North Carolina to provide EPSDT services to Medicaid eligible children was confirmed in the United States General Accounting Office report (GAO-01-749) dated July 2001. The results in the brief section of the GAO report states:

"The extent to which children in Medicaid across the country are receiving EPSDT services is not fully known, but the available evidence indicates that many are not receiving these services. A comprehensive view is not possible because annual state reports to HCFA on the delivery of EPSDT services are unreliable and incomplete...These and other studies have found that several factors contribute to the lack of services. Some involve program issues, such as inadequate systems for ensuring that services are provided. Others involve beneficiary issues, such as parents' being unaware of the need for or availability of covered services...Although many of the actions taken by one state to improve the delivery of services may apply to other states, HCFA does not have mechanisms in place for identifying and highlighting such actions...We are recommending that CMS work with states to develop criteria and a timetable for assessing and improving the reporting and provision of EPSDT services. We are also recommending that CMS develop mechanisms for identifying and highlighting practices that could be used as models for other states."

The report continues:

"...The federal government sets certain requirements for state Medicaid programs. Coverage of screening and necessary treatment for children is one of these requirements...For many children, especially those with special needs because of disabilities or chronic conditions, EPSDT is an important help in identifying the need for essential medical and supportive services, and in making these services available.

"The Omnibus Budget Reconciliation Act of 1989 (OBRA 89) made significant changes to improve the provision of EPSDT services to children in Medicaid. It required that the Secretary of Health & Human Services (HHS) set state-specific annual goals for children's participation in EPSDT...and imposed new reporting requirements...HCFA required, starting in 1990, that states submit annual EPSDT reports (known as the form 416).

"...A number of studies of limited scope indicate that many children in Medicaid are not receiving EPSDT services.

"State-reported data, upon which HCFA depends, are often not timely or accurate...The state's Medicaid agency has not imposed sanctions against noncompliant plans or providers, restrained in part by its reluctance to lose any providers given the shortage of providers willing to serve children in Medicaid....Simply, some states have problems tracking referrals and follow-up treatment services...in HCFA's 1998 compilation of state reports, seven states reported that no children had been referred for corrective treatments."

This confirmed the North Carolina report which listed no children referred for corrective treatment.

The GAO report continues with beneficiary outreach and education suggestions that include "designing clear and informative member handbooks, creating helpful and easy-to-understand materials to supplement member handbooks, developing programs to reach special populations such as children with disabilities, and conducting community outreach activities." These wonderful suggestions would help North Carolina finally make EPSDT services "enormously accessible," as the DMA director believes they already are.

According to the GAO report, "HCFA has reviewed only eight states since 1995 and has not established a mechanism for sharing lessons learned or innovative practices already in place among states. Since there is no HCFA requirement to periodically focus on and promote EPSDT on the state level, the decision to do so resides with management of each HCFA region...We found that regions typically have one staff person designed as EPSDT Coordinator, but with multiple responsibilities other than EPSDT."

The last section of the GAO report outlined legal actions taken throughout several states on behalf of children not receiving EPSDT services. This section reminded me of a North Carolina adoption practice that clearly violates the EPSDT provision. As my e-mail list grew I met a mom from the western part of the state who adopted a child with emotional disabilities. At the time of adoption the child was two years old. The trauma that this young child experienced in the first two years of life left her with many emotional scars. At two years of age the child became the responsibility of the North Carolina Department of Social Services (DSS). This North Carolina agency in turn sought adoption opportunities for the child. The adopting family was told that the child would keep her Medicaid card and that the income of the adopting family would not jeopardize the child's eligibility for Medicaid and all its services. However, the North Carolina agency never informed the family of any of the EPSDT Medicaid services available. Due to the trauma in the first two years of life, the child displayed a number of mental illness disorders, including post traumatic stress syndrome. As a result of North Carolina officials ignoring their responsibility of EPSDT and CMS allowing North Carolina to ignore their responsibility, this family (along with many others in the same situation) was left to find services on their own. Many times throughout their journey the child was placed in facilities outside her home. Through e-mails and many telephone conversations, I shared with this mom all I learned about EPSDT. Her diligent research led her to filing a formal complaint with the Office of Administrative Hearing (OAH). Because attorneys are expensive, this mom represented herself and her adopted daughter throughout the OAH hearing.

The Conclusions of Law by the OAH judge are as follows:

"7. Petitioners have shown a preponderance of the evidence in this case that such treatment services are medically necessary to correct or ameliorate the mental illnesses and conditions from which (Petitioner) suffers. All of the competent medical testimony from medical doctors in this case indicate that such treatment services are essential to the proper care of (Petitioner). All of her treating clinicians agree that without such services her illnesses and conditions will worsen and that she will be at greater risk without such services. The only testimony to the contrary was provided by a licensed psychologist...an employee of the Respondent Blue Ridge Center, who testified that while he agreed that crisis intervention and stabilization services were medically necessary for (Petitioner), the structure of those services as directed by the treating clinicians were not medically necessary. (The psychologist) is not a medical doctor nor a treating clinician to (Petitioner).

"8. Respondents are not relieved of this duty to provide the medically necessary treatments to (Petitioner) by simply attempting to refer (Petitioner) to such services. The EPSDT provisions of Medicaid impose a much higher duty on the state to assure access to EPSDT services than to other Medicaid services. Thus, in contrast to other Medicaid services, the state must not only cover needed EPSDT services but must 'arrange for (directly or through referral to appropriate agencies, organizations, or individuals) corrective treatment.'

"The federal statutory provision quoted above that the State must arrange for such services to be provided, either 'directly or through referral' is a clear indication that the State, in this case acting through the appropriate area program, must insure that the medically needed services are provided. The evidence in this case is that both the area program and the State have the knowledge and ability to provide these services directly, if needed. In fact, according to the Acting Head of the Child and Family Services Section of the Department of Health and Human Services, the State is planning to provide additional crisis stabilization capabilities in response to the evidence brought forward during this Hearing. That is commendable. However, the medically necessary needs of (Petitioner) must be met now in order for her to receive the treatment she is entitled to under the federal law.

"BASED UPON THE FOREGOING FINDINGS OF FACT AND CONCLUSIONS OF LAW, THE UNDERSIGNED MAKES THE FOLLOWING RECOMMENDED DECISION.

"It is recommended that Respondents' denial of Petitioner's request for therapeutically appropriate crisis intervention and stabilization services for (Petitioner) be **REVERSED**. Effective immediately, Respondents should provide to (Petitioner) 24 hour per day, 7 day per week crisis intervention and stabilization services in a form consistent with the direction of her treating physicians."

VICTORY! But whether or not this case will set a precedent for others remains to be seen.

It is an absolute shame that a service put in place over thirty years ago to help children with disabilities is so carelessly considered by state and CMS staff. Despite this victory and the embarrassing GAO report, the EPSDT question regarding its interplay with the waiver was still unanswered.

On August 9, 2001 I received a letter from the North Carolina DMA assistant director. The letter was in response to an e-mail I sent to a member of the CMS Baltimore staff. My research of the North Carolina Medicaid state plan uncovered a statement in the plan regarding the amount, duration, and scope of EPSDT services. The plan further stated "treatment of conditions found" is without limitation. The purpose of my e-mail to CMS was to understand why the EPSDT calculations were included in the overall waiver costs. The letter from the assistant director brought a new twist to the debate.

"In order to receive EPSDT benefits, a child must be Medicaid eligible by meeting income standards. Because income is treated differently for waiver participants, some people with higher incomes are eligible for Medicaid only if they are waiver participants. An expenditure upper limit applies to waiver participants. Individuals for whom cost of care exceed the limit, cannot participate in the waiver and may receive all other Medicaid services (including EPSDT services) only if they meet the income requirements under 'regular Medicaid' rules."

Upon receiving the letter, I sent an e-mail to the CMS Baltimore staff asking why my question was not answered by CMS staff and was delegated to the North Carolina staff. The CMS staff response was typical of the response families receive from bureaucracy staff at all levels. "I just returned from vacation so I apologize for the delay in my response." It is amazing to me how much vacation time is taken by those in the human service field. While we wait for people to return from vacation, our lives float in a state of limbo. There never is any backup staff. Just as the GAO report pointed out, one person is assigned to EPSDT and if that person is on vacation or on sick or medical leave, everyone must wait.

After the apology for vacation was out of the way, the CMS staff e-mail continued.

"In CMS (formerly HCFA) Central Office, I work in the area of EPSDT services. However, I do not work with HCBW (waiver) services. I have been involved in discussions with central office and regional office staff on the issues you've raised but I defer to the waiver staff to explain their areas of expertise since I am not qualified to do so."

In this situation she did not defer to CMS waiver staff. She deferred to the North Carolina DMA staff, who are not waiver experts.

"From the EPSDT perspective, eligible individuals must receive all medically necessary services that are coverable under Medicaid. States determine medical necessity and may not place arbitrary limits on services but may use prior authorization as a utilization control on some services. The services may be delivered under a waiver or as in most cases, as part of the state plan services."

This has become the EPSDT chant. But nobody seems to be willing to address the interplay issue. While continuing to ask the same question over and over again, I continued to study.

An issue brief written by an attorney with the National Health Law Program dated June 20, 2002 states the EPSDT benefit is "an important, but underused source of federal funding for early intervention services." Parents and professionals all agree on the importance of early intervention services. It is an absolute crime when families learn of early intervention opportunities when it is too late for their children. The attorney clearly points out in the brief that "many states and health care providers operate under the impression that only limited early intervention services can be covered through Medicaid. To the contrary, the Medicaid Early and Periodic Screening, Diagnosis and Treatment service can be used to cover a broad array of early intervention services...It is critical for health care providers who are treating young children to know the full scope of EPSDT...EPSDT benefits include all of the services that the state can cover under Section 1396d(a) of the Medicaid Act, whether or not such services are covered for adults...The service must be medically necessary; in other words, it must be needed to 'correct or ameliorate' a physical or mental condition."

Ameliorate is an important word in recognizing the full array of EPSDT services. *Ameliorate*, according to Webster, is to "make or become better; improve." Some disabilities will never be corrected. For example, cerebral palsy is a condition that is lifelong. However, physical therapy, occupational therapy, and speech language pathology are treatment methods that could ameliorate the condition. The word *ameliorate* is part of the Social Security definition of EPSDT services.

The brief continues with a case study involving the Eighth Circuit.

"On appeal, the Eighth Circuit held that a 'Medicaid eligible individual has a federal right to early intervention day treatment when a physician recommends such treatment.'

"The Court closed its decision with a reminder to the state that EPSDT provisions obligate it to inform recipients about the EPSDT services that are available to them and that it must arrange for the corrective treatments prescribed by physicians. The state may not shirk its responsibilities to Medicaid recipients by burying information about available services in a complex bureaucratic scheme."

This judge used all the right words: "The state may not **shirk** its responsibilities to Medicaid by **burying** information about available services in a complex bureaucratic scheme." Yet that is exactly what North Carolina has done and no one is holding the state responsible for its actions. It is very naïve to think that states are going to do the right thing simply because it is written into law. We constantly see the Individual with Disabilities Education Act (IDEA) tossed aside by many states. EPSDT is no different. Both are federal laws. If monitoring and accountability are not available to ensure the laws are properly implemented, states will operate according to budget and not according to responsibility. Strong monitoring and accountability ensures the budgets created by states accommodate the full provision of the laws for their citizens. So where is CMS in all of this? Where is the monitoring and accountability from the regional and federal offices? Is everyone on vacation?

The EPSDT battle began with my phone conversation with the ADAPT attorney in March 2001. At the time Danny was eighteen years of age. EPSDT provisions are available to children with disabilities up to the age of twenty-one.

Finally on January 28, 2005, four years after my telephone conversation with the ADAPT attorney, a letter was issued by the director of the North Carolina Division of Medical Assistance (DMA) to all DMA staff, fiscal agents, and contractors:

"Waiver services are available only to participants in the Community Alternatives waiver programs and are not part of the EPSDT benefit. A recipient under age 21 receiving waiver services who is financially eligible for Medicaid whether or not enrolled in the waiver may elect to receive necessary EPSDT services in addition to waiver services."

This final letter on EPSDT still did not clearly address the interplay between EPSDT and the waiver. According to Social Security Administration (SSA) criteria, a child becomes an adult at eighteen years of age. When my son turned eighteen I completed an array of documents with the SSA. An SSI check was issued to Danny because he was considered an adult by the SSA. No longer was my income considered by the SSA for Danny's benefits. At eighteen years of age he was on his own, "financially eligible" for Medicaid and therefore eligible for the complete array of EPSDT services according to the DMA letter. However, the waiver still added the cost of Medicaid services to the cost of waiver services. The waiver has a dollar limitation, thereby limiting EPSDT services. In addition, the letter from DMA was dated January 28, 2005. At the time, Danny was twenty-two years of age. He no longer qualified for

EPSDT, on or off the waiter.

EPSDT was an acronym now uncovered in North Carolina. When we first started down this road, people would get the letters confused. It certainly is a mouthful. Four years later we uncovered the mystery and exposed the injustice. At all levels EPSDT was being discussed. Parents were finally informed of its existence and hard questions were being asked of bureaucrats at all levels. It wasn't until the renewal of the North Carolina waiver in September 2005 that the full provision of EPSDT was recognized. The new waiver cost summary no longer had a Medicaid column that was added to the waiver dollars. This finally allowed for the unlimited EPSDT dollar provision that had been in existence since the passage of the Omnibus Budget Reconciliation Act of 1989. But this did not solve for all children the dilemma faced regarding EPSDT.

On February 27, 2006 I received an e-mail from the same mom who represented her adopted daughter in an Office of Administrative Hearing (OAH) battle and won. The e-mail referred to a friend of this mom who filed for an OAH hearing on behalf of her adopted son. The child was a minor with a Medicaid card and should have had available to him EPSDT coverage for medically necessary services and support. The subject line on the e-mail stated, "Outrageous! Why is it OK for DHHS and DMH to break the law????"

The e-mail stated:

"Read above attachment which includes a Motion to Compel, a court document filed in the General Court of Justice – Superior Court, because the DMH and HHS refuse to follow federal law and their own agency decision!!

"See the court order and the DMH agency decision AGREEING that crisis services, including facility services, are medically necessary... and AGREEING that under federal law (EPSDT), the state must provide these services.

"Read (the Secretary's) deposition testimony: 'Crisis facility services for children crucial.'

"Also read evidence from a MHDDSAS (Mental Health/Developmental Disabilities/Substance Abuse Services) publication that outlines the critical nature of crisis services for people with mental illness, including crisis facilities, which states: 'Others' however, will require brief hospital or crisis unit stays. When these clients' crises arise, the LME (Local Management Entity) must have the capability within its provider system.

"Also attached is a letter from an LME administrator directing the case manager to document a phony crisis plan without (the parent's) signature and instructing the case manager to falsely record that the plan 'accurately reflects services are available.'

"Read (the parent's) testimony that Western Highlands shamelessly attempted to create the 'appearance of a crisis continuum' for (the child) without the consent of the providers listed. Read documentation from those providers that they would not provide the services Western Highlands listed as available to (the child).

"THERE ARE NO CRISIS SERVICES FOR (THIS CHILD) AND IN FACT, TODAY (THIS CHILD) HAS FEWER SERVICES AVAILABLE TO HIM THAN HE DID A YEAR AGO.

"Now ask our legislators why our Department of Health and Human Services and the Division of Mental Health is permitted to break federal law by continuing to refuse to provide these medically necessary and legally required crisis services to (this child).

"Our legislators, our county commissioners, and all advocates must demand that the Department of Health and Human Services, the Division of Mental Health, and Western Highlands LME cease the stonewalling, stop the deception and immediately establish 'crucial' and medically necessary crisis facilities to (this child) and to people of all ages who need a full continuum of crisis care, which necessarily include a mobile team and a crisis facility."

And the madness continues....

Chapter 13

The Challenge for Community Life

By this time I had served on several committees as a staff member of Easter Seals North Carolina and project manager for one of the North Carolina self-determination projects. One of the many committees I participated in was the North Carolina Developmental Disabilities Consortium. The consortium consisted of many organizations that provided support to individuals with developmental disabilities. One of the organizations represented was the North Carolina Mental Retardation Association (MRA). The representative was an older woman about twenty years my senior. She was a parent of an adult living in one of the state-run institutions and she in no way wanted the institutions closed. There were many heated discussions during consortium meetings that involved the MRA on one side of an issue and the rest of consortium membership on the other. One day I decided to take this mom to lunch. I wanted to hear her story and find out firsthand why she was so adamant about the institution for her son rather than bringing him home.

Amazingly enough, her son's story is parallel to Danny's. Both our sons had childhood illnesses at six months of age. Her son had encephalitis and Danny had meningitis. The major difference was thirty years. Her son was born in 1954 and Danny was born in 1982.

Both parents were college educated. Her husband was a professor at one of the North Carolina universities. Tragedy struck their oldest child at six months of age. During lunch, as she told her story, her explanation sounded as if the events had just taken place. She remembered very clearly, just as I did, the day she asked her husband to focus on his career while she focused her attention on the children. Other children were born into the family before they realized the extent of the disability of the older child. Every time she had a doctor's appointment for her children the doctor would ask how *she* was doing. She always said she was fine but she was tired and was beginning to wear out. Finally she hit a wall, just as I did in Indiana. When the doctor asked her how she was doing, she cried and finally admitted she could not go on alone. The only help offered was the same help I was given in Indiana—a residential facility for the child. Doctors, friends, and relatives tell you this is the right thing to do. But your heart knows different.

Sister Mary Olivia, John's "mom," was the administrator at St. Mary's most of the years John lived there. Many times Mom and John would reminisce about life at St. Mary's. It was always fun to listen to the many stories of boys getting into all kinds of mischief. But Mom would also share the stories of the boys who cried for their parents and could never understand why they weren't with their families. Most of the boys at St. Mary's came from shattered homes where one or both parent had walked away from responsibility. Many of the boys were placed at St. Mary's by the New York Department of Social Services. After years of leading an organization that cared for over seventy boys, Sister Mary Olivia made a profound statement to me that I will never forget. She said, "Nothing can replace the family." God only knows how hard the nuns tried to make a family home for each of the boys at St. Mary's. But the truth remains. Family is powerful. Family is necessary. Family is irreplaceable.

The MRA president, along with thousands of other parents, struggled with the idea of out of home placement, but no other options were given. Her son has lived in the institution for over thirty years. Now the state had come along and said, "Oops! We made a mistake. Institution isn't the best thing. Community is the best thing." How do you do that to people? This mom knew family was the best thing for her son. She knew it in her heart in 1954 and she knows it now too. But she is over sixty years of age. How could she orchestrate this change for her son? Would she have the energy to see it through? Would she have enough years in this life to see it through?

139

As a parent of a young adult with significant disabilities living in the community, I ask myself the same questions. In addition I ask, *What happens to Danny if I die first?* All parents ask this question, including the parents of children placed in institutions. The parents of children placed in institutions, however, rely on the guarantee provided by the state that their loved ones will be taken care of for life. The integrity of a bureaucracy is faulty at best. Trusting a bureaucracy to guarantee security and happiness is futile.

I remember very clearly walking back to Danny's ICU room with the chaplain at Madigan Army Medical Center almost twenty years earlier. I cried, "Danny can't die." But now my thoughts have changed. I realize now more than ever I am not in control of life or death. When it is time to be born, you are born. And when it is time to die, you die. I could very well die before Danny. I've given my opinion to God even when He didn't ask for it. It would be much easier if Danny died before me. I orchestrate life for Danny and ensure he has everything he needs. I battle the bureaucracy on his behalf when it puts road blocks in our way. If I'm not here, who will do this for him? Danny depends on me and I depend on God. If I am out of the picture, isn't God big enough to replace me? God has never abandoned Danny. This is a young man who should not be alive. Doctors scratch their head in wonder every time they see Danny. It would be easier if Danny had died first, just as it is easier to allow a loved one to stay living in an institution rather than accept what you know in your heart to be true. Life was never meant to be easy. John and I have an extensive written plan of action in the event we die before Danny. This plan includes our will and a trust for Danny. It also includes guardianship for Danny that was at first with The Arc of North Carolina and is now with our oldest son. Before making this change, we sat down with John II and his wife, Christie, and asked them to spend time thinking about being Danny's guardians. Without hesitation, Christie responded first. "Mom, there is nothing to think about. Danny is family and we will do anything for him." John II said, "Mom, you didn't have to ask me. I will always be there for my brother." Although these two are young, as young as John and I were when we first headed down this journey with Danny, they portray the essence of love and the power of family.

In addition to our will, trust, and guardianship instructions, there is also a five-page letter written to my brother and a very close family friend who are the first and second trustees. The letter outlines in detail Danny's circle of friends, his needs, his wants, and all that is to occur on his behalf. Whenever John and I go on a plane together, we send my brother an e-mail putting him on alert. A thoughtful written plan and the trust of family and friends bring me the comfort I need to live life without fear or worry. This could never be replaced by any promise or guarantee made by the bureaucracy.

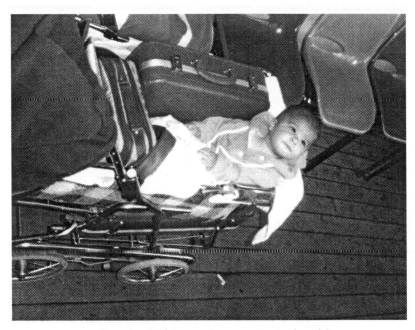

Danny ready for vacation – 5 months old.

Mercado family – Seattle, Washington – summer of 1982

Danny's 1st Birthday – March 1983 – five months after meningitis

The Mercado family
– US Army Officer
Candidate School (OCS)
Graduation – 1984

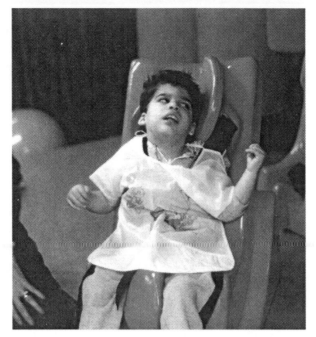

Danny receives therapy in Seoul, Korea – 1985

Danny and Mom after therapy session – Seoul, Korea – 1985

Family visits Danny at Silvercrest Developmental Center – New Albany, Indiana 1988

Mercado family vacation – Biltmore Estates – Asheville, North Carolina – August, 1992

Danny enjoys the ocean thanks to Easter Seals specialized equipment!

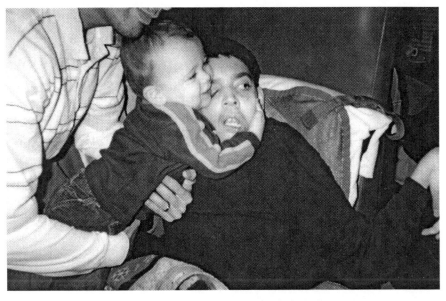

Danny gets a special hug from nephew, John III

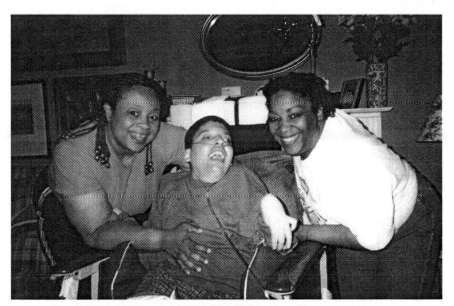

Danny with support staff – Donna & Bernie – 2002

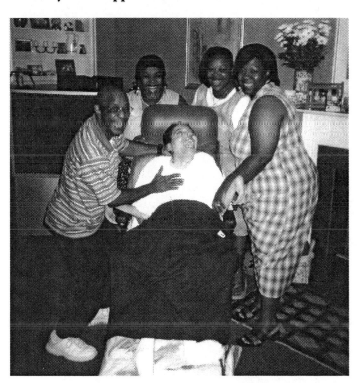

Danny with support staff – Rafael, Bernie, Paulette, Leslie – 2005

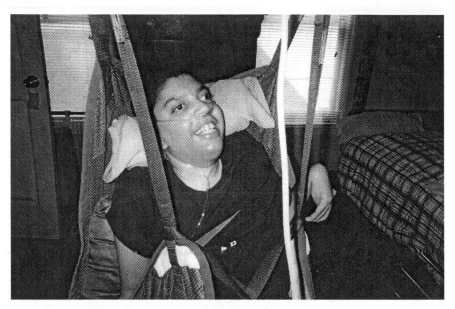

Danny trying out his new lift system – 2002

Danny's 21st Birthday!

Chapter 14

CAP Smart

The definition of the 1915(c) waiver is posted on the website of the National Association of State Medicaid Directors (NASMD). The definition reads as follows:

"Home and community-based waivers (1915(c)) are tools used by states to obtain federal Medicaid matching funds to provide long-term care to patients in settings other than institutions. Waivers must be approved by CMS and are good for three years, after which they may be renewed every five years. Home and community based care is increasingly being viewed as a preferable alternative to long-term institutional care, not only for the individual who may remain among friends and family, but also for the state, because **services maybe provided for less than the cost of institutional care**."

Toward the end of the EPSDT battle, the state announced a forty-million-dollar deficit in the CAP MR/DD budget. This deficit was announced shortly after the approval of an annual increase in the waiver from $68,000 to $86,058. By this time the self-determination projects were spinning their wheels trying to find ways to implement the self-determination principles. We were, however, learning to develop individual budgets for consumers. The flexibility of an individual budget in many cases provided cost savings. The announcement of the budget deficit added to the already pending EPSDT issue involving access to the full benefits of EPSDT services and the cost limitations of the waiver. One couldn't help but wonder if the deficit could be prevented by utilizing a more cost-effective method. I remembered very clearly how long it took for the state to remedy the high cost of diapers provided on the CAP waiver. The implementation of self-determination principles would not guarantee cost savings, but it could provide the flexibility needed to allow families control of the Medicaid dollars, which could very well amount to savings in many consumer budgets.

In an attempt to come up with a solution to the deficit situation, I contacted several waiver families across the state. These families provided me with their children's waiver cost summaries. Through a dialogue with the families, an individual budget was developed for each consumer. Our goal was to present this information to the North Carolina secretary of Health & Human Services. We were unable to secure an appointment with the secretary. However, with the help of the executive director of The Arc of North Carolina, an appointment was set with the assistant secretary on May 30, 2001 at 4:00 p.m.

By this time the injustice of EPSDT was exposed. In addition, every family throughout the state had adverse experiences with their school district in accessing an education for their child with a disability AND there were still over 6,000 people with disabilities across the state waiting for waiver services. The CAP MR/DD waiver is still a big secret in North Carolina. Although children are part of the school system and see pediatricians and other medical professionals on a regular basis, it is rare that waiver information is given to families from these sources. Families find out about the waiver just as I did in 1993: through conversations with other families. It is an understatement to say families are angry. Millions of taxpayer dollars pour into school districts and government agencies across the state for the purpose of complying with laws written to assist children with disabilities and their families. Families across the state experience non-compliance with these laws at every turn. Our anger is justified and we want the non-compliance to cease. Our children have lost valuable time as they continue to wait for services. Our families experience unnecessary stress beyond repair. Marriages continue to fall apart as a result of the unnecessary stress put on families. The stress is unnecessary because the rules, regulations, and laws are clear as to what should occur for children with disabilities and their families. But the bureaucracy is not properly monitored; nor is it held accountable for its actions. As I spoke with families, it was my goal to make sure the assistant secretary and the other powers that be understood the serious-ness of the issues presented and, more importantly, understood families were tired of the nonsense and wanted it to stop. To ensure they took us seriously, we invited the attorneys from the National Health Law Program to attend the meeting with us.

During our preparation for this meeting, I received an e-mail from a family in the western part of the state.

"Denise, you are a kindred spirit with Kathy and I. Thank you for being so crazy and doing all this, believing somehow it might make a difference. This is the big break we have been praying for and the Health Law Program attorneys seem heaven-sent. After years of beating my head against the wall, I have lost all hope that things will change by sitting at the table with state program officials. I think change will have to be legally forced."

When I first met with the director of the North Carolina Division of Medical Assistance regarding EPSDT, I presented my son's doctor's note as instructed by both the ADAPT and National Health Law Pro-gram attorneys. The fact that I took instruction from attorneys did not seem to move the director. If the mention of attorneys did not move the issue, then maybe their presence would make a difference. However, the executive director of The Arc of North Carolina disagreed. He believed an attorney's presence would put the assistant secretary on the defen-sive, not open to hearing what needed to be said. By the same token, without attorney support, we risked being disregarded. It was difficult in the middle of all that we had to deal with to come up with an effec-tive strategy that would get us what we needed for our children. The families discussed the issue and decided to invite the attorney despite the recommendation of the executive director of The Arc of North Carolina. However, the day before our meeting I received an e-mail from the National Health Law Program attorney stating she was unable to attend the meeting. She advised not to delay the meeting. "There are real plusses with an attorney not being there, given the state's history with litigation. There is a very real risk that our attendance could serve only to shut the discussion down." So, like it or not, we were on our own. However, the executive director of The Arc of North Carolina did attend the meeting with us.

Three moms, including myself, represented CAP MR/DD families.

151

Another mom represented families of children with Medicaid cards who receive little to no medically necessary services. The meeting with the assistant secretary was scheduled for 4:00 p.m. and would last no longer than one hour. We carefully planned our presentations. Each parent was limited to a ten-minute presentation, during which time he or she shared a picture of his or her child and told of the horror of accessing services.

After introductions, I explained to the assistant secretary that the reason for our visit was to make him aware of the reality we face as parents of children with disabilities in North Carolina.

During the presentation, we shared an e-mail from a DMH staff member that circulated throughout the state. It was dated May 22, 2001. The e-mail states.

"Due to the status of our budget for CAP MR/DD year ending 6/30/01, we will NOT be able to release any emergency slots for the remainder of the year, new or turn-over. Our average cost per person has climbed over the past three months based on actual billing to the point that we cannot bring additional people into service. If the legislature appropriates additional funds for the next fiscal year beyond what has already been planned, we will be able to resume new service. We will be sending out a formal communication to you all in the field. I am sure you are aware of several people in pretty dire straights right now waiting on this decision, so please assist those areas in making alternative plans. A final note, please make sure that children who are Medicaid eligible without CAP are receiving the full extent of EPSDT services they may need, known as Health Check in this state. If you need additional information about this program, let me know. As you know, only the legislature can make a difference right now. Thanks for your help."

This is really a continuation of the blame game. "Only the legislature can make a difference right now." Not necessarily so. Could there not be a better, more cost-effective way to spend taxpayer dollars? The budget deficit is a result of the bureaucracy pushing families into a corner with an unexpected push back from the families. When we pushed we exposed the injustice of EPSDT and the fact that the present waiver was not operating according to the current average cost of ICF/MR facilities. The bureaucracy is standing before us with its pants around its ankles, looking to the legislature to save it by throwing it more taxpayer dollars.

After presentations from the families, I presented to the assistant secretary a packet which focused on the CAP MR/DD waiver and the budget deficit.

Although the new waiver began April 1, 2001, the entire state was operating the waiver without a manual. By this time families understood the danger of trusting what was being said without anything in writing. We knew the manual would curtail inconsistencies from case managers and other area program officials across the state. A manual is a basic necessity to run any program and yet we waited months after the waiver was approved to see anything in writing. Our first request to the assistant secretary was to help us get a manual so we knew what should be occurring in this waiver. "I'll look into it and get back with you" was the assistant secretary's response to the manual concern.

The CAP MR/DD waiver was renewed again in September 2005. This time, however, a DRAFT manual was provided. Consumers, families, and provider agencies were told by state officials that the DRAFT manual was to be used as a "guide." The finalized version of the manual for the renewed September 2005 waiver did not materialize until January 2006.

The services in the 2001 waiver included four daily levels of supported living and an hourly supported living periodic service. Some of the other services included were day habilitation, personal care, and respite. Each service had very strict rules. For example, you could not have four hours of supported living periodic without at least one unit (fifteen minutes) of personal care. Each daily supported living level had a specific number of hours of service. For example, Supported Living Level I provided only four hours of service; Supported Living Level II provided up to six hours of service; Supported Living Level III provided up to seven hours of service; Supported Living Level IV provided up to eight hours of service. The level of service received was dependent upon the extent of the disability. This was determined through the North Carolina Support Needs Assessment Profile (NC SNAP). In addition, each service had a designated rate.

The purpose of our meeting with the assistant secretary was to show that the present system was not working for families and consumers. The presentation provided three pages of comments from families across the state.

The comments from families addressed necessary equipment not being funded by Medicaid along with equipment that takes over a year to arrive, such as augmentative communication equipment. Several families shared the tough decisions they made between services and medically necessary equipment such as feeding pumps, wheelchairs, ramps, and other recommended therapeutic equipment for children considered medically fragile. Despite obtaining prescriptions for medically necessary services and supports, children and adults with significant disabilities were not receiving the prescribed items. A single parent shared the difficulty working outside the home as she depended upon private providers to fill staffing needs during the summer months. Because families do not select, hire, and fire staff from provider agencies, parents shared the nightmare of finding workers asleep on the job. As parents reported the misconduct of staff to the provider agency, the parents were then reported by staff to the Department of Social Services for allegations that were almost always found to be false.

Several families shared concerns with scheduling restrictions to the respite definition which caused primary care givers to take a lesser number of respite hours then needed. One parent of a child with significant disabilities was also a former CAP MR/DD case manager who found the system to be extremely difficult to maneuver and understand.

As I listen to the concerns and issues of families throughout the state, I can't help but wonder if the parents of children and adults in the five state mental retardation centers have the same comments to make. For one thing, they certainly can never say they did not have enough respite!

The purpose of the waiver as described on the National Association of State Medicaid Directors (NASMD) website is "to provide long-term care to patients in settings other than institutions." The website further states that "home and community based care is increasingly being viewed as a preferable alternative to long-term institutional care, not only for the individual who may remain among friends and family, but also for the state, because **services maybe provided for less than the cost of institutional care**."

Does the state save money by ignoring the needs of the consumer? It certainly seems that way. The only alternatives offered to families of children with disabilities was ICF MR facility care or this crazy, unresponsive bureaucracy that holds families captive to a system that exploits rather than supports those in need. Our presentation to the assistant secretary provided a third alternative that would for the first time address the needs of the consumer while living at home.

As project manager for one of the North Carolina self-determination projects, I learned the concepts of the employer of record and fiscal intermediary services. With this knowledge I developed individual budgets for twelve CAP waiver consumers. Every budget developed had two standard line items. The first line item was entitled Individual Assistant. This line item was designated for the support-staff hours needed. The second line item was entitled Case Management/Support Broker. The term *support broker* was the self-determination term for case manager. Other line items in the budget were based on the specific needs of the consumer.

At the time, Danny was nineteen years old. The services he received were personal care at 56 hours per week, supported living periodic at 28 hours per week, and 225 hours per year of respite. The rate for personal care and respite services at the time was $13.44 per hour. The rate for supported living periodic was $22.28. This totaled $74,600.96 for direct care staff support. The direct care staff are crucial to the support of people with disabilities. It is very difficult for a family to care for the intense needs of a son or daughter without the support of others. Despite this high rate for services, wages for the direct care staff were $8.00 per hour with no benefits. For computation purposes, the 225 hours of respite were calculated at four hours per week. This totaled 88 hours per week of service. Taking into consideration payroll taxes and mandatory worker's compensation insurance, an $8 hourly wage for three staff members in an 88 hour work week without any overtime would be an approximate wage of $720 per week. This multiplied by 52 weeks in the year is a total of $37,440. The difference between the actual cost of wages for the staff and the rate provided by CAP funding is $37,160.96. This means that the overhead of provider agencies equaled 50 percent of the Medicaid waiver rate.

The concept of employer of record and fiscal intermediary services requires a shift in control of dollars. As fiscal intermediary, the provider agency would channel Medicaid dollars to the family according to the individual budget. As employer of record, the provider agency would ensure direct care staff met all Medicaid and Department of Labor requirements. Taking into consideration these two major functions and other possible functions required by the waiver, the provider agency would establish a fee schedule.

For the individual assistant line item, I asked families how many hours of direct care staff they needed per week. I also asked what wage they would offer and if they would offer benefits.

At the time I was working full time in Raleigh, North Carolina. Travel time from Fayetteville, North Carolina to Raleigh, North Carolina was an hour and a half each way. I needed twelve hours per day of care for Danny in order to maintain my work schedule. On weekends I usually took less than twelve hours of care, but for computation purposes in this individual budget I allocated twelve hours per day for the entire week. In addition to regular hours needed, 250 hours of respite per year were allocated. I calculated my direct care staff wages at $12 per hour. Including payroll taxes, worker's compensation insurance, and medical benefits calculated at $50 per week, the total wage for the year, not including overtime, was $57,600. At the time, the fiscal intermediary and employer of record fees were being calculated at approximately $5,000 per year. This totals $62,600 per year for direct care staff. If the fiscal intermediary and employer of record fees were doubled at $10,000 per year, the cost would be $67,600. The comparison in just this one line item indicated a $7,000 savings. As a result of shifting control to the family, the direct care staff was paid higher wages and received benefits.

The CAP MR/DD budget also had a line item for case management. The cost was $6,108 per year. Many of us didn't know what these dollars provided. Once a month an assigned case manager came to visit. He or she also typed up the annual plan of care and any revisions needed. This didn't seem like $6,108 worth of work. In the individual budgets presented, the case management/support broker line item was reduced to $4,000 per year.

Although I felt confident the cost of Danny's supplies and equipment could be decreased if given the opportunity to shop around, I thought it best to keep the costs the same when developing the individual budget. Other line items added to Danny's hypothetical individual budget were cell phone, vehicle repair/maintenance, recreation, and vacation. Oh, I can hear the bureaucrats now! "We can't use taxpayer dollars for a consumer's vacation." Why not? Taxpayer dollars pay for bureaucrat's many long vacations—not to mention sick time and 401K benefit packages!

The individual budgets also took into consideration a 3 percent administration fee for the local area program to channel dollars from the state to the perspective provider agencies along with a small start up fee for fiscal intermediary and employer of record services. The total of Danny's hypothetical individual budget was $77,907.05. The total of Danny's CAP budget was $86,058. In the $86,058 CAP budget, wages for staff were lower and there were no staff benefits. Although the individual budget showed a lower allocation to the consumer, it offered higher wages and benefits for direct care staff and other line items to support the consumer to live successfully in the community.

In one of the eleven individual budgets developed, the family designated $1,800 per year for food supplements. Another budget included horseback riding therapy and day camp fees. Each of the budgets included higher wages and benefits for direct care staff. In some cases families were able to access more direct care staff hours per week.

The total CAP dollars allocated to each of the twelve consumers totaled $667,360.80 per year. The total dollars for the individual budgets for the same twelve consumers totaled $606,336. The comparison showed a savings of $61,024.80.

The key to the individual budget is the flexibility of dollars. Families decide the wages for staff. They also have the ability to move dollars throughout the budget. For example if $5,000 is designated for equipment and the family shops around and finds the equipment needed for $4500, the difference can then be added to another line item such as direct care staff support.

We made our presentation with such high hopes that we would be heard. The system needed to be fixed. It needed to be more consumer friendly in order to meet the needs of the consumer in the community. The families believed that the cost of quality care for a child or adult with significant disabilities would certainly be less than institutional care and in some cases less than what was presently being allocated. This proposal, if acted upon, could allow the state to serve more people who were simply waiting for a slot. We waited, we prayed, but there was no response. Finally on July 2, 2001 I sent a letter to the assistant secretary.

"It is with great concern that I write this letter. On May 30, several parents met with you to discuss the reality we face as parents of children with disabilities in North Carolina. It has been over a month and despite phone calls and e-mails to your office, we have received no response to any of the issues presented to you on May 30.

"It was in good faith that we met with you in the hopes that our issues would not fall on deaf ears. I realize we are facing trying times in our state, but our children are still waiting. So, once again, we ask these questions:

"How do children with Medicaid cards access EPSDT services (Health Check) in the state of North Carolina?

"When will we see flexibility in the service delivery system that will ensure cost effectiveness for our state and quality of life for people with disabilities in North Carolina?

"I ask you, sir, what is it going to take to get answers to these questions?"

On July 17, 2001 a follow-up phone call was made to the assistant secretary's office to confirm that the letter was indeed received. The reality was simple. We were being ignored. Our issues and a possible solution weren't important enough to move the bureaucracy. However, the bureaucracy was quick to announce its deficit. It may be that the purpose of the deficit announcement was not to find a solution to the problem, but to instill fear in the hearts of the people it serves in order to generate a sense of gratitude for the inadequate solutions that were finally provided.

In the meantime, documents continued to come across my desk that would boggle my mind on the inadequacy of services provided. In October 2001 the state conducted a consumer survey of all the area programs. The survey in its entirety can be found in Appendix A. This survey was divided into four sections with the following results:

Overall Satisfaction with Services – 93% of consumers surveyed indicated overall satisfaction with the developmental disability services provided.

Access to Services – 93% of consumers surveyed indicated developmental disability services were accessible.

Appropriateness of Services – 92% of consumers surveyed indicated developmental disability services were appropriate.

Self-Assessment of Outcomes – 80% of consumers surveyed indicated that they were doing better as a result of the developmental disability services provided.

Of the thirty-nine area programs that participated in this survey, nineteen area programs did not list a percentage in any of the sections in the survey. Instead the code "N/A" was indicated with a footnote stating the following: "N/A indicates that there were less than ten responses so the data is not shown for the area program." If nineteen out of thirty-nine area programs did not have enough consumer participation to be counted in the survey results, then how can you conclude 93 percent of consumers with developmental disabilities statewide are satisfied with services provided? It would seem to me that fiscal responsibility of taxpayer dollars would require survey participation from at least 75 percent of all consumers receiving services from the developmental disabilities section of each of the area programs. In Cumberland County there are over 225 individuals receiving CAP MR/DD services. CAP MR/DD is only one aspect of services provided to individuals with developmental disabilities in an area program. If 75 percent of CAP recipients participated in the survey, over 170 responses should have been received. But according to this survey, less than ten responses were received. My son is one of the CAP MR/DD recipients in Cumberland County. I never received the survey. I checked with several other CAP MR/DD families across the state. None of us received the survey. Yet I am sure the bureaucrats believe the survey is but another "enormously accessible" document.

In an attempt to solve the waiver deficit issue, families decided on a new strategy that involved state legislators. The CAP SMART campaign was the result of this new strategy. Our purpose was to show legislators that there was a smarter way to spend taxpayer dollars while serving children and adults with significant disabilities in their homes. While gathering statistics to support the campaign, the April 1, 2000 study from the Office of the State Auditor was reviewed. The state auditor indicated in the study, "Although a lot of money is involved, money, by itself is not the answer. In fact, we believe that the current amount of

State spending is not necessarily to blame for system problems, although North Carolina can do better. The problem is that the spending patterns are not aligned with the directions the system should be taking. Too much money is being spent on too few clients."

On January 17, 2002 a letter was sent by families to the director of the Division of Medical Assistance (DMA), the acting chief of the Division of Mental Health/Developmental Disabilities/Substance Abuse Services (DMH), and the director of the North Carolina Developmental Disabilities Council (NCDDC). These three directors were referred to as the state partners. By this time a new director for the Division of MH/DD/SAS was being recruited. The letter sent read as follows:

"For the past two and one half years, families of children with disabilities and adults with disabilities presently served on the CAP MR/DD waiver have waited patiently for the birth of Self-Determination in our state. After more than $400,000 in DD Council and state funding, the Self-Determination Pilot Projects have failed in supporting people presently on the waiver according to the principles of self-determination. This failure is due in part to the lack of advocacy generated by the pilot projects. It is also the result of a lack of cooperation between the state partners in developing a self-determination waiver as promised at the beginning of the projects' existence.

"Families of children with disabilities and adults with disabilities recognize the importance of the CAP MR/DD waiver. Without these services, many of our children and adult citizens with disabilities would reside in public and private ICF/MR facilities away from family and friends. Although appreciative of these waiver services, families of children with disabilities and adults with disabilities also recognize the inefficiencies of this program. Recipients of waiver services do not have flexibility within the waiver to implement the principles of self-determination. As a result of numerous rules and regulations, this waiver has reached crisis proportions with a deficit of more than $40 million.

"With this waiver in jeopardy, families of children with disabilities and adults with disabilities fear the repercussions of the deficit will be additional cuts in services or the total loss of the CAP MR/DD waiver. We, therefore, propose a shift in the way the CAP MR/DD waiver is presently operated."

The letter continued with the same concept presented to the assistant secretary along with the individual budgets developed for twelve families. By this time the makeup of the twelve families had slightly changed. Of the twelve families presented, two would require higher funding than presently received. However, the other ten families provided a savings of over $84,000. The total savings for these particular twelve families was over $82,000. A copy of this letter was also sent to the governor, the secretary, and the assistant secretary. The letter was also e-mailed to parents and self-advocates across the state along with the director of the self-determination center in Michigan.

Immediately after the letter was sent to the state partners, a packet was developed with a cover page stating,

"IMPORTANT INFORMATION FROM YOUR CONSTITU-ENTS!"

The packet included the letter sent to the state partners along with the names, contact information, and counties represented for each of the twelve families. The packet also included the proposed individual budgets for the twelve families along with a copy of an e-mail from a mother in Wake County sent to her state legislator on January 7, 2002.

The email stated the mother's understanding of the budget concerns and the freeze on the CAP MR/DD program. The email also clearly indicated that this was a middle class family of a two-year-old with significant disabilities. The child has a seizure disorder, is fed with a feeding tube, has visual impairments, and needs specialized equipment the family cannot afford.

The mother explained in the e-mail that she was having difficulty caring for her daughter, "as she is getting too heavy for me to lift daily." At one point institutions were suggested to the family, but the mother learned of the Katie Beckett story and knew institutionalization was not the only option. Like so many of us, this mother begged for help.

Our goal was to put the packet in the hands of each of our state legislators. The packet was eighteen pages long. Unfortunately we had no official support from any developmental disability organization. What we were embarking on was considered radical and revolutionary. In order to meet our goal, we passed the hat among the twelve families and asked for contributions to cover the cost of printing over sixty-five packets for state legislators. In order to curtail costs, we hand-delivered the packets to each legislator's office. A packet was also delivered to the office of the Fiscal Research Division at the legislative building and the Budget Management Division. Packets were sent to several Raleigh and Fayetteville media sources. Parents across the state were instructed to meet with their local media sources to review the packet and request coverage. Our request for coverage even stretched as far as the famous television program *60 Minutes*. Unfortunately we never heard from anyone regarding our request for national television coverage.

In the middle of the CAP campaign, the Division of MH/DD/SAS announced the selection of its new director. We heard lots of good things about this new director, particularly that he had understood and implemented the principles of self-determination in another state. There is an old saying that holds true to our first encounter with this new director: Never judge a book by its cover. Another parent and I made arrangements through several sources to meet the new director the day before he started his new job. As we sat in the restaurant waiting for the new director to arrive, we sized up every male who entered. We did not know what this guy looked like. At one point we saw a distinguished gentleman with salt-and-pepper hair walk in with nice kaki pants and a preppy type sweater. He looked like he was looking for someone and we were convinced he was our guy. After approaching the gentleman, we realized we were wrong. Just then a big, burly guy in kaki pants, a shirt, and tie came barreling in. He too was looking for someone. But this couldn't possibly be our next director. This guy had a ponytail! Never in a million years had I expected the conservative state of North Carolina to hire a male with a ponytail as a director of any government agency! In many ways I saw hope. This guy looked like a liberal and maybe that's what we needed to make change. But the ponytail unfortunately was nothing more than a façade. Over lunch we shared with the director the CAP campaign. He immediately said, "This would make a great project." We were so excited to have someone finally listen to us. The twelve families met and decided to hold a welcome party for the new director. The party was held at one of the twelve family's homes on February 15, 2002. Again, this was a pure family endeavor with donations taken at the door.

The new director seemed true to his word. On February 20, 2002, a meeting was held with the twelve families and several division staff members. At the meeting the director stated, "I want your sons and daughters to have a life like I choose to have in my community...I need the system to learn how to do that—to be supportive of that...I want to work closely with the DD Council...I want the four self-determination pilot projects to learn...I personally want to follow these twelve families." He further explained that self-determination begins with the person-centered planning process. He wanted the plans for each of the twelve families to be all-inclusive of what was needed. As a result he assigned division staff to each of the twelve families to serve in the role of case manager. He also insisted that the twelve families remain twelve families and that no other families be added to the project. Our agreement to this limitation was a fatal mistake to the success of this campaign. We made a similar error with the Director of the North Carolina Division of Medical Assistance during the EPSDT battle. He didn't want doctor's letters determining medical necessity of services coming to his office because, as he put it, "it would bog down the system." But the system needed to be bogged down so that he would understand the urgency of the need. The same held true here. Unfortunately we did not recognize the mistake made during the EPSDT battle. Therefore, we willingly agreed to accept the limitation of the "twelve-family project."

In the meantime, the January 17 letter to the state partners generated letters of support from the North Carolina TASH organization and The Arc of North Carolina. In addition, only one of the state partners responded to our letter. That response came from the director of the North Carolina Council on Developmental Disabilities. The letter began with a history of over six years of council participation in state developmental disabilities reform efforts.

"Since that time, to this end, we have invested over a million dollars in a series of statewide, multi-project initiatives, spanning systems change, advocacy and leadership, and capacity building activities."

Six years and a million dollars later and we still don't have self-determination!

"We do not believe that the (Self-Determination) projects or their partners have failed. We believe that the initiative is poised to act. It is seeking leaders— leaders like yourself, and the self-advocates, professionals and policymakers who are, or are yet to become part of, the energy for change surrounding these four sites."

I do not understand a bureaucracy that used lack of leadership from the people they were in business to serve as an excuse for their lack of movement. If family and self-advocate leadership was so vital to ensure change, where were our paid staff positions? The bureaucracy expects families to be the natural support for their loved ones and to volunteer in a number of capacities throughout the bureaucracy in order to help it do its job. If the members of the bureaucracy need that much help doing their jobs, then maybe they don't belong in their positions.

The twelve-family project met on a somewhat regular basis with the division staff. The meetings were not productive in any sense of the word. For every one of our meetings, families traveled from all corners of the state with no reimbursement for mileage. The families knew that flexibility of dollars was what was needed to make the change effective. The families requested over and over again that the current rate structure be waived to allow families to implement the individual budgets that indicated the savings needed. At one meeting the director showed up for less than five minutes, stating he was needed at the General Assembly. He turned the meeting over to his assistant director, who spent the next thirty minutes whining, pissing, and moaning about all the work the division had to do to "turn the ship around." At no time was any consideration given to the sacrifices parents were making to attend the meeting. One of the twelve parents drove nine hours from Murphy, North Carolina to Raleigh for each of the meetings. In addition to the sacrifices parents made to attend the meetings, most of the twelve families had children with significant disabilities, like my son. We would leave our children with paid staff support and drive to Raleigh to help foster change—change that unfortunately, to this day, has yet to materialize. Over and over again, families would ask, "What is the timeline?" Every time we look in the eyes of our children, we see time ticking away. Our children's life-expectancies are longer than they were fifty years ago, but it is not the same life-expectancy as your and mine. Will they ever see decent services that will promote quality of life?

The twelve-family project kept us busy with busy-work. Decisions were made on who would be the division staff member assigned to each family and what type of person-centered planning process would be used. The twelve families represented ten area programs throughout the state. The division director wanted buy in from each of the area programs. It took a lot of caressing and hand-holding on the part of the division staff to get the area programs to agree to participate. As we witnessed the finessing, the twelve families watched in disbelief. Why doesn't somebody put their foot down and say, "This is what is going to happen"? In addition, another goal of the division was to use the twelve families to identify barriers in the CAP MR/DD waiver. The Microsoft Excel computer program was used in a number of ways by the division staff to display the numerous barriers identified by the twelve families, but solutions were nowhere in sight.

In an e-mail from one of the twelve families, the frustration and confusion was clearly stated.

"I am a bit coffee deprived this morning. I can never seem to get enough these days, but I would really like some feed back and help sorting my thoughts out about all the CAP SMART stuff.

"I am beginning to have more and more concerns, feeling that this whole thing is just becoming another bureaucratic nightmare. So here are some of my thoughts:

"1. We now have 'trainings' to go to on at least four days. This was not mentioned when we started this. I feel this is a tremendous time commitment, and I am not sure how 'person-centered' it is if we all have to do it with no regard for our individual needs and lives. Will we be kicked out if we don't go? And who will pay for childcare and transportation?

"2. My partner (Ann) seems very agenda oriented. (First we do this, then that, etc.) She is really pushing (although gently) for me to learn all the methodologies and then pick one and then pick a person off a list who can do this method. YUCK!!!!! My whole being rejects this. We don't do formal methods in our family very well, especially with strangers.

"I get the feeling that this is more about demonstrating the different methods than it is about real person-centered planning.

"3. When I told Ann that I had already decided that the person was as important as the method and I wanted Gail (an excellent support broker well versed in person-centered plans, and someone Amelia knows and trusts), it was almost as if she didn't hear me. She just went back to asking if I knew all the different methods and the PATH. So, I'm thinking that she is not being very person-centered herself at this point, but I agreed to look at the video she is going to try to send me.

"4. Amelia is at the age that she needs a transition plan and when I ask who will help and coordinate that, I get no answers from anybody. The case manager says it's the school's responsibility. The school has not a clue. Ann dodges the bullet. I know we need to start bringing in voc rehab and services for the blind and visually impaired, but are there other agencies, resources? Am I jumping the gun here? And once the 'plan' is done someone will miraculously appear and coordinate all this?

"5. What is in this for my family? So far all I see is huge time commitment and no goodies at the end—except that the state can say it has now used such-and-such a methodology, etc. Our lives are already so hectic and full of meetings and appointments. So now we have to set up a meeting to meet everyone and perhaps choose a method, then a facilitator. So when do we do the plan? And who helps implement it? Or is this just another one of those times when we get to dream and then are told, 'That's very nice, dear, but you know we can't do that, or help you figure out a way to do it.' In other words, WHERE IS THE IMPLEMENTER?

"6. I keep thinking of all the money they are spending on this and that it is money that is not going to really directly help anyone. So they get to go home at night excited about the changes they see coming and we get to stay up all night wondering how those changes are going to affect us.

"And then I see in the paper today that the secretary is proposing to close two mental health facilities and there is resistance. From whom? The staff!!!! Where is the article about how the consumers feel about this? It is such a blatant example of people turning things upside down. Now people with MH/DD are there to provide jobs for others and job security is more important than helping people. It sure helps me to understand why the provider agencies are so powerful, along with ICF MRs. The state needs to protect the jobs of all those people, hang the needs of the people they are serving. It's the employees that count. I am so disgusted with the whole thing!

"Please let me know what you all think and help me find some ray of hope and a reason to stick this out."

Once again time was ticking away. Months were passing and little to no progress was being made to relieve the budget deficit. The new director had been on staff for three months when he wrote a seven-page open letter to advocacy organizations and people with disabilities.

"I have concluded my first three months as the Director of the Division of Mental Health, Developmental Disabilities and Substance Abuse Services. A great deal of changes are occurring as part of reforming our state's system of specialty supports and services (mental health, developmental disabilities and substance abuse supports and services) for people with disabilities. I want to take this opportunity to speak briefly about two key concepts: consumer involvement and community capacity."

"Consumer Involvement…one of the fundamental principles of the State Plan is the need for people with disabilities and their families to take active ownership of the support and service system. This is particularly the case for the state and local public systems, but also applies to private provider systems as well. This active ownership is to occur at the 'micro' (individual) as well as the 'macro' (systems) level.

"At the micro level, the principle is person-directed/centered practice. This practice places the individual with the disability at the center of the process of defining real life outcomes and methods of support so they may best achieve their desired ends…This practice promotes the voice of the individual and supports choice…This practice requires people with disabilities to assume control and power in the decision making process as well as the corresponding responsibility.

"At the macro level, there are a variety of opportunities that are intended to ensure voice and systems ownership for people with disabilities and their families. This includes community-based planning efforts, such as involvement with the development of the Local Managing Entities (initially, the development of the local Business Plan). People with disabilities and their families should be afforded opportunities to be involved in the actual management of the community-systems. Remember that the newly emerging Local Managing Entities (LMEs) are intended to be public organizations that are not an 'organization in the community' but are part of a 'community of organizations.' Therefore, the involvement of people with disabilities in areas such as planning, access, quality improvement, rights protection, provider development efforts and monitoring, as key examples, is essential.

"Community Capacity – The challenge for the state and local systems is very clear – how do we best manage finite resources to respond to what seems to be infinite need. Therefore, in order to best focus efforts, there is a need to look very closely at whom we support and serve as well as the manner we support and serve people.

"As a simple definition, community capacity involves local communities' abilities to respect and value people with disabilities. This includes ordinary resources such as housing, employment and education as well as opportunities for developing friendships, social interactions advancing spiritual desires and exercising civic interests. Therefore, part of community capacity involves developing a community's desire to embrace people with disabilities as full citizens."

People with disabilities will never be accepted as full citizens as long as the educational system is allowed to get away with continued segregation of children with disabilities. When you are born you enter a family, a neighborhood, a community. Your citizenship continues when you enter school. If you are a child with a disability and are automatically segregated because of the disability, if you are sent across town to a school that has the "special program," you will experience an uphill battle toward full citizenship. If it is the goal of the North Carolina Division of Mental Health/Developmental Disabilities/Substance Abuse Services (DMH) to build communities that embrace people with disabilities as full citizens, then it must recognize the injustice in the education system and address this issue with its sister bureaucracy.

The benefits of person-centered planning at the micro level are dependent upon the ability of the consumer or family to insist that the plan is centered around the person with the disability and not anyone else. Every planning team must have a team member strong enough to keep the entire team focused on the person with the disability. When the disability involves cognitive impairments, the responsibility to focus on the person with the disability almost always falls to the parent or legal guardian. If the parent isn't strong enough in this role and no one else on the team steps in to fulfill the role, the person-centered planning process will be nothing more than a façade and needed services and supports will not be obtained.

At the micro level, the director stated that "people with disabilities and their families should be afforded opportunities to be involved in the actual management of the community-systems." The North Carolina General Statutes specifically outlines the structure of the area program board of directors:

GS122C-118.1(b) – At least 50% of the members of the area board shall represent the following:

(1) A physician licensed under Chapter 90 of the General Statutes to practice medicine in North Carolina who, when possible, is certified as having completed a residency in psychiatry.

(2) A clinical professional from the fields of mental health, developmental disabilities, or substance abuse.

(3) A family member or an individual from citizens' organizations composed primarily of consumers or their family members, representing the interests of individuals:
   a. With mental illness; and
   b. In recovery from addiction; and
   c. With developmental disabilities.

(4) Openly declared consumers:
   a. With mental illness; and
   b. With developmental disabilities; and
   c. In recovery from addiction.

The statute clearly involves people with disabilities and their family members as part of the area board. As board members of the area program, consumers and families are involved in the actual management of the community system. Unfortunately politics is also very much involved in the makeup and effectiveness of an area board. However, it is within the structure of the area board that decisions are made that directly impact the management of the area program. If this system is not working, it needs to be fixed. Instead the new director established consumer and family advisory committees (CFAC) consisting of consumers and family members throughout the area program system. The responsibilities of CFAC are to:

- Comment on state and local plans and budgets
- Help identify under-served populations and gaps in the service array
- Participate in the monitoring of service development and delivery
- Advise on the development of additional services and new mod-

els of service delivery
- Participate in quality improvement projects at the provider and LME level

Consumers and families have been participating in and advising the bureaucracy for years. Involvement in the actual management of the community system is not at the CFAC level but at the area board level. If consumers and families are complaining about services provided by an area program and the area board is not responding to the complaints in a timely and effective manner, then it should be the responsibility of the state to intervene. The intervention should include hard questions about the area board composition and decision-making processes. It should always be the goal of the state to ensure quality service delivery to all its consumers. I believe the state would agree that its goal is to ensure quality service delivery across the state. However, this bureaucracy reeks of the plantation mentality. In an attempt to respect the aristocracy of the area program system, the state will spend a countless number of hours talking, meeting, forming committees, and holding conventions to convince area programs to do what is right and provide quality services to people with disabilities and their families. In the meantime, consumers are thrown bones and expected to show appreciation for services rendered.

It was obvious from the new director's seven-page open letter that he was truly a bureaucrat despite the ponytail. Instead of addressing the entities that already existed, he chose to create new entities, resulting in a lot of activity but very little change. While consumers and families waited patiently for the new director to fulfill his promises, life continued in all aspects.

At this point Danny was nineteen years old. Considering his many physical and mental limitations, Danny was a healthy kid. Danny got colds like the rest of us. It took him a little longer than most to get over a cold, but he eventually did without any complications. I took pride in Danny's health. It was one of the few positive attributes in the situation we faced. It was very difficult when I first heard someone refer to Danny as medically fragile. Those words took my breath away. Unfortunately it was the last fact of reality that needed to be faced. For nineteen years I took pride in the fact that Danny never had pneumonia. Many children like Danny suffer from continuous bouts of pneumonia, but not

Danny.

In March, 2002, shortly before Danny's twentieth birthday, Danny became ill. When a person is unable to communicate with words, it is very difficult to understand what is wrong. The process of elimination always takes time and sometimes our conclusions are wrong. Danny showed signs of constipation. This was typical for Danny. To help with this we would keep a stool chart. If on the third day there was still no bowel movement, we would give Danny a small glass of prune juice via G-tube. This almost always worked. The doctor knew of our procedure and recommended that if at any time the prune juice did not work to use a fleet enema. It was very rare that we had to use an enema, but when we did it always provided positive results, except this time. It was late Sunday evening. The prune juice hadn't worked. Two fleet enemas hadn't worked. Danny was miserable. Nothing I did for him provided comfort. I called the advice nurse at the hospital. After explaining our situation, she recommended I bring Danny to the emergency room for a soapsuds enema. John and I bundled Danny up and traveled to the Womack Army Medical Center emergency room. In the examination room, the doctor greeted us. I explained very confidently that we were there for a soapsuds enema. She asked questions about Danny and then said very calmly and firmly, "Mrs. Mercado, we are going to start from the top of his head and work our way down." She immediately took out a penlight flashlight and began looking into Danny's eyes. Slowly she moved down his body, thoroughly checking every square inch. She listened with her stethoscope to his chest and stomach and then ordered X-rays. "What do we need x-rays for?" I asked. Again she said very calmly and firmly, "Mrs. Mercado, we are going to start from the top of this head and work our way down." In my mind I thought, "When the hell is she going to get to his butt? He needs an enema for crying out loud." The x-ray was taken and Danny was resting quietly on the gurney while we waited for the results. I was standing by Danny's side when the doctor came in and announced that Danny had pneumonia. My legs gave out as I fell in the chair. John and I looked at each other with tears in our eyes. We both feared pneumonia for Danny and believed it would be the one illness that would bring him down. "What happens now?" I asked the doctor. "We are going to admit him." She then continued her examination until she reached Danny's toes. She did exactly what she said she would do: she started at the top of his head and work her way down.

By this time it was Monday morning. As arrangements were being made for Danny's admission, John and I made phone calls to clear our calendars for the next several days. One of my Monday appointments was to meet with several families and the National Health Law Program attorneys regarding the twelve-family project and the state's lack of response to our concern of the deficit situation. The twelve-family project was going nowhere. The busy-work we were given was to develop with our state-assigned case managers a thorough person-centered plan. But first we had to decide which method of person-centered planning we each wanted to use. We were also to identify the system barriers. Well, one of the most important barriers is not the development of the plan but the implementation of the plan. The meeting was held without me, with one of the new parents taking copious notes. As I read the minutes from this meeting, I was amazed at the brainstorming had taken place. "Where do we go from here? What is the best strategy? Do we file a lawsuit? Do we push for an amendment to the waiver?" The parent taking the notes was new to our group and had ended her minutes with a personal comment. "Glad to be in the war zone with such great comrades. You guys are kicking major ass and I don't even think you know it."

For the next several days our focus was solely on Danny. Danny's pneumonia was complicated by the scoliosis. The doctor described Danny's lungs by referring to two paper bags full of air. He stated one lung was good but the other lung had collapsed due to the pneumonia and was unable to regain full capacity because of the scoliosis. In addition, Danny developed pockets of fluid around the lung. A chest tube was inserted to help drain the fluid, but because of the pockets it was impossible to reach all the fluid. We were told the pockets were like little incubators. The slightest germ could get in a pocket and cause another case of pneumonia. If this were to occur, there would be no way to get medication to the pocketed areas. After more than two weeks in the hospital, Danny was sent home with hospice services.

Due to Danny's chest tube, a lift system was critical for Danny once he was home. During his hospitalization I had spent countless hours trying to motivate a case manager who had no clue where to turn. Two years earlier Danny had been hospitalized for reflux. Medication was given and his G-tube feedings were drastically increased. As a result, Danny gained thirty pounds in one year. Although our case manager visited monthly and witnessed myself and the support staff manually lifting and transferring Danny to different equipment, it was not until my husband hurt his back and I hurt my arm that she recommended a Hoyer lift. I didn't even know what a Hoyer lift was. In order to find out what equipment was appropriate and available to us to support Danny at home, I recommended an assessment be done of our home and Danny's needs. That took over sixty days to materialize. Finally on February 27, 2002, an occupational therapist and physical therapist from one of our state-run facilities came to our home with an equipment vendor. A report was written by the therapists on March 1, 2002 specifically outlining equipment needed throughout our home. The report reads as follows:

"Daniel Mercado is a 19-year-old non-ambulatory client who has a diagnosis of profound mental retardation, cerebral palsy, spastic tetraplegia (right side more affected than left side), hydrocephalus, gastroesophageal reflux disease, chronic bilateral hip dislocation and seizure disorder. Also, he is status post two femur fractures and has a C-shaped scoliosis convex to the left; however, no attempts at surgical correction are being considered, secondary to stridor respirations.

"Daniel has lived with his mother and father all of his life in a single-family dwelling, and it is hoped that they can continue to provide his care. He requires round-the-clock supervision, as he has no voluntary movements and depends upon others to meet all of his needs.

"On February 27, we met with Daniel; Mrs. Denise Mercado, mother; Cumberland County Mental Health Center (CCMHC) case manager; and representative from Rehab Solutions, Inc. to determine appropriate assistive technology to meet Daniel's medical needs.

"Due to improved nutritional status, Danny has gained thirty pounds in the past year and currently weighs 80 pounds. Both his mother and father have sustained injuries from the repeated transfers that Danny undergoes each day. We recommend that a ceiling mounted lift and track system be purchased and installed in Daniel's bedroom. This would allow for ease in transferring Daniel to and from his bed, shower chair, and wheeled chair. Danny's bedroom, originally intended as a dining room, is very small, particularly since a bathtub/shower combination has been added to the room. A portable lift system would be too hard to maneuver in the small area, and has no place to be stored when not in use. If the track system is approved, only a single straight track of approximately ten feet would be needed.

"Daniel requires an O2 nasal cannula at night. He spends approximately 12 hours per 24-hour period in bed. His bed was constructed by his father, and stands approximately four feet off the floor on a stable base. Egg crate overlays are used for skin integrity, two or three pillows are placed under his head, and several others are used at his legs for positioning. When Daniel coughs, his head is sometimes pulled off of the pillows, and he is unable to reposition his head. In addition, the modified bed does not allow for the recommended 30 degree of elevation to lessen the effects of his recently diagnosed GERD. Therefore, we recommend a hospital bed to allow for proper elevation. To decrease the risk of pressure sores on Daniel's still-bony frame, a foam mattress and alternating-air mattress overlay are also advised. Padded side rails are essential to ensure safety.

"Daniel and his family need the lift system and hospital bed without delay. Because such items will be specifically catered towards his health needs, it represents an effective and appropriate use of program funds. In addition, this request must be given a high priority. Every day that passes without the recommended durable medical equipment increases the risk of further injury to a caregiver, as well as gastric upset and poor positioning for Daniel.

"If you have any questions, please feel free to contact us…"

This letter came thirteen days before Danny was hospitalized with pneumonia. The request for the equipment was considered by the therapists to be a high priority before the bout of pneumonia. The hospital bed was received almost immediately. However, the lift system was another story.

While in Danny's hospital room, I spoke with the case manager, administrators at the local area program, state employees at the division level, and the National Health Law Program attorneys, trying to get the equipment in our home that Danny would need. When Danny was discharged the lifting system was nowhere to be found. It took two people to lift and transfer and provide the care Danny needed. Finally on April 24, 2002, a letter was sent from one of the National Health Law Program attorneys to "request a hearing on a denial of medically necessary equipment for Daniel." Every time I called to ask the status of the lift system, the response was the same. "We're working on it, Mrs. Mercado." But when I asked for specifics I was told they were stumped on how they would pay for the $4800 piece of equipment. I was back to looking at Danny's cost summary. Now more than ever I could not give up the direct care staff. I needed the staff to help me with Danny. Without the lift system there needed to be two people to transfer him. The letter from the National Health Law Program attorney was written to the case manager and copies were sent to several staff members of the Cumberland County Mental Health Center, the director of the North Carolina Division of Mental Health/Developmental Disabilities/Substance Abuse Services (DMH), and several other DMH staff. A response was received on April 26, 2002 from an attorney providing legal counsel to the Cumberland County Mental Health Center. The letter was addressed to the attorney at the National Health Law Program and stated the following:

"This letter is in receipt of your faxed letter to (case manager) on April 24, 2002, concerning request for hearing on Daniel Mercado. I serve as legal counsel for the Cumberland County Mental Health Center.

"It is my understanding that this issue is being addressed on an ongoing basis with mental health staff in collaboration with State officials. They are exploring every appropriate resource available in an effort to resolve this matter and will continue to keep Mr. and Mrs. Mercado updated.

"In the future, please direct all legal correspondence to my office."

So adding attorneys to the mix did not help the situation. Why was this taking so long? Why were we given no timelines? Were they waiting for Danny to die? After all, he was now a hospice patient.

My daily conversations regarding this matter were primarily with those individuals at the state. The assistant director of North Carolina Division of Mental Health/Developmental Disabilities/Substance Abuse Services (DMH) seemed to take this challenge on as a personal project. Finally on May 3, 2002, we received a letter from the O'Berry Center Foundation. O'Berry Center was one of the five state-run mental retardation centers. The letter informed us that the foundation had approved the request to fund the lift system for Danny. On June 15, 2002, three months after Danny's hospitalization, the barrier-free lift system was finally installed in our son's room. In the meantime, the new DMH director still wanted the twelve families to identify barriers in the system. How's this for a barrier?

The Cumberland County Mental Health Center (CCMHC) serves over 225 CAP MR/DD recipients. At the time the cost for case management services per month was $509. The area program received $509 per month for each of the CAP MR/DD recipients served. This was an annual revenue source of $6,108 per consumer. $6,108 times 225 recipients equals a revenue source of $1,374,300. There were seven case managers on staff at the CCMHC when Danny was hospitalized with pneumonia. If all seven case managers were receiving an annual salary of $35,000, which was high for this area, the total salary expense would be $245,000. Even if you doubled that to accommodate the supervisory staff and threw in an extra $100,000 for payroll taxes, worker's compensation, and health benefits and another $100,000 toward other overhead costs, there still was over $680,000 in annual revenue unaccounted for. How was it that an area program with this kind of revenue source could not find $4800 to support an adult with significant disabilities to allow him to remain at home in his community? In addition, why was the caseload for case managers so high? Why were more case managers not being hired?

All of these concerns and more were brought to the next twelve-family meeting held on April 18, 2002.

We began this meeting by restating our goal. The "CAP Smart" goal was to obtain fiscal control of CAP dollars. We particularly wanted control of support-staff dollars so we could offer higher wages and benefits for staff support. Our goal was to provide a different way of doing business that would result in a better quality of life for those served and would possibly provide a much-needed savings to share with those still waiting for services. All of this would require systemic change. We thought the state had heard our concerns and goals. The solutions offered thus far included person-centered planning (PCP), determining individual budgets, funding the individual budget using waiver dollars and other funding resources, and identifying system barriers.

After review of our goals and what had been proposed thus far, we asked the following questions:

Is the individual budget part of the person-centered plan (PCP)?

We learned that the individual budget is part of the PCP; however, this is not necessarily done by the person who facilitates the plan. In addition, no one seemed to know who the developer of the individual budget would be.

What is the present status of the person-centered plan (PCP) process for each of the families?

Each of the twelve families seemed to be at a different stage in the process. Interestingly enough, not all the state case managers assigned to the twelve families were present at this meeting. Similar to the EPSDT dilemma, this was an added job duty that did not seem to take priority. Yet there was a forty-million-dollar deficit in this waiver. That, in and of itself, should have made this issue a priority.

What influence does the state have on the area programs in pursuing a special project? If the state wants to pursue a special project, what incentive does the area program have to participate?

The rest of the meeting focused on the barriers identified by the twelve families.

After much discussion around these questions, the twelve families requested a letter be written to the ten area programs involved, stating that their participation would be looked at favorably during a review of their perspective business plans. The development of a business plan by the area programs to be reviewed and accepted or rejected by the state was a new concept that many had difficulty completing. Unfortunately the director of DMH was unable to attend this meeting. The assistant director gave the standard response, "I am unable to write any of these letters, however, will bring these ideas forward to (the director)." During a telephone conversation between myself and the director that evening, he agreed (and had on several occasions mentioned to some of the ten area programs) that involvement in the twelve-family project would be a plus regarding the business plan. However, I shared with the director that he needed to do this with all ten area programs and that it had to be done in writing. He agreed.

The meeting then focused on the lack of effective case management. Now, there was a sore subject—especially after what we had just experienced when trying to obtain medically necessary lift equipment for our home!

Vacant case management positions existed in each of the area programs. Those in case management positions were overworked with huge caseloads. In Cumberland County alone there were over 225 CAP MR/DD recipients. At $509 per month for each recipient, this equaled over $1,370.000 in revenue. After approximate payroll and overhead costs, there should have be over $680,000 in revenue remaining. There was no excuse for vacant positions to continue to exist. The twelve families suggested that if a case management position remained vacant for more than thirty days, the state should remove ten slots per position and serve the CAP recipients from the state office. Case management in this situation would be contracted locally. One of the DMH staff members was quick to state her dislike of the idea. The assistant director—the more experienced bureaucrat—quickly interjected with a typical bureaucratic answer. "I'll be sure to share your suggestion with (the director) and get back with you." The same inexperienced DMH staff shared what she referred to as a "bizarre" request from a family on CAP. The request was that the child needed a swimming pool at their home. The family even had a doctor's prescription. The staff member, with a smug chuckle in her voice, shared that Medicaid could not pay for this and that the family had been told this. The issue, she stated clearly, had been dropped.

How do you do person-centered planning with bureaucrats who tell you to dream and then laugh at you when you do so? When doing person-centered planning (PCP), you ask the family and the person with the disability to dream. If their dream is a little farfetched, you do not laugh at them and share their "bizarre" request with the rest of the state. What you are supposed to do is continue dreaming with this person to find out what the person really is trying to convey. This encounter reminded me of what I read about one of the founders of the PCP processes known as Circles. The founder has quadriplegia with only purposeful head movements. As a student at a university in Canada, several of her classmates and professors started brainstorming with her to help her get out of a nursing home. During the process, they asked the individual with the disability what she wanted to do with her life. She stated that she wanted to be a truck driver! Imagine that. A quad driving a truck! No one laughed at her. Instead they continued to talk with her. During these talks they realized what she wanted was the freedom to travel. In her mind, truck drivers had a great life. They did on a daily basis what she had great difficulty doing. She wanted to see the world and travel to many places, which is not an easy feat for someone with extensive needs. The group was challenged but brainstormed and helped her reach her goal.

When the DMH staff member shared the "bizarre" request at the meeting, I looked immediately at the assistant director and waited for a response that never came. How far up the chain of command did this attitude go? I did not address this issue at the meeting any further but discussed it in detail with the director at a later date. The director agreed that this was not the way person-centered planning should be done. While I discussed the issue with the director, one of the other twelve moms sent an e-mail to the assistant director.

"I have been thinking about our meeting last week when you met with several of the twelve families…There was much discussed and much to think about, but there is one point in particular that I feel I must comment on further. I am referring to (the staff's) remark about the request by a family on CAP for a swimming pool. As you recall, she remarked that there was 'even' a doctor's prescription for it. She stated that Medicaid would not pay for such a thing. The family was told this and the matter was dropped. I don't know the circumstances of the family, but upon reflection, it occurred to me that the swimming pool might be financially advantageous— not a 'bizarre' request. I know from experience that Medicaid pays for pool therapy at Duke, which can run well over one hundred dollars a session. If the family was needing pool therapy for their child on a regular basis, the cost could run thousands of dollars quite quickly, not even taking into consideration time, scheduling, and transportation issues. Perhaps the family was actually asking for something quite reasonable, given their situation and needs. Beyond the dollars and cents, (the staff's) comment reflects an attitude that families are trying to milk the system for all its worth. It is my belief and hope that as we move toward a more person-centered way of doing things that comments and attitudes like the ones made at the meeting must stop. They serve no purpose beyond highlighting the attitude that families are not to be trusted to ask for what they need, but rather what they can get away with. This incident underlines my concern about who makes the final decision as to what is 'reasonable' to need and want. We are being asked to be truthful and honest in our needs and wants. But this is a scary thing to do when we see that there is an attitude among the people who have the final say that what we need and want might not be okay according to them. I look forward to your comments concerning this."

What an excellent e-mail! This mom, like the rest of us, was offended by the *bizarre* story presented by the DMH staff. And more importantly, we were literally floored that no comment came from the mouth of the assistant director. With great boldness, the assistant director responded to the e-mail.

"Without getting into perceptions and discussions of 'this was said, no, this is what I meant,' I would like to share my honest reactions with you. The forum for such a concern should not be based in an e-mail after the fact. The appropriate forum to state those concerns was in the meeting itself, and you missed the opportunity to challenge an individual if you thought they were out of line."

The twelve moms sitting in that room were not the only ones who missed an opportunity. This **ASS**istant director, and I emphasize the first three letters of his title, also missed an opportunity if in fact he thought his staff was out of line. In saying nothing he said a lot! His e-mail continued, "I feel badly using the e-mail to respond, because the dynamics of dialogue are absent. I believe that the discussion about a pool is taken out of context. It was not an example of someone's dream or example of self-determination, it was in the context of the discussion of costs that Medicaid would pay for. (The staff) showed no disrespect or insensitivity to this issue, it was a discussion of facts, reasonable or not, this is not something that Medicaid would pay for. It is most unfortunate that you come to a conclusion that (the staff's) attitude 'must be stopped.' Our staff has dedicated its talent and energy, and such a personal presumption is not at all fair. We are committed to work in a positive and productive respectful manner, and I would chastise my staff if they were out of line. As stated earlier, if this is what anyone felt, you lost an opportunity for dialogue, resolution and closure at that meeting. I pledge to you our continued effort to work in changing the system, and ask you to assist in a positive fashion because we are in this together. The road is a difficult one, but when traveled with mutual respect it makes the journey easier for all. Thank you for listening, and let's continue our efforts as friends and instruments of change."

I forwarded both the mom's e-mail and the assistant director's e-mail response to my husband and asked for his opinion. He responded, "Do not allow him to get away with this. Let him know that you think his e-mail attack on (this mom) was uncalled for and that he needs to rethink his stand on 'his staff's dedication, talent, and energy' because if one family member is feeling this way, then there is a 'perception' that some or maybe all other family members are seeing. Let him know that trust is a two-way street. We as families need to see his trust and his staff's trust before he can receive our trust."

This same assistant director called me on the phone months later. "Denise, do you have a minute?"

"Sure. What can I do for you?"

"I'm going to put you on speakerphone. I'm here with (one of my staff)."

He then proceeded to chew out my ass for all the e-mails I sent and for sending copies of all e-mails to CMS and other federal officials. As I listened to him scream at me over the phone, I could feel my body shake. I had taken the call in my bedroom. I sat slowly on my bed, trying to get control of myself and my thoughts. When he finally took a breath I said, "You must have me confused with your staff. I do not work for you. Therefore, you have no right telling me what to do and no right to call me and chastise me for my actions."

"Do you realize what you are putting us through?" he screamed. "We are trying to make the changes you want and you've got people breathing down our throats at all levels."

"Okay", I said with my voice trembling. "I see your point. What do you suggest?" I was angry and scared. Never before had someone considered a "professional" screamed at me like this. I didn't see his point but I needed more time to get my thoughts together. He took a breath and calmed down and proceeded to tell me what he wanted me to do. I don't remember any of the details of what he wanted. I really was not paying attention to what he expected me to do. After he was done I said, "If you really feel this needs to be done, I suggest you do it yourself. I don't work for you; therefore, I do not take direction from you." After a long silence, I said, "Hello." He said, "Yeah, I'm still here." Again there was silence. Finally we said goodbye to each other and hung up the phone. I really wanted to hang up on this guy, but I didn't want to give him the right to say that parents were difficult to work with. I remembered very clearly what John taught me. One of many military tactics is to always probe the lines for a weakness to exploit. I was not going to be this man's weak link and bow down to his demands. I did not hang up on him. Instead I lobbed the grenade back in his lap. Several weeks after this encounter, I attended a North Carolina Council on Developmental Disabilities (NCCDD) function. As I spoke with the executive director of The Arc of North Carolina, the DMH assistant director approached rather quickly. He interrupted my conversation with a smile and a big hug and said, "I owe you an apology. Will you forgive me? What can I say? I'm Polish!" We smiled and laughed and got through the meeting. His behavior had nothing to do with being Polish. His behavior had everything to do with being a bureaucrat! Bureaucrats need to control the situation. He took a gamble and tried to corral one of the lead moms in the state and he lost.

The discussion at the April 18, 2002 twelve-family meeting continued regarding inadequate case management. All twelve families experienced case managers trying desperately to do their jobs with primitive work tools. In Cumberland County, with over $680,000 in excess case management revenue, the case managers on duty shared computers. They had to coordinate their schedules and make an appointment to have computer time to type the plans of care for the individuals on their caseload. Many times, case managers would come to my home with paper, pencil, and a calculator in hand trying to figure out the cost summary page of the plan of care. Math is not a positive attribute of case managers. Case managers are people persons. They do not like math and they do not do it well. We live in an age of technology that equips us with computer programs like Microsoft Excel that can do the math for us. Why ask case managers to do a job we all know they are not good at? Why not give them the supplies they need so they can spend their time helping the person with the disability live successfully in the community? Obviously, money is not an issue with $680,000 in excess revenue! Again, we got the typical bureaucratic answer. "We'll have to get back with you." It wasn't until the September 2005 waiver that the cost summary attached to the plan of care was finally developed on an

Excel spread sheet. Now case managers multiply the number of hours an individual will receive by four in order to get the number of units (fifteen-minute intervals) for each service. The number of units is then entered into the Excel spreadsheet. The rest of the calculations are done by the computer program. Wow! Progress at last!

Another barrier presented at this meeting included the Medicaid payback fear factor expressed by the area programs. In order to help alleviate the fear factor, the families suggested the state audit the twelve families using personal outcome standards rather than the present paper-driven model. Another great idea, which to this day has yet to materialize!

It is amazing to me that twelve moms can come up with common sense solutions. Common sense is key to cost-effective planning. Moms take seriously what happens to their children. More importantly, we understand the responsibility and appreciate the support of taxpayer dollars. In no way do we want to exploit those dollars.

On June 20, 2002, as promised by the DMH director, a letter was sent to the ten area programs inviting them to a meeting with the twelve families on July 11, 2002 at the state office. The follow-up letter, dated July 17, 2002, contained the minutes of the July 11 meeting. The letter stated:

"As you can see from the attached summary, we have achieved benchmarks, but we are still faced with obstacles as we move our system towards a true person-centered focus in the provision of services and supports to individuals with disabilities and their families. Your efforts are providing an opportunity for families, future LMEs and the Division to explore a variety of creative strategies for supporting the development of a participant-driven system that reflects the principles outlined in the State Plan. To encourage your efforts, we have decided to exclude the waiver recipients in this effort from our fiscal audit processes for this year."

Despite the achievements and progress initiated by the twelve families, the project was dismantled in the summer of 2002. Families were tired and the progress was entirely too slow. In a last-ditch effort to help the bureaucracy understand the barriers that exist, I re-sent on July 29, 2002 a six-page letter to state officials. The letter was originally sent in February 2000 at the request of a North Carolina Division of Medical

Assistance staff member. The letter speaks to my experience with the Cumberland County area program in achieving a slot for my son in the CAP MR/DD waiver. The letter, like this book, is very important in identifying what needs to be changed in our current system. The bureaucracy, in its wisdom, operates through committees and unending meetings. But change will only take place when the bureaucracy takes the time to listen to the people it serves. The bureaucracy must be willing to meet with families where they are. It must be willing to leave the state capitol and meet with families in their homes and observe their surroundings and the sacrifices they make and the struggles they endure. The bureaucracy believes it is doing just that when it organizes public meetings throughout the state. This is not the same as picking up the phone, calling a family who receives services, and asking to visit. It is an eye-opening experience when you sit in the home of a family of a child or adult with severe disabilities. When you sit in their living rooms you can see the home taken over by equipment and technology. You can hear unidentified outbursts, but to your surprise, no one moves because these outbursts are an everyday occurrence. You can see and feel the emotion, the love, the frustration, the hurt, the grief. Only then can you understand the plight of families and only then can you set up a system that will meet their needs.

The twelve families stood before the bureaucracy and forced it to open its eyes and see the reality of its system. A bureaucracy that exists as a result of taxpayer dollars should not be forced to listen to the people it is in business to serve. Families and people with disabilities on the CAP MR/DD waiver still do not have fiscal control of Medicaid dollars in North Carolina. Wages for direct care staff are still in the hands of provider agencies that take entirely too much overhead, resulting in continuous staff turnover and unrest for the individuals being served.

Chapter 15

PCSS Is Born!

After receiving my degree in the summer of 1999, I took a full-time position with Easter Seals North Carolina. My job duties varied throughout my three years with the organization. At first I was the project manager for one of the North Carolina self-determination projects. When that project was disbanded I became the project director for the Partners in Policymaking (PIP) class. This was truly an honor. I was a graduate of the first North Carolina PIP class in 1993. As I studied and learned about the intricate details of the PIP program, I realized the North Carolina program was falling short. The original PIP program contained eight weekend classes. Up until this point, the North Carolina program never had eight full sessions. The last session of the original PIP program covered community organizing. During this session, participants learn to rally for change. It seemed the conservative state of North Carolina did not think this was such a good idea. Although state officials wanted to be considered progressive in their thinking, they thought it best to revise the PIP program and leave out the radical parts. As I read more and more about community organizing, I realized this was an important component to foster change. The push for the full array of PIP sessions added to my already aggressive frustration regarding the self-determination projects— all of which were primarily funded by the North Carolina Council on Developmental Disabilities. Needless to say, by the end of my three-year tenure with Easter Seals North Carolina, it was a great relief to all parties concerned when I announced my resignation.

During my tenure with Easter Seals, I met so many families across the state. Regardless of whether we were families from the eastern, western, northern, or southern part of North Carolina, the cries and frustration of the people being served were the same. While at Easter Seals I also had an opportunity to participate in Project Leadership. This was a national version of the PIP program that involved parents and individuals with disabilities as representatives of their perspective states. Again, the war stories and battle scars were the same. While on vacation in Jamaica, John and I met a couple from England who shared the same frustration in accessing services for their thirty-five-year-old daughter with disabilities. I am not sure why civilized countries cause so much frustration and heartache for families and people with disabilities. However, one thing I have learned is that some things do not require permission.

In 1997 I was part of a threesome of moms that orchestrated a coup of the defunct Arc of Cumberland County. After leaving The Arc of Cumberland County as executive director in 1999, I lost contact with the two other moms. In the summer of 2002 I received a phone call from Mary, one of the ringleaders of the takeover. After small talk, Mary said, "Denise, I think you and I should go into business." I almost dropped the phone. We made arrangements to meet for lunch the next day. During lunch I listened as Mary shared how she had established an agency that served only her daughter.

Mary's background allowed her a level of business confidence that I lacked. We both had gone to college immediately after high school and had left for different reasons. Finally, years later, we went back to school and completed our degrees. Mary and I are both Campbell University graduates. Mary obtained a Bachelor of Business Administration degree with a minor in accounting. She graduated summa cum laude—seventh in her class of 277 students! Shortly after graduation, she worked for the Social Security Administration in Fayetteville and then took a position in Washington DC as a naval auditor. She eventually came back to Fayetteville, where she worked as an accountant for a prominent CPA firm. After battling several illnesses with her daughter, she realized working out of the home was next to impossible. She then took all she had learned in business and applied it to her daughter's situation by creating a Medicaid agency that supported only her daughter.

I listened in amazement as this fireball of a woman said several times throughout the conversation, "We can do this! We can do this!" I did not have the same business confidence that Mary had, but I couldn't help but wonder, "What if she is right?" I heard my mother's voice inside me: "Nothing ventured, nothing gained." So I agreed. Shortly after, Mary and I began meeting at Barnes & Noble in Fayetteville on a regular basis. The agency Mary had established for her daughter was a Limited Liability Company (LLC). We established a separate LLC with a new name: Person Centered Supports Services, LLC (PCSS). We converted the basic policies and procedures from Mary's original LLC, but we wanted this agency to be different. We established a business model that incorporated the principles of self-determination as much as the crazy North Carolina system would allow.

PCSS focuses solely on the CAP MR/DD waiver. A person-centered operating budget, similar to the individual budget concept, is established for each consumer served. All consumers are expected to operate within their budget limitations. Once the LLC was established and a Medicaid number was obtained, Mary's daughter, Joanne, was transferred to PCSS in September 2002. In November 2002, my son Danny was also transferred to PCSS. Although we used our children for several months as guinea pigs, we kept a close watch on the business model established and the effects of its implementation. Within the first year of operation we found it necessary to modify the person-centered operating budget by taking out the startup fees and slightly raising the PCSS operating fee. Because we choose to work out of our homes, we do not have the extensive overhead affiliated with brick and mortar. Therefore, our operating fee is far less than that of the traditional provider agency. Although PCSS is a for-profit agency, its business model resembles that of a true nonprofit agency. We knew from the beginning that PCSS would need to serve several individuals to receive the same profit a traditional agency would receive on one, but our primary goal is never to exploit the consumer or the family. The PCSS mission is "to provide fiscal control of Medicaid dollars allocated for support staff for recipients of CAP MR/DD through Fiscal Intermediary and Employer of Record services." Although PCSS is not an official fiscal intermediary (FI) and employer of record (EOR) agency, it operates as such. PCSS bills Medicaid on behalf of its consumers for hours worked by direct care staff and for hours and services authorized by Medicaid. These dollars are the revenue source for the person-centered operating budget.

As EOR, PCSS hires and trains individuals selected by consumers and families for hire. The services PCSS provides to consumers and families include the following:

- Payroll Processing
- Federal/State Tax Deposits Based on Employee Wages
- File all Federal/State Monthly/Quarterly/Annual Reports
- Establish/Implement/Monitor Supervision Plan
- Regular Communication with each Employee
- Work with Consumer/Family/Staff to Develop a Backup Plan
- Develop Scenarios Based on Person-Centered Operating Budget to Assist Consumer/Families in Determining Wages for their Direct Care Staff
- Process Employee Raises
- Regular Communication with Case Manager
- Regular Communication with Consumer/Family
- Monitor Services
- Review/Approve Service Documentation
- Set up Medicaid Billing Documentation
- Complete Medicaid Billing as a Direct Enrolled Provider
- Provide Consumer/Family Monthly Revenue/Expense Statement
- Provide Updated Employee Training as Needed
- Establish Co-Employer Agreement with Consumer/Family
- Establish Consumer Needs Account
- Develop Job Description
- Assist in Writing Ads/Fliers
- Process Advertising Invoices
- Review Applications with Consumer/Family
- Assist in Interview of Employees as Needed
- Assist in Hiring Decisions
- Conduct All Background Checks
- Review Health Check Registry
- Complete Reference Checks
- Provide Offer for Employment

- Set up Personnel File for All New Employees
- Complete All PCSS Employee Paperwork
- Set up Payroll Documentation
- Complete Training Requirements for All Employees
- Participate in the Development of the Plan of Care/Continued Needs Review
- Develop Appropriate Strategies for Outcomes as Outlined in the Plan of Care

The PCSS vision is "to reduce the stress of staff turnover by allowing the individual and/or family to set wages within the constraints of their Person Centered Operating Budget." When I finally was permitted to set wages for my staff, salaries increased from $8 per hour to $12 per hour.

The individual budget concept was an idea The Arc of North Carolina established shortly after the self-determination projects disbanded. The Arc Alternative, a subsidiary of The Arc of North Carolina, provided similar aspects of the PCSS model; however, it was not as accurate when establishing budgets. When Danny joined The Arc Alternative model, we were told the request for $15 per hour for support staff was acceptable within the individual budget. This unfortunately was a drastic mistake that caused my budget to remain in a deficit state for the entire length of time with the agency. When we moved Danny to PCSS, it was realized these wages could not be accommodated. This in turn caused a rift between my family and one of my long time staff members. Mary, as an accountant and auditor, understood the ramifications of inaccurate calculations. She, therefore, developed a consumer friendly Microsoft Excel document that clearly indicated all revenue and expenses.

In addition to the FI and EOR concepts established in the PCSS business model, PCSS also has a strong advocacy stance. This is so, because of our role as parents. Mary and I can relate to each and every family we meet. We understand their emotions and frustrations. Both Mary and I were labeled the "difficult parent" along with many other adjectives. We continue to wear these adjectives as a badge of honor.

Mary's daughter Joanne and my son Danny were both born in 1982. Joanne began receiving services from the CAP MR/DD waiver in 1989. Danny began receiving services from the waiver in 1995. Mary and I both remained in the dark for a long time before any waiver information was brought to light. We both then waited on lists and begged for services. As a result of our experiences, we established within our business model a respite fund whereby a portion of our profit is set aside to provide respite services to families of children with disabilities who receive no services.

An underlying goal of PCSS is to empower consumers and families so they can make informed choices. We constantly teach families their rights. Our presence brings a modified, one-on-one Partners in Policy-making session to the families we meet. Whether the family presently receives waiver services or is introduced to us as a result of the respite fund, families are learning what we know. Services for people with disabilities are obtained by maneuvering within a large bureaucratic maze. Mary and I have learned a lot through our years of experience with our children. We want to share what we learned. In return, families spread the word about PCSS. If families are satisfied with the PCSS model, we want them to share it with others so that we can reach as many families as possible with a unique way of doing business.

Chapter 16

Fight for Independent
Case Management

Shortly after the start of PCSS in June 2002, Mary and I took a long, hard look at the case management services our children were receiving. Up until this point, the area program/LME had a monopoly on case management services. There was no choice. Case management was a required waiver service. When an individual was approved for waiver services, he or she was assigned a case manager. If the case manager assigned was inadequate, another was assigned from within the area program/LME.

The definition of case management according to the April 1, 2001 CAP MR/DD manual is as follows:

Section 6.3 – Case Management (W8188)

Case Management is a service that assists individuals who receive waiver services in gaining access to needed Waiver and other State Plan services, as well as needed medical, social, educational and other services, **regardless of the funding source** for the services to which access is gained.

Case Management is locating, obtaining, coordinating, and monitoring social, habilitative, and medical services as well as other services related to maintaining the person's health, safety, and well-being in the community. The Case Manager's responsibilities are discussed throughout this manual in regard to specific topics. Primarily, they include:

- Coordinating and monitoring the screening of the CAP MR/DD funding recipient to be sure that they are eligible for CAP MR/DD participation.
- Obtaining input from the person/providers/significant others about the service delivery process and seeking information from anyone in an effort to obtain needed services/supports on behalf of the person.
- Developing the Plan of Care, preparing notices for planning team meetings, **facilitating person-centered planning**, circle of friends, mini-planning teams, revising the Plan as needed and securing approval of the Plan.
- Locating and coordinating sources of help...Completing application forms to assist in receiving community and other formal service supports.
- Facilitating the service delivery process...
- Monitoring the individual's situation to assure quality care as well as the continued appropriateness of the services and CAP MR/DD participation...
- Observing the person's educational services, including attending IEP Meetings and school transition meetings and referring/linking to services.

In Section 15.5.2 it states, "...It is essential that the case manager fully utilize all resources to allow the individual to stay in the community...This may include seeking assistance from community groups, private individuals, public agencies, and other entities."

As we reviewed the definition, we realized that our assigned case managers were not fulfilling their role and responsibility to our children. We moms were the true case managers for our children while someone else got paid for it.

Section 11.1.2 of the CAP manual indicates the case manager role in person-centered planning.

"The Case Manager becomes a key change agent to move toward a Person Centered Planning process and away from an individualized program planning approach."

The last bullet in this section states:

"The case manager will understand that a key role is the assurance that the focus individual and his/her family can make knowledgeable decisions. They must understand all options in order to make real choices."

At the time, case managers worked directly for the area program/ LME. This bureaucracy is a reactive bureaucracy. There is nothing proactive about it. In order for individuals to make informed choices, a case manager must inform families of options available. They must also have the foresight to inform families of what may be needed in the future. For example, if a child uses a wheelchair or purchases his first wheelchair from CAP MR/DD funding, it would only make sense for the case manager to inform the family of funding available through the waiver for vehicle modifications so that the family can make trans- portation decisions. My case managers—there were several—watched for years as I lifted Danny into his car seat and folded his wheelchair into the trunk or back end of the van. Not once did they talk to me about funding for vehicle modifications. Yet we sit at person- centered planning meetings for our son and once again the case manager asks, "What do you need?" If I know enough to put the transportation issue on the table, then I may get some information, but if I fail to identify this as a concern, then it is assumed that life is going well. Most of us are thrown into the disability world. We don't know what is available to us. We don't know anything about lift systems and modifications. We need someone to tell us what is available so that we can then make informed choices. We are back again to the same dilemma. "Tell me what you have and I'll let you know if I need it!"

Another responsibility of the case manager as outlined in the man- ual is to "observe the person's educational services, including attending IEP meetings and school transition meetings and referring/linking to services."

Not once did a case manager from the area program take an inter- est in Danny's education. They requested a copy of his IEP for their files, but there was no support or interest in what occurred for Danny in the educational setting. We were truly on our own. Sometimes in one twenty-four-hour day a family can deal with both bureaucracies. I've sat at grueling IEP meetings in the morning and then had a visit in the afternoon from my case manager, who would ask, "Does Danny need anything?" Too emotionally exhausted to play the guessing game, I would simply reply, "Everything's fine."

If case managers performed as indicated in the CAP MR/DD manual, individuals with disabilities and their families would receive not only quality services through the waiver, but also quality services within the educational system, the workforce, and the community at large. Mary and I both believed case managers were compromised in performing their job duties because of their employment connection to the area programs/LME.

On December 12, 2002, John and I met with the area director and Developmental Disabilities (DD) director for the Cumberland County Mental Health Center. Interestingly enough, the DD director at the time was Danny's first case manager. This was the individual who had done an assessment of my home in 1993 instead of an assessment of Danny and his needs. At that time, she had asked, "What do you need for Danny?" I quickly replied, "What do you have and I'll let you know if I need it." Obviously her tactics were in line with the bureaucracy's plan, because she had been rewarded to the highest DD position in the area program.

During the meeting with the area director, we requested the area program contract Danny's case management services with The Arc of North Carolina. According to Section 6.3 of the CAP Manual, **"Lead agencies may contract for Case Management Services."** The area director was taken aback by the request and immediately shared revenue concerns and the decision made by the area program to keep case management services in house. If I were the area director, I would certainly want to keep this lucrative revenue source. The monthly case management fee at the time was $509 per month per CAP MR/DD recipient. Cumberland County area program served over 225 CAP recipients. This is a revenue source of over $1,370,000. However, if the revenue source is so valuable, then the criteria and expectations in receipt of the revenue must be attained. Our experience clearly showed that the case management criteria and expectations outlined in the CAP manual were not evident in the job performance of the Cumberland County case managers assigned.

By this time Danny's assigned case manager had asked to be reassigned. The area director offered me an opportunity to interview all the area program DD case managers and choose from within the agency. I agreed to do this as long as the area director agreed to meet with me and The Arc of North Carolina regarding the contract issue. After several rounds of e-mails, a meeting was finally scheduled for January 10, 2003. On January 9, 2003, I had a telephone conversation with the head of program accountability at the division level. The chief of program accountability suggested that I let the area program know that we had spoken. He explained that the program accountability section handled investigations on such matters. Although it would be best to obtain resolution at the local level, the chief of program accountability assured me that if this was not possible, the program accountability section would "be there for us." The chief further stated that he believed we had a choice to go outside the area program for case management services and referred to the child mental health case management arrangement. He explained that there would be two issues that program accountability would address. First was the right to choose case management outside of the area program; and second was a review of the case management services provided to Danny.

During the January 10 meeting with the area director, the director acknowledged the area program's right to contract case management. He stated that some of the area programs had taken this option, but the contract was for all case management, not just one client. The area director further expressed a concern about setting a precedent and reiterated his initial concern about a loss of revenue. He stated boldly that he would welcome an investigation because he believed the services provided by his case management staff were of high quality.

Upon leaving this meeting, I recognized several things that needed to be accomplished. First, I needed to interview the area program case managers to select one for Danny, since his present case manager asked to be reassigned. Second, I needed to bombard the e-mail system with questions regarding choice for case management provider agencies. Third, I needed to file for an investigation with program accountability.

The interviews with area program case managers were held on January 17, 2003. To prepare for this, a list of interview questions was presented to the area program for approval on January 13. The interviews were held at the area program office in the presence of the DD director. Those interviewed were selected by the DD director. In hindsight, I realized this was a mistake. The interviews should have never taken place without Danny. The interviews should have been at my home rather than the mental health center. But I was given a list of individuals to interview by the DD director along with a time and place where the interviews would be held. I did not think to challenge this but at the time was focused on getting the job done.

Interviewees:

Candidate #1 – caseload 30

Candidate #2 – caseload 25

Candidate #3 – supervises 5 case managers with a case load of 25 each. Candidate #3 was also Danny's case manager from 1997 to 1999.

Candidate #4 – Hab Tech Trainee; caseload 8

Before asking questions I introduced myself and shared that my son Danny was an adult CAP recipient with significant disabilities.

1. What experience do you have in serving adults with significant disabilities?

Candidate #1 – Not much with adults; lots of experience with adults with MR and MI (mental illness). In Boston I worked with adults with disabilities who also had MI, but not severe and not total care. I have worked with CAP MR/DD children that were total care.

Candidate #2 – Most of my experience is with children. I have adult experience but not with adults with significant disabilities.

Candidate #3 – I have worked with Danny before. Even before my time with Mental Health, I worked with adults. All my early experience is with adults and then I moved to children. Haven't done case management since 1999.

Candidate #4 – Graduated from college about a year ago. Been a Hab Tech trainee since September. No experience with case management. I have a medical documentation background.

2. What resources have you utilized in the past to assist adult consumers to live successfully in the community?

Candidate #1 – I have been here for two years and have not worked with adults here. I have placed children in the community when they could no longer live at home—placed them in DD (developmental disabilities) homes that were available.

Candidate #2 – The adults I serve are mostly in school. I have assisted a parent with the Cerebral Palsy (CP) Foundation as far as a resource. That is the only outside source that I have used in helping a parent. Everyone is usually helped under CAP (the waiver).

Candidate #3 – I have dealt more with children and getting them placed in group homes, but not with adults.

Candidate #4 – Began case management last week; have worked so far with VR (vocational rehabilitation).

3. a. What type of person-centered planning methods have you been trained in?

Candidate #1 – Unsure of method trained on.

Candidate #2 – I am working with the agency and family on the Greenspan training.

Candidate #3 – Circles and ELP (essential lifestyle planning).

Candidate #4 – Received training from local CAP approval office. Have contacted DDTI (Developmental Disabilities Training Institute) for the schedule for ELP training.

b. Which do you use on a regular basis?

Candidate #1 – I meet with the family, the provider, the teachers and bring all information together; no special process used.

Candidate #2 – Everything I do is centered around the person, not necessarily using any specific method.

Candidate #3 – ELP.

Candidate #4 – (Couldn't answer; too new.)

4. Without breaching confidentiality, share a successful experience with the person-centered planning process.

Candidate #1 – Fourteen-year-old client; at risk of being removed from the home because of behaviors; able to get her CBS services. Behaviors have diminished. She is now still at home.

Candidate #2 – Person could not walk due to TBI (traumatic brain injury). She can now do that because of CAP services—because of the one-on-one she receives.

Candidate #3 – Adult consumer living in a group home chose to move back home with parents. The team questioned this but supported his decision.

Candidate #4 – I sat in on a CNR (continued needs review) meeting and facilitated a CNR meeting. Met with aide and consumer for their input. It was a good experience and a good meeting. We developed a plan. The new plan has just been put in place; working on new goals.

5. Without breaching confidentiality, share a frustration/disappointment you experienced with the person-centered planning process and how you handled it.

Candidate #1 – Client last year who had MR/MI wanted to live with another family. She lived in a group home and wanted to move in with a family. I brought together the team. She was placed in Lumberton with an AFL (alternative family living) family. It did not work out. She went through several placements— group homes, hospital, AFL. (She is) still not where she wants to be.

Candidate #2 – I do not have a lot of frustrations. My frustrations come a lot with agencies when they do not cooperate or with families when they are looking only for babysitting.

Candidate #3 – My frustration would be when the team comes around the table and there is very little input from the service provider or from the caregiver to help meet the needs of the consumer. A lot of responsibility falls to the case manager. If everyone is on the team, then everyone should have input. Case manager is responsible for generating the document. It should be information from all key players.

Candidate #4 – (Couldn't answer; too new.)

After the interview questions, the following scenarios were presented.

1. The legal guardian of an adult consumer on your caseload has made decisions for the consumer you believe are causing frustration and unhappiness for the consumer. What would you do to assist the consumer?

Candidate #1 – I would speak with the other players involved in the consumer's life. Would talk with the parents and present some of the options. Might call a meeting. I would look at what is medically necessary for this service since this is Medicaid. I would look at the consumer's goals and where the parents want them to be.

Candidate #2 – Will sit down with the legal guardian and the consumer and discuss those frustrations. If the consumer could not speak, I would on his behalf talk with the guardian and try to interpret for him. I would then go to the agency with the QDDP (qualified developmental disabilities professional) and the guardian and see what we could come up with.

Candidate #3 – I would make the legal guardian aware of the frustrations that I have seen. If the person was verbal, would help consumer make his wants known to the guardian. I am always very careful to not overstep my boundaries. It may be the consumer's choice, but the legal guardian does have rights. I try not to overstep my rights as a case manager. I will do whatever I can to ease the frustrations—try to find a happy medium. There is a line I cannot cross.

Candidate #4 – I would want to approach the guardian with my concerns. I have to believe that the guardian's vision in regards to the care of the client are the same as mine. I am sure we could come to some kind of agreement on how we could best serve the client. PCP (person-centered planning) is about what the client wants. That has to be (at) the forefront. This is what I would stress to the guardian.

2. You have facilitated a person-centered planning process for an adult consumer on your caseload. This is a new experience for this consumer and the only people included in this process besides the consumer are his parents. One of the consumer's goals is to live in a place of his own. The consumer and his family have made it clear that they will not consider a group home or other congregate setting. The consumer wants a place of his own. What steps would you take to pursue this goal?

Candidate #1 – I would have to see the skill level and needs of the consumer and if the needs could be met with the CAP program. I would contact providers of CAP and find out about facilities for CAP. If there was a provider for these services, it would probably have to be twenty-four-hour care since your son is total care. You can only do what you can do.

Candidate #2 – I don't have adult consumers that are looking for a place of their own. I do not have any idea. Would go to supervisors for support.

Candidate #3 – We will need to sit down with the family and consumer and decide on an area to live, a cost limit, accessibility, close to bus route, doctor's appointments. Would need to find out what kind of support system would be needed; who will live with them. Is the person going to need some assistance? How much? How many hours per day? Probably would have to cover budgeting. How are we going to pay the rent and utilities; furniture for the apartment? After establishing what is needed, then this would determine where we go from here. Contacting utility companies and see if there are any discounts for people with disabilities. Fayetteville Urban Ministries could probably help with furniture. Donations from Salvation Army, both monetary and whatever. Getting the housing or the apartment would probably be the hardest fit. (I asked this candidate if she had ever dealt with Section 8 housing vouchers before. She replied she had not).

Candidate #4 – If the guardian is involved, must include the guardian. I would first want to evaluate and see if it is realistic in terms of the client being able to live on his own. We have to be realistic in what the client is capable of doing. Would look into independent apartment living where there is at least supervision; something to consider. This will all depend on the client's capabilities. We would have to stress safety.

3. During one of your monthly visits to a consumer's home, you notice that the consumer is in need of a piece of equipment. Although the consumer has room in his CAP budget to accommodate this equipment, you have been instructed by your supervisors to only pursue costly equipment purchases when the consumer or family request it. How would you handle this situation?

Candidate #1 – Might just make a suggestion to the consumer/family if what was needed was obvious. It is usually up to the guardian to actually get them an evaluation and letter of medical necessity. If parents are limited in their ability, I have helped them with that.

Candidate #2 – I have mixed emotions on that. To be honest, with the state crunch about this, if the family or physical therapist says it is needed then I would go forward and pursue it. In the past I have waited for the parent or the PT to say it because the state is in a crunch.

Candidate #3 – As a case manager, it is your responsibility to look at the health, safety, and well-being of the consumer. So if there is a need I would make sure that the occupational therapist/physical therapist or other professional that would have to make an assessment is aware of this.

Candidate #4 – As a case manager we have to advocate for the client. It is a delicate situation. I would approach the supervisor. You can advocate for the client, but if the supervisor has other fiscal knowledge then you can't do it. I can't imagine this scenario happening. If I see a need and the budget allots for it then I will pursue it.

Throughout this entire interview process, the DD director did not speak. She did not participate in any way. She brought to the meeting piles of paper to work on during the interviews. At times I wondered why her presence was even necessary. As I listened to the candidates, I hoped she was paying close attention to their responses. After all, she was their supervisor.

4. a. Same Scenario as #3 except the consumer's CAP budget is maxed out. The piece of equipment the consumer needs costs $5,000. What steps would you take to assist the consumer?

Candidate #1 – Grants would be places to pursue. Would talk with other case managers. Would try to find other agencies that would fund the equipment. As a last resort, I would go to the Mental Health Auxillary, probably church groups, and maybe even the Internet.

Candidate #2 – Depending on how bad the consumer needs the equipment; if they could wait. Also depends on the birth month. CP foundation could help. If it is not an emergency situation, I would see if they would try to wait.

Candidate #3 – We will try to see if we could get someone to donate the amount of money. Would contact human relations committee to see if they had any money. Would explain need and situation. It might take two or three places to cover the cost. Would look for agencies that could donate.

Candidate #4 – I would access community resources. We have a handbook. There are a lot of well-seasoned case managers to go to. Would ask for contributions.

By this time, Danny had recently received funding from the O'Berry Foundation for his lift system. The O'Berry Center is one of North Carolina's five mental retardation centers. Not one candidate mentioned the O'Berry Foundation as a possible funding source. I couldn't help but wonder, if staff meetings were held regularly, what information, if any, was being shared?

b. Continuation to #4 – You've made several good referrals for this consumer. However, none of them have met this consumer's needs. The consumer's situation is getting worse and the equipment is desperately needed. What are your next steps?

Candidate #1 – I would talk to the family about cutting back services to fit it into the CAP budget.

Candidate #2 – We could write an exception. Would seek supervisor's support to put together an exception to get the equipment and then go to the next steps.

Candidate #3 – I did have a situation where we contacted the UCP (United Cerebral Palsy) and applied for a grant. I would try to look for grants. I would try to do all that I could and as quick as I could. Would have to stay on it and make as many contacts as I could to make sure the consumer's needs are being met.

Candidate #4 – Advocacy: going to my supervisor and advocating for the equipment. With experience comes knowledge of the opportunities available in the community. I would rely on supervisors and seasoned case managers: great resource.

After the scenarios, I posed the following questions.

Please share the method or system you use to meet the needs of ALL consumers on your caseload.

Candidate #1 – I have a list of all consumers. I write down meeting times. Those getting CBS services must be seen one time a month. But the person who talks the loudest gets the most attention.

Candidate #2 – I do my visits, sit down with parents if I can and go over their plans. I try to find out from families what it is that they want to get from CAP. I like to have a relationship with the aides. I get to see everyone one time per quarter.

Candidate #3 – My supervision style is an open-door policy. A lot of time you set aside for your staff. I would make it clear to my staff that I have a caseload and would have to be out of the office. The supervisory role gets to be hectic. Somehow you get to it all.

Candidate #4 – There is an overall system required of all case managers. There is a tickler system so no one is forgotten. We are also allowed to develop a system on our own. I maintain a folder with the client's number, plan of care, cost summary, revisions. When I go out for visits I write down their needs. I utilize the e-mail system that flashes messages. I use a paper backup system. As I gain knowledge I think it will make me better.

Last question – As I have shared with you, my son has significant disabilities and requires total assistance. This could be a very challenging situation. Why do you want to serve my son?

Candidate #1 – I like challenging cases. My specialty is working with children with autism and behaviors but I have served well children with total care.

Candidate #2 – It would be part of doing the job and hopefully making a difference in getting the things he needs and (making sure) that his CAP services are meeting his needs.

Candidate #3 – I pride myself on being a good case manager and we have to realize that as case managers it is our responsibility to meet the needs of the consumer and to meet the needs of the parents, no matter what they are. Our job is to meet the needs of the consumer and to make sure the health, safety, and well-being are in tact. I know that we like things done in a timely fashion. The need may be immediate but our ability to access it may not. The consumer and family need to be reassured that I did not drop the ball. I need to stay in contact with the family.

Candidate #4 – I am an honest person. It wouldn't necessarily be because I wanted to serve your son. I went to school to get a degree because this is what I want to do. I consider this a blessing and a challenge—to be able to do something for someone. The attitude I have toward your son will be the same toward all my clients.

After reviewing the responses from each of the candidates, I chose Candidate #3. Candidates #1 and #2 reminded me too much of the DD director back in 1993. When my case manager requested a transfer, I received a letter in November 2002 assigning me to Candidate #2. I am glad I had an opportunity to meet Candidate #2 before being assigned. This was certainly someone I did not want in Danny's life. Candidate #4 was too new to the system. She hadn't been tainted by the bureaucracy and therefore had potential. However, this would be an uphill battle considering her supervisor was Candidate #3 and the DD director. Candidate #3 knew what I wanted to hear. She had all the right answers. She was once Danny's case manager. She was about as good as the rest of them. We researched information on our own and help was not given until we hit a wall. I had hoped there would be someone on staff to provide adequate case management; however, that did not seem to be the case. My focus was to obtain true choice.

Once again e-mail distribution lists were used to disperse and obtain vital information. The question posed was simple: "Do families/consumers have the right to choose case management providers in the same way they have the right to choose all other service providers?" E-mail responses came from all over the country including Maine,

Wisconsin, and California. It seemed case management monopolies existed in other states and choice was not an option provided to people needing case management services.

The choice question was also posed to the National Health Law Program. Its response:

"Short answer is this: Unless the state has obtained a waiver of the 'freedom of choice' statutory requirement from the federal government, then it must allow a recipient to have free choice of qualified providers. Now, this can get complicated by state licensing requirements that limit providers, but that is the next question. I'll be interested to see what responses you get from Medicaid officials."

An e-mail conversation with CMS began on January 11, 2003 as follows.

January 11, 2003

"Enjoyed speaking with you yesterday regarding my Medicaid question on case management. About a year ago, I asked a question regarding EPSDT and the waiver to a number of individuals at CMS. I still do not have an answer to my question. I hope this question does not take that long to answer. I need a response as soon as possible. I have spent the past several months battling our area program over the lack of case management services. As a result, my husband and I have made a formal request to our area program to have our son's case management services contracted out. The area program absolutely refuses. Here is my question, 'Is it illegal or against federal regulations for an area program to monopolize on case management and not contract it out, in essence, not give people choice?' In the meantime, I have filed a complaint with our state's program accountability office and requested an investigation. I am sometimes baffled as to why it takes so long to answer a family's question. Please realize that my son's life is on hold until the answer is given. Would appreciate an answer within the week."

January 14, 2003 – CMS Response

"The answer to your question has to do with particular language in the waiver, i.e., provider qualifications can be defined in different ways. We now need to look at your waiver and will call you when we have that info."

January 14, 2003 – My Response

"How long is this going to take? Remember, I'm the parent waiting over a year for an answer to my EPSDT question. I don't mean to sound harsh, but it baffles me that my questions take so long to answer. Please be considerate of the fact that my son and many other children and adults with disabilities in our state await your response."

January 15, 2003 – CMS Response

"You did make it clear that you are in a hurry, in a number of ways. How long it is going to take depends on what we find. Perhaps I was not clear – your question has evolved. Challenging a policy takes longer than asking about a policy. You asked about rules governing provider choice in case management. Our reply was that provider choice is satisfied by choice of individual case managers within an agency. This answer was not acceptable to you, and we agreed to look more specifically at the particular waiver you are participating in. In addition, because of your question, we are examining our policy and practice on this issue. For an operating waiver, CMS Regional Offices work with states to interpret guidelines such as what constitutes choice. We therefore are talking with the relevant parties about the basis for the practice of designating the area agency as the provider. We will report to you whether or not we feel that the waiver is within current policy on choice of provider. However, to avoid any misunderstanding, I am sure you will understand that if any additional steps are required, significantly more time may be needed."

January 15, 2003 – My Response

"I appreciate your reply. However, I want to make it clear that under this waiver families and consumers DO NOT have choice of individual case mangers within the area programs. We are assigned case managers by the area program. Therefore, rules governing provider choice in case management ARE NOT satisfied. I am pleased to know that you are examining your policy and practices on this issue and that you will provide an answer to my question. I am concerned with no timeline to work with. Therefore, may I ask that you send me an e-mail within the next two weeks with at least an update of the status on this issue. Again, I need to make it clear that there is a sense of urgency in obtaining an answer to the question because children and adults with disabilities in our state are receiving poor case management services because the area programs have a monopoly on a service that is pivotal in the development and implementation of person-centered planning."

January 16, 2003 – CMS Response

"We will definitely get back to you with a status report before January 30. The policy issue you raise is being taken very thoughtfully, and a number of people are engaged with it. If I recall correctly, you did manage to secure choice of individual case managers for yourself, but you point out that the problem is not solved for others. As you know, compliance issues are dealt with at the state or regional level, so the complaint process you have started would be the place to deal with the issue of choice of individual case manager. However, as currently approved, the waiver does not require choice of agency, so that is not a compliance issue, and we are looking into that."

January 17, 2003 – My Response

"Look forward to hearing from you on the 30th."

January 29, 2003 – CMS Response

"I promised an update for you by 1/30, so here is the latest. You complained to me about lack of information from us in the past. And I think everyone is better off when we are straightforward. However, following is the status of this issue from my personal perspective, as general information to you, and does not represent CMS official view. I was actually composing a response to you, on Friday. However, one of the several people working on the question noticed that our approach was not consistent with another aspect of Medicaid policy, so we have to try again. While this takes more time than you desire, it is certainly better than having to retract something later. To explain a little about why this issue takes time….I know you want more choice in your particular case, but as an advocate, you are also very aware that policy statements effect entire programs across the country. Case management is not just one of many waiver services, it is directly tied to how programs are administered. The unexpected consequences of a hasty change would threaten programs and jeopardize access to HCBS (Home & Community Based Services waivers) for beneficiaries in situations different than your own. I would be curious to know if The Arc you mentioned as a contractor in other counties provides case management in addition to the area agency, or in place of the agency? i.e., is there a choice for consumers, or does The Arc become the only case management provider in that jurisdiction?"

Several allies were interested in seeing the January 30 response from CMS. When I forwarded this to the director of the self-determination project in Michigan, he replied, "There is no response here. I think you are raising a question that obviously has put them in a quandary. I don't know what their final response will be but I will bring it to CMS and the folks I am working with in DC. Ask him for the regulation that allows 'choice' of case manager."

January 30, 2003 – My Response to CMS

"I've just read your e-mail and I am sitting here shaking my head in disbelief. I honestly do not know what to say. This is the second time I have been through this kind of response from CMS staff. Please tell me how much more time you are going to need to answer this question. I would like another timeline set. This time, you pick it. Also, please forward me the regulation that allows 'choice' of case managers. Contact information for The Arc is listed below. They can best answer your Arc questions about case management. Look forward to your response."

In the meantime, on January 10 I sent an e-mail to the chief of Program Accountability requesting an investigation on two issues. First, our son was not receiving adequate case management services; second, our request for independent case management and choice of providers had been denied. Several phone messages were left with division staff regarding the investigation. It wasn't until February 14, 2003 that we finally received instructions on how to request the investigation. The application was completed, signed, and faxed to the appeal office on February 14, 2003. Mary also completed and faxed her form on the same day. In the application, we both requested an impartial local review while waiting for the hearing date. On February 19 I received a phone call from a member of the Cumberland County Mental Health Center staff, informing me that the impartial hearing date was scheduled for February 27, 2003 at 1:00 p.m. In addition, I was told there would be a three-member panel and that the panel members would make their decision after the meeting. I was also told that the decision would be sent to me within six to seven days after the meeting.

Shortly after, I received a phone call from Program Accountability. I was assigned an investigator and instructed to send any materials for review in the case. On February 26, 2003 a packet was put together and mailed to the investigating officer. At no time did the investigating officer come to our home to meet us or Danny. However, he did have a meeting with the area program and the case management staff.

To prepare for the local review meeting, Mary and I met frequently to discuss strategy. Somewhere along the line, Mary received a faxed copy of an e-mail that came from an Atlanta CMS staff member. This e-mail traveled throughout the state before Mary was able to get her hands on it, but as she put it, "It was our ticket out of jail." The CMS e-mail was dated February 5, 2003 and was sent to the North Carolina waiver point of contact at the Division of Medical Assistance. The e-mail was copied to several CMS staff members at both the regional and federal offices. The e-mail reads as follows:

"Even though your CAP MR/DD waiver was approved having a lead agency as a case management provider agency, there should be a process to enroll providers who meet the qualifications as case manager as outlined in the waiver. The 'enrollment' could either be one of a contractual arrangement with the lead agency or one using your SOP (Standard Operating Procedure) for qualified providers enrolling directly through your agency."

Now here is the most important part of this e-mail:

"If you want to restrict providers of case management services, you may want to consider amending your State Plan and CAP MR/DD waiver to include targeted case management in the Plan for the waiver population and remove this service from the waiver."

We were both very puzzled by the last paragraph of this e-mail, but we continued preparing for the local review. This e-mail, although distorted from being faxed to so many places, was one of the items we brought with us to the local review.

The local review meeting was held as planned on February 27, 2003 at the Cumberland County Mental Health Center offices. Once again we were sitting across from a panel of representatives from the Cumberland County Mental Health Center to include a DD representative. Mary and I attended with our husbands. We brought with us several documents to include the February 5 e-mail from CMS staff. We stated our case as clearly as possible. We wanted choice in case management services. We wanted quality services for our children. We were tired of being the case manager for our kids while someone else got paid for it. Despite the parent taking the responsibility of the case manager when the case manager fell short of his or her job duties, there was a tremendous amount of taxpayer dollars spent on this service, regardless of who did the job and how well it was being done. Sometimes the case manager would simply type the plan of care and make a one-time visit per month for about fifteen minutes. My last case manager from the Cumberland County Mental Health Center would make her visits when she knew I wasn't home and would spend fifteen minutes talking to Danny. In addition, most of the case managers on the DD staff were assigned at one time to each of our children. Needless to say, we were not impressed with the services provided thus far.

After the local review, we heard rumors that the North Carolina division director sent a memo to all area program directors regarding the CMS e-mail. It seems that while we were in the local review, the director's memo was coming off the fax machine in the next room. The memo was dated February 27, 2003. Excerpts are as follows:

"We have recently received communication from the Centers for Medicare and Medicaid (CMS) indicating that consumers receiving waiver services should be allowed the option of choice with regards to case management, including the option to request that their case management services be provided by a contract agency rather than the area programs. This represents a change in the direction and interpretation that has been provided in the past. This change is effective immediately."

It is amazing to know that the bureaucracy does not understand the phrase **"effective immediately"** even when it comes as a directive from the division director. In many areas of the state, it took several years for contracts to materialize. The area programs absolutely did not want to give up this revenue source. Although their job performance in providing quality case management was inadequate at best, their focus seemed to be the revenue generated and not the service provided.

The memo continued.

"The duties of case management for waiver recipients are described in the CAP Manual, Section 15 with some additional changes as described in the Memorandum to Area Directors of December 2, 2002."

The December memo referenced reduced paperwork requirements for case managers. However, despite the memo instructions, to this day, too much case manager time is spent on review of Medicaid documentation instead of assisting the individual as defined in his or her person-centered plan.

The February 27, 2003 memo continued.

"Area programs retain the responsibility for all the duties associated with lead agency status as described in the CAP Manual, Section 19.

"The current CAP case management rate of $509 per month is a blended rate that includes payment for both administrative functions as well as the direct services of a case manager. An area program may contract for the full amount of the direct services but retain the administrative cost fees from the rate."

Of course, there was no further explanation given, therefore leaving the division of the rate in the hands of the area program. This is what prolonged the contract process. Many area programs wanted to keep as much of the $509 fee as possible, claiming administrative costs were high. This left nothing for the case manager who actually provided the hands-on work for the person with the disability. It is very similar to the dilemma faced by other direct care staff. The so-called administrative fees and overhead costs of provider agencies are so high, leaving low wages for the direct care staff.

Finally, on March 7 I received the following letter from the Cumberland County Mental Health Center.

"On February 27, 2003 an Impartial Review Committee was convened to review the request by the parents of Daniel Mercado for CAP MR/DD case management to be provided by an agency other than Cumberland County Mental Health Center (CCMHC)…

"Both sets of parents (referring to Mary, myself and our husbands) are requesting that they be allowed to transfer case management to an agency other than Cumberland County Mental Health Center (CC-MHC) CAP MR/DD case management personnel. They provided several documents which they believe support their ability to make this change:

1. Title 42 (Public Health) Sec. 431.51 Free Choice of Providers.
2. Section 504 of the Rehabilitation Act of 1973
3. An internal memo from DMH staff to CCMHC staff containing an opinion on the subject from CMS staff
4. An excerpt from the Federal Register; Decision 27, 2002 (Volume 67, Number 249) re: Notice of Hearing: Reconsideration of Disapproval of New Jersey State Plan Amendment 02-10
5. North Carolina CAP MR/DD Manual 4-1-02 Section 6-9

"The Committee heard from all interested parties and the following pertinent observations are made:

"1. Daniel M is a 20 Y.O. male who resides at home with his parents and is currently under the care of Hospice.

"2. He is currently funded through CAP MR/DD funds in the amount not to exceed $86,058 and mother states that if not for his currently being involved with Hospice this amount would be insufficient.

"3. Due to client currently being involved with Hospice all his needs are being fully met with no additional expenditure to family and mother states he meets medical necessity criteria for this level of care.

"4. Mother states she met with the Area Program Director reference this issue and he declined the request to change the case management to another agency.

"The Impartial Review Committee after assessing carefully all the information available in this matter, giving consideration to documentation presented and upon receipt of a new directive regarding the provision of CAP case management services from the Division of MHDDSAS, approves the request to change case management services to an agency other than Cumberland County Mental Health Center.

"Cumberland County Mental Health Center will continue to provide appropriate case management to this client until an orderly transition can be accomplished should that continue to be the parents decision."

Upon receipt of this letter, arrangements were made for The Arc of North Carolina to provide case management services to both Danny and Mary's daughter, Joanne. Since we did not know anyone in the area qualified to provide this service, I contacted the North Carolina Developmental Disabilities Training Institute (DDTI) and asked for referrals. After interviews were conducted, we chose an individual who had extensive training in person-centered planning and came highly recommended by the DDTI. For the next six months Danny had the best case management services possible. There was a team approach with the case manager as the leader. I was no longer in the lead role. I remember the first meeting the team had with our new case manager. The case manager came prepared with paper and pen in hand and asked good questions about Danny's likes and dislikes and services provided and needed. She also took copious notes as the team answered her questions. This was so refreshing. For years I had to pry information out of people or redirect them because they did not take into consideration what Danny liked or didn't like. In the past I was the note-taker. Even when I encouraged them to take their own notes, there were still so many important facts missing from the plan of care. Unfortunately the new case manager did not last long. After a very short period, The Arc of North Carolina offered this individual a team leader position in the Durham, North Carolina office. Although she remained Danny's case manager throughout her time with The Arc, her extensive job duties as team leader prevented her from devoting the time necessary to meet Danny's many needs. As a result I slowly moved back into the position of case manager. Fortunately my relationship with all The Arc of North Carolina case managers selected was a good one. This provided a much better arrangement and allowed the plan of care submitted to the area program to fully contain all Danny's needs, wants, and desires. But as far as connecting Danny to community activities, that was a case manager responsibility that unfortunately remained with me.

With the case management battle over, I collected all my notes and arranged them neatly in a three-ring binder. In doing so, I once again came across the CMS e-mail instructing North Carolina on the provision of choice regarding case management. The last paragraph of the e-mail was very disturbing.

"If you want to restrict providers of case management services, you may want to consider amending your State Plan and CAP MR/DD waiver to include targeted case management in the Plan for the waiver population and remove this service from the waiver."

Why would CMS instruct a state on the restriction of providers? Everything in the last paragraph of this e-mail has come to fruition. The state has even gone one step further and put in place job qualifications for the case management position that make it difficult for parents and other qualified individuals to fulfill this role. The first announcement of the educational requirements came after The Arc of North Carolina had established several case management contracts across the state. The initial requirements stated a case manager had to have a four-year college degree in the human service field. That knocked out over 50 percent of the present case management population. One might think that maybe the case management services were inadequate because the case managers had the wrong educational training. However, most parents don't have any training in this field. Many of us don't have degrees. Some parents only have a GED. Despite our limitations, many of us write our children's plan of care, connect our children to community sources, and provide the best advocacy. We understand the advocacy needed and the importance of community connection and involvement. The case management service was inadequate not because case managers had the wrong educational training. Case management services were inadequate because case managers worked for a monopoly that mastered all elements of control. The advocacy efforts of The Arc of North Carolina resulted in a "grandfathering" of those case managers without a human service degree with a requirement that a human service degree be obtained within five years.

To date, contract case management agencies exist throughout the state. Case management, however, for the most part, is no better than the former arrangement. In many instances, individuals with disabilities are still being assigned case managers from within the case management agency. Many parents do not know they have the right to interview case managers or select another agency. In addition, the requirements for contract agencies make it impossible for new agencies to exist. Parents, after years of firsthand experience, are unable to secure a contract for case management services, because they are unable to obtain $1,000,000 in professional and general liability insurance. Another deterrent to quality case management is that when the contracts were issued, case managers simply changed employment from the area program to the contract case management agency. Even if adequate training on how to effectively provide case management services existed, the area program still maintains control of the contract. Effective advocacy can sometimes ruffle feathers. If the feathers of the area program are ruffled in any way, it could mean the demise of the contract, therefore putting the contractor out of business.

My request for a hearing on the case management issue was twofold. The request for independent case management and choice of providers was resolved with the memo from the division on February 27, 2003. However, there is a big difference between independent case management and contract case management. PCSS is a provider agency of direct care waiver services. We bill directly to the state for the services we provide. This eliminates area program control. If the state doesn't like our advocacy style or if it feels we are pushing too hard, it cannot take our contract away, because there is no contract to take. The state has decided that targeted case management will replace waiver case management. Supposedly, targeted case management will be a direct bill service. This has yet to materialize. In the meantime, case management continues to be inadequate even when provided by a credible organization like The Arc of North Carolina.

My second request for a hearing involved inadequate case management services provided to my son. In order to prepare for the investigation, a packet was prepared and submitted to the investigator assigned on February 26, 2003. The packet included the following summary sheet.

PROGRAM ACCOUNTABILITY INVESTIGATION

Issue: Inadequate Case Management Services

My request for Independent Case Management is a result of inadequate case management services. Attached are copies of Sections of the CAP MR/DD manual that outline the role and responsibilities of the case manager.

Danny has received case management services from the Cumberland County Area Program under the CAP MR/DD waiver since 1995. Throughout these eight years, case management has fallen short in meeting the case management responsibilities outlined in the CAP manual. One of the examples involves the lift system that was needed for Danny.

In March 2000, Danny was hospitalized with reflux. Once the reflux was resolved, it was decided that Danny would be on a continuous feed pump at night and receive two cans of Nutren. This was done to increase his weight gain. It worked very well. In one year, Danny went from 50 lbs. to 80 lbs. Our family never had a lift system for Danny. We really didn't know what a lift system was. No one ever told us that this was an option despite the fact that a case manager visited our home on a monthly basis and witnessed us and Danny's staff lifting him.

Finally, in December 2002, I approached the case manager and shared injuries my husband and I attained while lifting Danny. The case manager immediately said, "Do you need a hoyer lift?" I told her I did not know what a hoyer lift was and thought it best to have someone come to our home and do an assessment of Danny and our home to determine equipment needed.

On February 28, 2002, a Physical Therapist and Occupational Therapist from O'Berry Center came to our home to do the assessment. Also present was the case manger and a representative from the equipment supply company.

Shortly after the February visit, the Physical Therapist and Occupational Therapist submitted a report outlining recommendations to include a ceiling lift and track system along with a hospital bed with padded side rails to ensure Danny's safety.

On March 12, 2002, the case manager notes stated the "mother was very vehement that this writer start revision immediately." I was vehement because both my husband and I sustained injuries caring for our son while our case manager withheld information about equipment that would not only have kept us safe, but would have also provided for our son's safety.

On March 14, 2002, Danny was admitted to Womack Army Medical Center with pneumonia. This was the first time Danny ever encountered pneumonia. It was a frightening and tough battle. While we sat by our son's bedside watching him fight for his life, we were making phone calls to our case manager and others at the state level to get the lift system that was recommended in our home by the time Danny was discharged. We felt it was absolutely critical that we obtain this equipment because Danny had a chest tube during his hospital stay. Although the tube was removed upon discharge, we knew it would be difficult to lift him without hurting him.

On March 22, 2002, Danny was discharged from the hospital as a Hospice patient. We had the hospital bed, but there was no lift. It took two people to lift Danny from his chair to his bed. We have private insurance for Danny and Danny also has Medicaid. There was absolutely no coordination support between the case manager and our private insurance or any other funding source to obtain this lift.

Shortly after Danny arrived home from the hospital, I requested a meeting with the area program to discuss finding a way to obtain the lift. Those present included the Area Director, the Assistant Director, the DD Director, the CAP MR/DD Coordinator, the CAP MR/DD Supervisor, the Local Approval Specialist, and my CAP Smart case manager assigned by the state.

The area program made it very clear at this meeting that they already did everything they could to obtain the lift and that they were very sorry it was not here.

I learned a long time ago to never rely on one source. While I tried to get the area program to respond to this need, I shared the need with several state employees and also approached an attorney with the National Health Law Program. The attorney sent a letter on Danny's behalf on April 24, 2002 requesting a hearing regarding this issue. We did not receive the hearing. Instead a letter was received dated April 26, 2002 from an attorney representing the area program. This letter instructed our attorney to direct all legal correspondence to his office. Shortly after this letter was received, funding for the lift was received. This funding was obtained not by our case manager or anyone from our area program. The funding was received by a state employee. The funding obtained was from the O'Berry Center Foundation. O'Berry is the Mental Retardation Center in Cumberland's catchment area. This is another example of how case management has failed in 'utilizing ALL resources to allow the individual to stay in the community' as outlined in the CAP manual.

Two letters dated March 21 and March 25 indicate what our area program was doing while we were desperately looking for a lift.

- Letter dated March 21 from Local Approval Specialist addressed to case manager states, 'Please submit a statement from the Physical Therapist/Occupational Therapist who did the assessment that the pads/bumper guards are not likely to cause suffocation or strangulation.'
  - o We have no idea if this was ever obtained.
- Letter dated March 25 from Local Approval Specialist addressed to case manager states, 'Please be advised that the request for the bed rails pads/bumper guards under Code W8151 is denied. Please refer to Section 25 of the CAP manual for appeal rights related to CAP MR/DD Denials by the Local Approval Office.'
  - o This letter was dated three days after Danny was discharged. Hospice is now in our life. We need two people to lift Danny so we do not hurt him and this is what we get from

our area program!

As you can imagine, I was in no frame of mind to deal with appeal rights three days after my son came home from the hospital with Hospice nurses visiting on a regular basis. To this day, I still do not have the bed rail pads that were recommended by the Physical Therapist and Occupational Therapist to ensure Daniel's safety.

I am happy to report that the ceiling lift was installed in May 2002. Danny is now safe and so are his caregivers.

This is only one example of what we experienced with case management from the Cumberland area program. We have gone through a similar situation to obtain van modifications.

What brought me to request an investigation began with a letter I received on November 12, 2002 reassigning our son to yet another case manager. The sequence of events is as follows…

My seven-page summary continued with the series of events that led to the filing of the investigation. Attached to the summary was a copy of the CAP manual sections regarding case management along with copies of case manager notes obtained from Danny's file at the Cumberland County area program. It was very difficult reading some of the case manager comments, as I am sure it will be difficult for some case managers to read this book. Many case managers believe they are providing an outstanding service to families. But that isn't always true. Despite excellent evaluations from supervisors and promotions to DD director positions, our family and many others experience inadequate case management services.

Copies of the following documents were also added to the summary document for the investigator:

- Letter from physical therapist and occupational therapist dated March 1, 2002
- Attorney letters dated April 24, 2002 and April 26, 2002
- O'Berry foundation request
- March 21 and March 25, 2002 letters from local approval specialist regarding bumper pads
- Letter dated November 12, 2002 reassigning Danny to a new case manager
- Case manager interview questions and responses – January 17, 2003

On May 16, 2003 I received a letter dated March 28, 2003 regarding the results of the investigation. The postmark on the envelope was May 16, 2003. It took over two months for a copy of this letter to be sent to me. The letter was addressed to the director of the Cumberland County Mental Health Center. The letter was sent by the acting chief of Program Accountability Section and the chief of Developmental Disabilities Section. The letter reads as follows:

This is to provide you the results of a Medicaid investigation that was conducted at the Cumberland County Mental Health Center (CCMHC) in response to a complaint that was received by the Division of Mental Health, Developmental Disabilities, and Substance Abuse Services.

COMPLAINT

The complaint was initiated January 27, 2003. Ms. Denise Mercado requested an investigation of the CAP MR/DD case management services that her son has received since 1995 from CCMHC. She stated that case management services have been inadequate.

- The case manager withheld important information about her son's benefits under the Waiver and failed to advocate for her son to ensure that he receives the person-centered services that he needs and is entitled to receive under the Waiver. The case manager and area program appear to be more focused on conserving funds due to State budget problems than in meeting the client's needs under the Waiver.
  - o The case manager saw both parents struggling for years to lift and transfer their son in and out of bed and failed to inform them about his eligibility for lift equipment…
  - o For four years, both parents had to physically lift their son and strap him into the van on their own. Ms. Mercado reported that she had learned that their son was eligible for $10,000 for van modifications to make it wheelchair accessible. No one at the area program volunteered this information.
  - o Two years ago, state increased the Waiver rates for service, but not the $68,000 annual limit under the Waiver. Because her son's cost of care was already at the annual limit, the case manager asked the parents what services they wanted

reduced in order to stay within the annual limit…

- The case managers at Cumberland County Mental Health Center consider only CAP MR/DD services and do not pursue all possible public and private resources and funding sources 'outside the CAP box' in order to meet her son's treatment/habilitation and support needs. As an example, she cited problems with funding the lift that her son needed…

- Ms. Mercado also requested an investigation of the area program's denial of her request for an independent case manager. Because of the above referenced inadequacies, Ms. Mercado had requested that she be allowed to choose an independent case manager outside of the area program to better represent her son's interests and to ensure that his needs are met. She reported that the area program initially denied her request preferring to keep case management in-house…

- Ms. Mercado reported concerns with case management being billed in January 2003 during the time she was negotiating a replacement case manager with the area program. She indicated that no case management was provided that month.

CONDUCT OF INVESTIGATION

Investigator was assigned on February 18, 2003 to investigate the complaint.

- On February 24, 2003 the investigator spoke with Ms. Mercado to obtain information about the complaint.
- Between March 3, 2003 – March 28, 2003, the investigator:
  - Reviewed documents that Ms. Mercado provided via mail, e-mail, and fax
  - Spoke with Ms. Mercado via the phone,
  - Interviewed Cumberland County Mental Health Center staff (Deputy Area Director, Finance Officer, DD Director, and the Case Manager assigned between 6/15/01 – 2/18/03). Prior case managers were not available to be interviewed,
  - Interviewed CAP MR/DD specialists at the Division of MH/DD/SAS,
  - Interviewed the Advocacy and Customer Services Section team leader at the Division of MH/DD/SAS who had as-

219

        sisted Ms. Mercado with one of her complaints, and

    o Reviewed the client's record and case management notes at Cumberland County Mental Health Center.

During the course of the investigation, area program staff were very cooperative and welcomed the investigation as an opportunity to receive useful feedback to ensure that they are in compliance with Division and Medicaid requirements and to identify opportunities to improve their services.

FINDINGS

Based on a review of documentation and interviews with Cumberland County Mental Health Center and Division staff:

- It could not be substantiated that the case manager or area program intentionally withheld information about the client's benefits under the Waiver or failed to advocate for or arrange person-centered services as required in the CAP MR/DD manual...

- It could not be substantiated that the case managers at Cumberland County Mental Health Center consider only CAP MR/DD services and do not pursue other public and private resources and funding sources 'outside the CAP box' in order to meet the client's treatment/habilitation and support needs...

- It could not be substantiated that Cumberland County Mental Health Center was in violation of the Division Director's February 27, 2003 memo informing area programs of guidance from CMS that consumers receiving Waiver services should be allowed the option to request that their case management services be provided by a contract agency rather than the area program...Based on the organizational and financial structure of single-county area programs and the steps needed for the county to approve and implement the budget revision, the area program acted appropriately to implement the Division Director's memo...

- During the course of the investigation, the concern about case management billing for January 2003 was resolved. At the time the complaint was initiated on January 27, 2003, case management had not yet been provided during that month. It was noted that a billable case management service was provided on January 31, 2003.

- While the investigation did not result in a finding of non-compliance with rules, it did provide a valuable learning opportunity for area program and Division staff and underscored the importance of paying attention to and taking appropriate action in the following areas:
  - o Recognizing the impact that variations among case managers in their experience, knowledge about community resources, level of initiative, degree of proactiveness, size and demands of case load, and other factors can have on their effectiveness and on consumer satisfaction with case management services.
  - o Ensuring that case managers receive appropriate training...
  - o Promoting communication and sharing information across the state between the Division and area programs/local management entities, public and private service providers, and service/support agencies in the community in order to identify and coordinate the appropriate use of all available resources.

NONCOMPLIANCE

None were substantiated.

CORRECTIVE ACTIONS REQUIRED

None are required.

After reading and rereading this report, I sat at my dining room table with tears in my eyes, thinking of the insanity of it all. The most unfortunate part of this report is that one of its authors was the state employee who had secured the O'Berry Foundation funds for the lift system. He knew firsthand that the Cumberland County Mental Health Center staff was not doing its job. Yet this individual signed his name to this report indicating **NO NONCOMPLIANCE AND NO CORRECTIVE ACTION REQUIRED.** This report confirms yet another character flaw of the bureaucracy. The bureaucracy will stick up for itself and do whatever it has to in order to protect itself, even to the point of grossly stretching the truth, as indicated in the findings of this report.

Chapter 17

The PCSS Family Grows

In December 2002, PCSS enrolled its first family from the Rocky Mount, North Carolina area. As the word got out to families, our business grew by leaps and bounds. People wanted something different. They understood the element of control and were concerned they had lost control when accepting services. With our business model, families understand and are willing to take on the responsibility of a co-employer relationship. In this relationship, families select direct care staff for their loved ones. They also decide wages for direct care staff within the established person-centered operating budget. Families are responsible for scheduling staff according to the amount and type of services authorized. They are also responsible for reviewing and signing all Medicaid documentation prior to submission to our office. In return, PCSS hires staff selected by families as long as all hiring criteria are satisfied. In addition, PCSS handles all payroll functions for all staff. Medicaid billing is also a responsibility of PCSS. This includes all Medicaid required functions such as implementation reviews and audits.

As we met new families across the state, we began to realize the hurt, despair, and frustration of those receiving services. In the summer of 2003, one of the CAP Smart families introduced us to a group of families in the far western part of North Carolina. Since I was not a native of North Carolina, building this business became a fun way to see this beautiful state. Murphy, North Carolina is a small town in western North Carolina with Georgia and Tennessee on its borders. It was a wonderful and exciting trip to Murphy through Asheville and the Nantahala Gorge. What a beautiful part of the state! One of the first families we met in Murphy had a twenty-nine-year-old daughter with significant disabilities. The diagnosis was gangliosidosis type II. This disability is a degenerative brain disorder. In talking with the mom, we were told that there was another sibling with the same disability who had died at nineteen years of age. This twenty-nine-year-old woman was the oldest in the country to survive with this disorder. The mom was the primary care provider for her adult children. As a result, she could not work outside the home. In order to provide an income for her family, the mom became a foster parent. Eventually the family extended on their home and took care of two more individuals with significant disabilities on the CAP MR/DD waiver. The individuals served in this home were very much like my son, Danny. They each used wheelchairs and other extensive adaptive equipment, including hospital beds, oxygen, and suction machines.

Mary and I had an opportunity to review the plan of care (POC) for the twenty-nine-year-old prior to our meeting. The POC should depict a clear picture of the individual's strengths, needs, and preferences. We had several conversations with the mom prior to meeting with the family. We knew based on our conversations that a lot of pertinent information was missing from the POC. In addition, we were concerned with the minimal amount of services authorized.

When I walked in the home and saw the twenty-nine-year-old in her hospital bed, I noticed contractures, oxygen use, and a feeding tube. Although I called her by name several times, there was no response. The mother informed me at that time that there was also no vision. At that point I looked at the mom and said, "Do you have enough services?" Her response was chilling. "That is all Smoky will give me," she said. Smoky Mountain Center (SMC) is the area program/LME in the western part of the state. I looked back at this young woman and thought, *What in the world happened to person-centered planning?* At a meeting in Raleigh several years earlier as person-centered planning was being introduced, I raised my hand for clarification as to which person the plan would center around. There was a slight chuckle from those in attendance. The person leading the meeting assured me that the person with the disability would be the focus person for the development of the plan. If that were true, then why did the mom respond the way she did? If true person-centered planning existed with the focus being around the person with the disability, the answer to the question would have been, "That is all we need."

Immediately Mary and I shifted into an advocacy role. As parents we are advocates for our children whether they have a disability or not. We speak on behalf of our children until they are able to speak for themselves. Unfortunately many children with disabilities continue to require an advocate in their lives even into adulthood. All people, regardless of significant disability, communicate their needs and their wants but many times have the inability to fight for the amount, duration, and scope of services necessary. This is what this twenty-nine-year-old individual was facing. It was now our job to educate her parents so they could make informed choices on her behalf.

As we moved forward in sharing facts about the CAP MR/DD waiver, one of the first emotions to surface was fear. The family was afraid to challenge SMC. The SMC had convinced the family they could move the other two individuals living in their home to another home. The SMC used a little *Godfather* mafia tactic and "made them an offer they couldn't refuse." Once again the bureaucracies tactics can be compared to the plantation model: "Be grateful for the bones I throw you because it is better than nothing. Remember, I have control to send you to worse places." In other words, SMC gave the twenty-nine-year-old the minimum it could, keeping its budget down. There was nothing the family could do to challenge that, because the SMC had convinced the family the other two consumers would be moved if they tried to challenge them. At the time, the other two individuals had been at this home for over ten years. The family was in love with these consumers and together they made one big family. The income from the care provided to these two other consumers also provided the livelihood for the family. Our first job was to convince the family based on facts. We spent time talking about the role and responsibility of legal guardians. The SMC was not the legal guardian for either of the consumers in this home. We made copies of the CAP manual and highlighted important sections for them to read. We made it very clear to this family and all our families: "Stop **listening** to the area program! If they can't back it up in writing, it probably is not true!"

The fight for appropriate services for this twenty-nine-year-old led us all to an Office of Administrative Hearing. Because the consumer was an adult, the legal aid office in the area was able to assist. Unfortunately legal aid attorneys are not always knowledgeable about waiver issues. However, this legal aid attorney was more than willing to learn. On our trips to Murphy, Mary and I would spend an extra day with the attorney, bringing him up to speed on the CAP world. Once again inadequate case management services were part of the reasons for the denial of services. The plan of care was missing so much vital information. In addition, the denial referred to the "absence of natural supports." In other words, the SMC knew the family was providing care to their adult daughter as a natural support and could not understand why, now at twenty-nine years of age, they wanted paid staff support. In addition, they wanted to make sure the parents would not be the paid staff support. This is not only disrespectful to the family, but also to the adult consumer who has the right to choose her own paid staff. As we watched all of this play out, we couldn't help but wonder how an area program/LME could objectively implement a person-centered plan of care with this mindset.

The hearing for this consumer was held in Murphy on January 8, 2004. One of the requests of the legal aid attorney was that the law judge visits the consumer in her home. Due to an ice storm in the central part of the state, Mary and I were unable to attend this hearing. I understood from speaking with the family and attorney after the hearing that during the first part of the hearing, the judge seemed to side with the SMC. However, the judge, family, and attorneys on both sides visited the consumer in her home during the lunch hour. The second half of the hearing was a turn-around for the judge. He now fully understood not only the paper presented, but the extent of the disability of the individual receiving the services.

It took ninety days to receive the judge's decision. The Conclusions of Law were as follows:

1. The Office of Administrative hearings has jurisdiction in this matter...
2. This Decision is rendered pursuant to N.C. Gen. Stat. 150B-34...
3. The proposed Plan of Care contains a supporting diagnosis for

Petitioner's tranquilizing medications and Respondent's reasons for denial based thereon are **erroneous**.

4. That due to the condition of Petitioner and her need for total care on a continuous basis with many tasks required to be performed at varying times and not on a set schedule renders her situation atypical and therefore the reasons for denial by Respondent pertaining to timing of tasks and repetitions of tasks are **erroneous** and **Respondent failed to use proper procedure**.

5. Tasks, care, and supervision that are naturally occurring are present in the proposed Plan of Care and the same were acknowledged by Respondent's letters of denial and therefore the reasons for denial on such basis are **erroneous**.

6. The NC SNAP is congruent with the MR2 and the Plan of Care; therefore Respondent's reasons for denial based thereon are **erroneous**.

7. There is justification in the Plan of Care for the amount of paid supports in the Plan of Care and therefore reasons for denial based thereon are **erroneous.**

8. The policy memorandums of Respondent, Petitioner's Exhibit 7A, are not contained in any applicable statute or regulation, have not been adopted pursuant to the Administrative Procedures Act, and are not contained in the CAP MR/DD Manual and therefore any reasons for denial based thereon are **erroneous**, and **not upon proper procedure.**

9. b. Violation of 42 USC 1396a(a)(10)(B) and 42 CFR 440.230 by failing to provide Petitioner services that are sufficient in amount, duration, and scope to achieve the purpose of the waiver, and by **denying to Petitioner the services that are provided to a similarly situated person residing in the same residence and requiring essentially the same services**...

c. **Violation** of the 'statewideness' requirement....which has not been waived in the North Carolina CAP MR/DD waiver.

d. Discrimination in **violation** of the Americans with Disabilities Act...**Petitioner's needs are not being met with appropriate waiver services in the most integrated setting due to budgetary restrictions** putting her at risk of institutionalization in order to have her needs met.

e. **Violation** of the provisions of the CAP MR/DD manual requiring that during a Continuing Need Review, services are added, changed, or deleted according to the person's current situation.

10. There is no requirement that any change in condition be shown in order to be awarded different or additional services than were contained in a prior year Plan of Care...

11. The proposed Plan of Care includes natural supports...

12. The proposed Plan of Care set forth that the family would provide natural supports for Petitioner's needs not provided by paid supports...

13. **Respondent's denial** of Petitioner's proposed Plan of Care constitutes **failure to act as required by law or rule**...

14. The Respondent acted **arbitrarily and capriciously** by denying the proposed Plan of Care based upon budgetary considerations contained in a policy not adopted pursuant to law and without any guidelines to determine the amount of hours of CAP MR/DD services that are appropriate for a person needing twenty-four hour care.

15. Respondent acted **erroneously, failed to use proper procedure, acted arbitrarily and capriciously, and failed to act as required by law or rule.**

16. **Petitioner's rights have been substantially prejudiced by Respondent** and Respondent has deprived Petitioner of property.

17. The proposed Plan of Care for Petitioner herein should be approved.

18. The services set forth in the Cost Summary...being 373 hours per month of MR Personal Care Services and 290 hours per year of Respite services, are appropriate for CAP MR/DD to provide to Petitioner, as established by testimony of qualified **expert witnesses and should be approved.**

NOW, THEREFORE, BASED UPON THE FOREGOING FINDINGS OF FACT AND CONCLUSIONS OF LAW, THE DECISION IS AS FOLLOWS:

1. Petitioner's proposed Plan of Care is approved.

2. Petitioner shall receive the services as set forth in the Cost Summary…

ORDER

It is hereby ordered that the agency serve a copy of the final decision on the Office of Administrative Hearings, 6714 Mail Service Center, Raleigh, NC 27699-6714, in accordance with North Carolina General Statute 150B-36(b).

NOTICE

The decision of the Administrative Law Judge in this contested case will be reviewed by the agency making the final decision…

The agency that will make **the final decision** in this contested case is the North Carolina Department of Health and Human Services, Division of Medical Assistance.

This is the 19th day of April, 2004.

The document was signed by the presiding judge. I do not understand why the judge's decision was not final. For five months we held our breath, wondering how the Division of Medical Assistance would respond to the judge's decision. Finally on September 28, 2004, we received a fax from the legal aid attorney.

"In accordance with G.S. 150B-36, and upon consideration of the record in this matter from the Office of Administrative Hearings including the transcript of the hearing held January 8, 2004 and the exhibits submitted therein, decision of the Administrative Law Judge dated April 19, 2004, and the exceptions filed on behalf of the Respondent, the undersigned determines the following (finding, conclusion, and decision paragraphs of the Administrative Law Judge (ALJ) which are not adopted have been **modified through the use of strike out of deleted material and italics** for added material with an explanation in the 'Basis for Change' following such paragraph; findings or conclusions without an objection are accepted as adopted by the ALJ; typographical and grammatical errors were left as in the administrative law judge's decision unless they affected the meaning)."

The final decision was signed by the director of the Division of Mental Health/Developmental Disabilities/Substance Abuse. By this time the division director was a bureaucrat with more than thirty years involvement in institutional care. Before accepting the position as division director, he presided over one of the five state-run mental retardation centers. Parents across the state wondered upon his appointment what life had in store for individuals choosing community life.

The administrative law judge's decision was fifteen pages long. The final decision from the division director was twenty pages long. The material in italics added five extra pages.

"There was **no evidence** to show that Petitioner was likely to go to an ICF-MR without the increase in funding. The request for approximately double the funding level from the prior year was not supported by a showing of a marked increased need nor by a change in the family's ability to provide the care that they had been providing...The budgetary limitations referred to in the letters attached to the denial letter did not cause the denial. They did cause the area program to review carefully for justification for the increase. There was **no evidence** that the health, safety, or welfare of Petitioner was in jeopardy. In fact, the evidence showed that Petitioner was receiving excellent care at the existing funding level. There was **no evidence** that Petitioner was not receiving sufficient services. There was **no evidence** of an actual violation of 'statewideness.' There was **no evidence** that Petitioner was at any risk of being institutionalized. There was **no evidence** that the provisions of the CAP MR/DD Manual were violated...

NOW, THEREFORE, BASED UPON THE FOREGOING FINDINGS OF FACT AND CONCLUSIONS OF LAW, THE DECISION IS AS FOLLOWS:

Respondent's denial of Petitioner's Plan of Care for 2003-04 is upheld."

The document was signed by the director of the Division of Mental Health/Developmental Disabilities/Substance Abuse and was dated September 21, 2004.

I can't help but wonder what the presiding administrative law judge thought when he read this final decision. Throughout the document, the director focused on natural supports and no reason given as to why the parents could not continue to provide support to their twenty-nine-year-old daughter as they were doing all along. There is absolutely nothing "natural" about a parent diapering a twenty-nine -year-old daughter. The director's comment about the area program being justified to look

at the situation harder due to budgetary constraints made me wonder about budget priorities. The cost of institutional care is far higher than the cost of community life. Yet no one says to the families of those residing in institutions, "Sorry, due to budget constraints, you will have to take your child home and become her natural support."

Shortly after this bizarre experience, the PCSS business began to flourish in the Gastonia, North Carolina area. During my tenure as the executive director of The Arc of Cumberland County, I visited Holy Angels in Gastonia. This facility is run by the Sisters of Mercy. As I toured this facility, I was introduced to the individual responsible for establishing the organization. She was a middle-aged individual with significant physical disabilities and was given to the sisters at a very young age by her single mother, who could no longer care for her. The child was never expected to live. The child's needs were extensive. The sisters took turns giving her the best care possible. As a result of that care and much prayer, this child grew to be a beautiful young woman. I was introduced to her while she performed her part-time duties as receptionist for Holy Angels. As the sisters took care of this young child, they wondered if there were other families in their community who needed help caring for children with disabilities. This wonderment led to the establishment of Holy Angels in the mid to late 1950s.

As I walk through facilities like Holy Angels, I wonder what information, if any, families had about their options before they made out of home placement decisions. Are they in the dark, like I was in Indiana? Are they given only one option: to care for their child completely on their own or placeing him or her in a residential facility? Is the waiver ever discussed?

One of our consumers in Gastonia, also born in 1982, spent seven years of her young life at Holy Angels shortly after her parent's divorce. The waiver, although it existed in North Carolina in the late 1980s, was never discussed and never presented as an option. Weekend after weekend, this mom would visit her daughter. With tears they embraced and with tears they departed. It seemed that the CAP MR/DD waiver was an option unknown to the sisters as well. Somehow, years after this child's admission to Holy Angels, information about the waiver was shared with the sisters. During one of the mom's many visits, one of the sisters shared the newfound information and provided assistance

in maneuvering through the system. Finally the young girl was back home with her mom and older sister. However, the nightmare was just beginning. Every year there is a battle for the amount, duration, and scope of services. Every year this mom becomes the case manager and writes her daughter's plan of care.

A similar situation occurred more recently for a family in the Rocky Mount, North Carolina area. This family, after thirty-two years of institutional life, wanted desperately to bring their son home. When I first met this mom, she shared with tears in her eyes how happy her son was to see her every time she picked him up from the institution for a weekend visit. But going back to the institution was a very different story. She said he would begin to shake the closer they got to the building. He would sometimes come home with bruises or marks, without any explanation, no matter how often they inquired. Although their son is nonverbal, he was certainly communicating his discomfort and fear of his living environment. Finally the family learned of the waiver and on September 1, 2005 their son came home. In just a short time he showed improvement and seemed so much more content to be with his family. But once again the battle began with the area program regarding the amount, duration, and scope of services. Despite the person-centered plan that was developed by the team, the family found themselves in a room, represented by an attorney, with the assistant attorney general representing the area program/LME. A negotiation process then ensued. The family simply wanted to know, "What will you give us to help us keep our son home?" The negotiations even went as far as the area program stating it would allow the parent to be the paid staff only for 50 percent of the hours authorized. After consulting their attorney, the family counter-offered 60 percent of the hours authorized. The area program agreed to this only after reducing the type of service from an enhanced service to a regular service. In addition, respite services were taken out of the picture. The area program/LME stated that respite would be provided when the staff were working and that therefore it was not needed. So why do we need a person-centered plan if it's going to come down to negotiations? Why ask us what we need only to tell us no? Why not save us all a lot of time and aggravation and just tell us what you can give us?

I always wondered why services for people with mental health, de-

velopmental disabilities, and substance abuse problems were housed under the same agency. After maneuvering through this system on behalf of my son and watching others do the same, I understand completely the logic behind the agency structure. Seeking services through this bureaucracy for developmental disabilities may cause you to eventually need services from all three sections.

Despite the insanity of it all, the PCSS family continues to grow. There are always new people to meet and new challenges to master. One family in Cumberland County approached us in tears. It seemed that the mother's daughter was receiving CAP MR/DD services from a local provider agency. However, because the daughter received a social security benefit as a result of her father's death in Desert Storm, she was obligated to meet a six-hundred-dollar Medicaid deductible before CAP MR/DD services could be provided. The local provider agency was invoicing the single parent for services. After several years of service, the bill accumulated to over ten thousand dollars. Every year around Christmas and tax-return time, the agency would call the single mom and ask for a payment toward the bill. The mom simply could not do it anymore and needed relief. Needless to say, we were floored. Because our business model includes a person-centered operating budget, we were able to work out a system with the Department of Social Services so that no Medicaid billing took place for the first several days of each month that CAP MR/DD services were provided.

The person-centered operating budget is unique to each consumer served. The total amount of the budget is determined by the type and amount of services approved in the plan of care. The budget includes our operating fee and other direct costs such as annual criminal background checks for each employee, first-aid kits, and direct-deposit fees. A family is asked what they would like to pay staff. Different scenarios are developed based on the information provided by the family. The person-centered operating budget also contains a consumer needs account line item. I was first introduced to this concept while working with the self-determination projects. Under self-determination in some states, a "risk pool" account was established for consumers to assist with unexpected expenses. Following this same concept, the PCSS business model established a consumer needs account as part of the person-centered operating budget. Dollars are allocated to each line item within the person-centered operating budget to ensure all Medicaid dollars are utilized on behalf of the consumer. Each month, PCSS families receive a consumer needs account statement. The statement outlines the total Medicaid amount billed and received on behalf of their child, the amount of wages paid to staff, the overhead received by our agency, and the balance of the consumer needs account. At any time, families can access the consumer needs dollars by submitting a receipt or invoice to the PCSS finance office. This same Cumberland County family not only resolved their deductible issue through the person-centered operating budget, but was also able to purchase hearing aids for their daughter by utilizing the consumer needs account.

The person-centered operating budget allows families to maximize Medicaid dollars. Staff are paid higher wages through the person-centered operating budget than most traditional agencies. In addition, the consumer needs account allows families to purchase more traditional therapy services along with therapy services that are not paid for by the Medicaid system, such as horseback riding therapy, water therapy, and other specialized therapy programs for children with autism. The consumer-needs-account dollars must directly benefit the consumer. Flexibility in what consumers need is always taken into consideration. A family we serve in Lenoir, North Carolina recently purchased a used golf cart for their son. The family's new home sits on several acres of land. The consumer's grandmother and aunt live several acres away on a private country road in the mountains of Lenoir. This young teenage consumer has cerebral palsy. With the help of his support staff and his new means of transportation, he is learning independence. It would probably take an act of Congress and decades of advocacy for Medicaid to approve the purchase of a used golf cart. But rather than tax a Medicaid system further with added costs, the low overhead of our agency and the unique components of the person-centered operating budget provide a means for consumers to get what they need to live successfully in the communities of their choice.

Many families throughout North Carolina were active in the EPSDT battle. As a result my e-mail distribution list was extensive. When we started this business I shared the business goals with many of these families. Several came on board without hesitation. However, years later I received phone calls from families who wanted to know how PCSS was doing and if we were still taking on new families. A phone call came from a Lumberton family almost five years after the EPSDT battle. In North Carolina, families who choose to open their homes to individuals with significant disabilities receiving CAP MR/DD funding are known as alternative family living (AFL) homes. If the AFL home provides care to one adult consumer, the home does not require licensing. If the AFL home provides care to a child or two adults, the home must be licensed by the Department of Facility Services.

The mom I spoke with opened her home nineteen years ago to a young woman with significant disabilities. She did the same for another adult consumer over five years ago. Since there are two adults with CAP MR/DD funding in this home, the home must be licensed. Because of the additional requirements of licensure, the PCSS operating fee is slightly higher than that of the traditional family.

When a family is interested in PCSS as a provider agency, one of the first things we do is gather information to develop the person-centered operating budget. For each of the individuals served in this AFL home, the AFL family was receiving $40 per day or $280 per week. When PCSS ran the scenarios using the person-centered operating budget, the AFL family's income increased to $650 per week. When the scenarios were sent to the mom, she was stunned and requested a face-to-face meeting. With calculator in hand, we carefully went through each line item to show the mom the accuracy of the numbers presented.

Throughout our fight for services, we know the bureaucracy will throw bones to families and expect gratitude in return. They will also instill fear when gratitude is not received. Now, we know from this experience that these same tactics are used by some of the traditional provider agencies to ensure profit.

Bringing on new families is the most exciting part of building the PCSS business. As families join our agency throughout the state, we need to ensure the monitoring requirements for services provided are met. In doing so, we hired fourteen associate professionals throughout the state, most of whom are parents of children on the CAP MR/DD waiver. This more than satisfies the monitoring requirement. In addition, it brought a remarkable level of connectedness between families across the state. As a result of the existence of PCSS, we have met tenacious, formidable, relentless moms throughout the state. One of these moms single-handedly took down one of the most corrupt area programs in the western part of the state. This is my kind of mom and almost immediately when we met more than five years ago, we connected and recognized a kindred spirit. As we shared war stories over the phone and through e-mail, we would strategize our next move. We were all very tired and wondered desperately when all this madness would stop. But for me, there was one more battle to pursue. The CAP MR/DD waiver was being renewed and the bureaucracy was positioning itself to ensure more intense control over those choosing to live in the community.

Chapter 18

The New Waiver Fiasco

The CAP MR/DD waiver was up for renewal in 2005. Somehow we knew this would be the mother of all battles. To prepare for this, I reviewed e-mail addresses and other contact information for the entire chain of command clear up to the deputy director, waiver expert at the CMS (Center for Medicare & Medicaid Services) Baltimore office. I also obtained the names, addresses, phone numbers, and e-mail addresses for all members of the Joint Legislative Oversight Committee of the North Carolina Division of Mental Health/Developmental Disabilities/Substance Abuse Services (MH/DD/SAS). In reviewing old files, I came across a compliance review of the North Carolina Home and Community Based Waiver for Individuals with Mental Retardation and Developmental Disabilities. The review was conducted by CMS staff formerly known as HCFA (Health Care Finance Administration) from the Atlanta Region IV office. The date of the review was February 28 through March 3, 2000. The review consisted of five elements. One of the elements focused on plans of care and provider qualifications.

Factor B1: Assure that the State has in place a formal system to monitor quality of care and access to care by which it assures the health and welfare of the beneficiaries.

Finding: …Blue Ridge – Reports were provided for 1994, 1996, 1997, 1998, and 1999. The 1994 report indicated that a family was being charged for supplies that exceed the Medicaid rate; the area program, as an enrolled provider agreed to accept the Medicaid maximum allowable for payment; and any amount in excess of the Medicaid maximum allowable could not be passed on to the consumer. This item was not listed as an area found out-of-compliance. However, a recommendation was made for the area program to immediately cease requesting payment from the consumer's family and refund any money collected from the family. The corrective action plan only addresses the items listed as out-of-compliance. There was no documentation that a refund was made to the family and that the area program ceased requesting payment.

Recommendation: ...The Division of Medical Assistance should also determine whether payments were returned to the family of the consumer identified in the 1994 Blue Ridge report. Collecting payment above the amount paid by the Medicaid Agency violates provisions at 41CFR 447.15. The State may wish to review the procedures for determining items that require corrective action and follow-up...

State Response: Cannot refute findings for Blue Ridge...except to say we now have a new process in place to follow out-of-compliance issues...

Factor B3: Assure that the services specified in the plans of care necessary to safeguard the health and welfare of the waiver beneficiaries were provided and that waiver beneficiaries have access to appropriate services when needed.

Finding: The case manager indicated in a note in one of the records that there were budgetary concerns if the client was to have supported employment since Medicaid reimbursed a higher rate for supported employment versus community inclusion. It appeared that the decision was based on reimbursement rather than the client's needs. One record only included waiver reimbursed services. Several records indicated that clients received the wrong size diapers; one record reflected that it had happened on more than one occasion. Another client received a bathtub that was too small. One client record noted that the client was to receive therapy services at school. The client's mother informed the case manager that the services were not being provided at school and the case manager revised the client's plan of care to include therapy services at home. The note also indicated that CI (Community Inclusion) services would be reduced if necessary to allow for therapy services at home. There was no indication in the record that the case manager contacted the school to get the school to provide the services.

Recommendation: It is recommended that the State address these topics when training case managers.

State Response: The Division of Medical Assistance has requested more intense case manager training. These trainings should include instructions for plans of care, appropriate responses to problems such as services being inappropriate or not provided and reminders that need not reimbursement should drive the plan of care. We will follow up on this request and attempt to attend the trainings.

Although this report was written in 2000, five years before the renewal of the CAP MR/DD waiver, the same findings are still evident throughout our system.

While attending a training session in Washington DC several years earlier, I learned more details about the Home and Community Based Services (HCBS) waivers. The training session was conducted by a Baltimore CMS staff member. The handouts from this training detail the process that each state must follow when applying for a waiver.

- An application for a HCBS waiver program must be submitted by the state Medicaid agency.
- Day-to-day operation of the waiver can be delegated to another entity but Medicaid must maintain the overall oversight of the program.
- Consumers must meet an institutional level of care.
- State Medicaid Agency must assure that the cost of providing home and community-based services will not exceed the cost of care for the identical population in an institution (i.e. cost neutral).
- Medicaid Agency must document that there are safeguards in place to project the health and welfare of consumers.
- Central office (Baltimore office) has the lead for review of initial waiver requests and for reviewing amendments of initial waivers.
- Initial waivers are approved for a three-year period.
- Regional offices (for North Carolina the regional office in Atlanta) have the lead for review of waiver renewal requests and for reviewing amendments relating to a waiver renewal.
- Renewed waivers are approved for five-year intervals.
- All waiver submissions (initial waiver, renewals, or amendments)

are subject to a ninety-day review period.
- States are required to annually submit data on the utilization and costs of waiver services.
- Regional offices are responsible for review of waiver programs approximately one year prior to the end of the waiver year.
- Waivers can be amended at any time during the life of the program.
- There are no limitations on the number of times a waiver can be renewed.
- Approximately 262 active waivers in operation throughout the country.
- It is estimated that over one million individuals received home and community-based services in 2000.
- The federal expenditures for home and community-based services waivers in FFY 2000 were approximately 12.4 billion dollars, a 14.6 percent increase over FFY 1999.
- Examples of State Flexibility
  o Payment rates
  o Numbers served under a waiver
  o Family members as providers
  o Services offered under waiver program
  o Qualified providers

Preparation for the 2005 waiver began in early 2004. On January 12, 2004 the North Carolina Division of MH/DD/SAS posted to its website the proposed new CAP MR/DD service definitions. It was our first look at proposed changes to services that many individuals, including my son, relied on to live in the community. One of these most important services is personal care services. This is a very basic service that involves assistance with eating, bathing, dressing, personal hygiene, and other activities of daily living.

As I reviewed my old files in preparation for the waiver changes to come, I was concerned with the detail outlined in the Washington, DC presentation by CMS staff that focused on cost neutrality. The handout specifically noted that the "State Medicaid Agency must assure that the cost of providing home and community-based services will not exceed the cost of care for the identical population in an institution (i.e. cost neutral)." My research led me to a document published by the Thomson Medstat group in Cambridge, Massachusetts. The document was dated May 25, 2004 and provided statistical information on Medicaid HCBS waiver expenditures for FY 1998 through FY 2003 for all states (Appendix A). This information was compared to ICF/MR facility care for the same time period. The results outlined in the North Carolina chart were as follows:

The North Carolina HCBS Waiver for the MR/DD target population had the following expenditures noted:

FY 1998	$132,531,231
FY 1999	$149,910,940
FY 2000	$190,496,958
FY 2001	$235,232,775
FY 2002	$254,035.290
FY 2003	$263,186,889

Statistics were also listed for the total expenditures of both North Carolina public and private ICF/MR facilities. These expenditures were as follows:

FY 1998	$380,157,092
FY 1999	$393,413,325
FY 2000	$396,863,370
FY 2001	$400,129,463
FY 2002	$416,422.558
FY 2003	$418,466,631

The only question unanswered at this time is the number of individuals served for the above expenditures. The North Carolina CAP MR/DD waiver serves over 5,000 individuals statewide. Each individual has been identified to need ICF/MR level of care. The level of care for all people served on the CAP MR/DD waiver and in the ICF/MR facilities are the same. The dollar amounts are, however, excessive for the ICF/MR facilities. Is it possible that in FY 2003 the CAP MR/DD waiver served over 5,000 individuals for $263,186,889 while the ICF/MR served another 5,000 individuals with the same level of care for $418,466,631? Were there more or less than 5,000 individuals in the public and private ICF/MRs in FY 2003? If one half more individuals were served in ICF/MR facilities in FY 2003, the number served would be 7,500 individuals. If 7,500 individuals were served in private and public ICF/MR facilities in FY2003, the expenditure noted in this chart is still far more than what it would have cost to serve the same number of individuals on the CAP MR/DD waiver. For the same 7,500 individuals on the waiver, the cost would be $394,780,333. It seems to me that maintaining cost neutrality in a waiver is easy to do with the excessive dollar amounts expended on ICF/MR facilities.

Despite these statistics, the threat of budget cuts to the CAP MR/DD waiver program was again a hot topic. E-mails were flying in all directions from families to their House and Senate representatives, begging that services provided by the CAP MR/DD waiver not be cut. Also, articles written in several newspapers were sent via e-mail throughout the state. Below are excerpts from an article that appeared in a Raleigh newspaper on May 28, 2004.

"In the last ten months, Ethan has learned to talk so his parents and others can understand him. He has learned to sit in a restaurant and wait for his food. He can stand in line without throwing a tantrum. 'I would say he's an 80% different child,' said (Ethan's mother.) Ethan has Down syndrome and autism and is prone to 'meltdowns.' But those episodes happen less frequently now, thanks to a specialized worker who spends time teaching Ethan proper behavior. The change in Ethan came about because he began receiving CAP MR/DD funds, money provided by state and federal governments to care for people with disabilities in the community instead of in an institution…Advocates for people with mental illness, developmental disabilities, and substance abuse problems have been scrambling this week to persuade the state House of Representatives not to cut up to $35 million in state money for CAP (Community Alternative Programs) and other services…"

Excerpts from another Raleigh newspaper article entitled, "State Agency Silences Advocate for Disabled" was dispersed via e-mail on May 29, 2004. The article indicated that the "interim director of the Governor's Advocacy Council for Persons with Disabilities (GACPD) wanted to comment this week on what damage might be caused by proposed cuts to the North Carolina Department of Health & Human Services budget. In the past, she has been a strong advocate for people with disabilities. This week, though, she was silenced by the state Department of Administration…. The council is a protection and advocacy agency, mandated by federal law to be free from interference by state government. But (the Department of Administration) refused permission for (the GACPD interim director) to comment directly and referred questions on the proposed budget cuts to the council's board chairman, who is not an employee of the state. The Board Chairman called the department's order a restriction on (the interim director's) ability to advocate for people with disabilities. The council answers to the Department of Administration for administrative purposes. But it must certify to the federal government each year that it does not interfere with the activities of the office. 'I say it could be construed as interference if our staff is not allowed to provide advocacy,' he said. 'If they are prevented from talking publicly, they can't advocate for persons with disabilities.' (Spokesperson for the Department of Administration) said questions could be e-mailed to her, then she would forward them to (the interim director), who would reply back to her so she could 'approve' (the interim director's) comments."

This is a prime example of the bureaucratic control of the North Carolina Protection and Advocacy Agency. A family responded to this article with an e-mail to the GACPD interim director.

"It is sad to say that it has been my experience that this is 'business as usual' in North Carolina. While officials like to bemoan the lack of 'family and consumer' participation, the fact is that they do not like or welcome such participation unless the individual supports the political line or sits silently in the meeting like a stuffed animal. We have seen several family organizations that have had funding pulled when they rock the boat and we have seen individuals frozen out of the process and even witnessed character assassinations. We know that people with mental illness are afraid to speak out for fear they will lose what benefits they have, and we know that providers are afraid to speak out because they are afraid they will not be awarded contracts and/or referrals. From what we have seen, their fears are justified."

Finally on July 26, 2004, a communication bulletin was posted to the North Carolina DMH Web site from the division director. The memo stated clearly that "by August 15, 2004, the CAP MR/DD Waiver Team will have completed a final draft of a new CAP MR/DD waiver…Throughout this work effort, the CAP MR/DD Team will actively solicit stakeholder input. The final draft of the basic waiver will be available for review and comment no later than August 15, 2004."

On August 13, 2004 I received an e-mail from the CAP MR/DD program director of one of the eastern area programs. The e-mail distribution list filled an entire page. The subject line read, "New Waiver Update 8/11/04." The e-mail simply forwarded an e-mail from yet another CAP MR/DD program director from a different area program. The e-mail forwarded stated the following:

"Please forward to other CAP Coordinators in your region that I do not have in my e-mail group. Thank you."

The e-mail continued with the following:

"Hello all. I attended a meeting yesterday in which the Division had a consultant to the Division from the Oregon Technical Assistance Corporation present a summary of the new waiver to a group of stakeholders. Here is a summary of what we heard."

The e-mail was two pages long and full of bulleted details. The first bullet presented great concern.

- "A comprehensive waiver has been developed by the waiver team referenced in the Director's communication bulletin. DMH (Division of MH/DD/SAS) plans to submit this to DMA (Division of Medical Assistance) on 8/18/04 and is shooting for an implementation date of 4/1/05."

The division director's bulletin on July 26, 2004 indicated that the draft of the waiver would "be available for review and comment no later than August 15, 2004." We now hear from a somewhat reliable source through notes taken at an unannounced meeting that the waiver will be submitted to the Division of Medical Assistance on August 18, 2004, giving the entire state three days for comment.

The bullets continued:

- "The state is also committed to developing a new Independence Plus waiver that they plan to submit to the Division of Medical Assistance by 6/30/05 with implementation sometime after (will depend on how many questions CMS has and when they approve). The intent is to allow waiver participants an opportunity for self-directed supports.
- "The comprehensive waiver is to address the following needs: 1) a solid, work-a-day waiver that provides supports to individuals in the community, 2) supports the Olmstead decision and the

state's efforts to move individuals into the community, 3) aggregate funding (no more individual cost limits), 4) Utilization Review, 5) Comprehensive CQI process, 6) DMH will take over the eligibility process (has not been approved by DMA management yet but discussions have begun), and 7) a more user friendly manual.

This was an awful lot of information and change being proposed. How could we possibly address all the issues in a three-day period?

The e-mail continued:

"Some of the new limits/changes to the services in the comprehensive waiver will be:

- "Personal Care Services – one of the new limits is that it will not be allowed in unlicensed AFLs (Alternative Family Living homes) as well as in licensed AFLs and residential facilities. Cannot be provided in home of the provider or in office of provider agency.
- "Respite – if respite is provided by a provider in their private home, that home will be subject to licensure. Not used as a daily service. Not provided to individual's who live in group homes. Not provided on the same day that primary caregiver provides another waiver service to the individual (there was a lot of discussion/comment about this restriction). Not provided to individual's who live alone. Only for the waiver recipient.
- "Residential Supports – payments are not for room & board. Payment does not include payments to family members (directly or indirectly). Only in facilities with 8 beds or less (only in larger settings if the individual is already on the waiver at the time this waiver is implemented.) Cannot get Personal Care Services with Residential Supports."

The e-mail continued for another page and a half. At the end of the e-mail, it was noted that the participants in the meeting asked if the division "would post the draft documents (service definitions, UR tools, etc.) to the Division website. Hopefully they will do that soon."

How can a bureaucracy consider self-directed supports and orchestrate a waiver for the sole purpose of supporting individuals to live in the community with a barrage of restrictions? How do you say to an individual that "we will support you and give you what you need, but you cannot have personal care services, even though you need this service, if you choose to live in a licensed or unlicensed alternative family living home?" What an individual needs and where he or she chooses to live are two different issues. What gives the state the right to limit where people can live? Isn't that what we did fifty years ago when we said services for people with disabilities would be provided ONLY in institutions? Although the notes in the e-mail were extensive, they generated a number of questions. Residential supports was a new service. All we knew of this service was written in the notes in the e-mail. This was not enough and once again time was ticking away. Several families sent e-mails and made phone calls to the CMS Atlanta office. We wanted the draft waiver put on the website immediately. We needed time to review and comment on what was being proposed before it went to the Division of Medical Assistance and left the state for CMS approval.

Finally, and I believe as a result of the many phone calls and e-mails that were made by families to the CMS Atlanta office, a communication bulletin was posted to the DMH website by the division director on August 23, 2004, not August 15, 2004 as promised by the director in the previous bulletin.

The August 23 bulletin reads as follows:

"Attached is the draft of the comprehensive 1915(c) Home and Community Based Waiver. This draft is simultaneously being submitted to the Division of Medical Assistance and posted to the Division of MH/DD/SAS public website. It should be noted that the Quality Management Plan is in the process of reorganization to insure clarity in addressing the components of the Centers for Medicaid and Medicare (CMS) Quality Framework and will be posted to the web once this is completed. Effective this date there will be a 30-day comment period ending on September 23, 2004. Comments may be submitted by e-mail, fax or written communication. Due to resource, time and efficiency problems, feedback will not be responded to on an individual basis. Comments should be directed to…"

Unfortunately the letter gave no indication how the division would respond to comments made during the thirty-day comment period. The attachment to this bulletin contained the completed waiver application. Immediately I dove into reviewing the entire document page by page.

The first page of the document indicated the new waiver period would be for a three-year period rather than a five-year period. This was odd. Initial waivers were for three years. This was indicated on the application. The CAP MR/DD waiver was an already existing waiver and should have been renewed for a five-year period. However, the checkmark indicated a three-year period.

The ICF/MR level of care remained the same in this waiver, with the target population being individuals with mental retardation and developmental disabilities.

On page three of the application, the following statements were noted:

"The State will refuse to offer home and community-based services to any person for whom it can reasonably be expected that the cost of home or community-based services furnished to that individual would exceed the cost of a level of care referred to in item 2 of this request." *(Item 2 indicated ICF/MR level of care.)*

"Through the implementation of aggregate funding versus slot funding individuals will receive the waiver funding that they need. Waiver funding does not replace other informal or formal supports that are available to the individual."

I continued to read this application, shaking my head in disbelief. The bureaucracy thus far had never given us what we needed without a fight. This certainly would be no different.

Attached to the application was Appendix B, outlining the services to be provided. One of the first big changes noted was that case management would no longer be part of the waiver. The waiver application specifically noted that "targeted case management will be provided to individuals participating in this waiver through the State Medicaid Plan." As I read this I immediately remembered the February 5, 2003 e-mail from the Atlanta CMS staff, which stated:

"If you want to restrict providers of case management services, you may want to consider amending your State Plan and CAP MR/DD waiver to include targeted case management in the Plan for the waiver population and remove this service from the waiver."

The next big change came in the restrictions posed on personal care services. Page three of Appendix B stated that "Personal Care Providers may be members of the individual's family. Payment will not be made for services furnished to a minor by the child's parent (or step-parent), legal guardian of minor, or to an individual by that person's spouse. Family members who provide personal care services must meet the same standards as providers who are unrelated to the individual." This part of the definition had not changed. This information was part of the previous waiver. However, despite this verbiage in the approved application and in the present CAP manual, parents of adult consumers across the state are being asked to provide justification as to why they are to be paid staff. In some cases, like the family in Rocky Mount, North Carolina, parents find themselves negotiating with the attorney general's staff over the amount of paid hours they will provide.

The personal care services definition in the application had not changed from the previous waiver. The definition is as follows:

"Personal Care Services include support, supervision and engaging participation with eating, bathing, dressing, personal hygiene and other activities of daily living. Support and engaging consumer participation describes the flexibility of activities that may encourage the person to maintain skills gained during active treatment and/or habilitation while also providing supervision for independent activities of the consumer. This service may include assistance with preparation of meals, but does not include the cost of the meals themselves. When specified in the plan of care, this service may also include such housekeeping chores as bed making, dusting and vacuuming, which are incidental to the care furnished, or which are essential to the health and welfare of the individual, rather than the individual's family. Personal Care also includes assistance with monitoring health status and physical condition, assistance with transferring, ambulation and use of special mobility devices. This service also provides assistance in the workplace with activities not already required or funded by other sources or services, including travel assistance."

The change to the personal care services definition came under the service limitations section.

"Individuals who live in licensed residential facilities, licensed alternative family living homes, licensed foster care homes or unlicensed alternative family living homes serving one adult may not receive this service."

If the individual requires personal care services in order to live in the community and chooses to live in one of the settings listed above, what service will be provided to him or her in place of the needed personal care service? The answer to this question is the new service entitled "residential supports" listed on page seven of Appendix B under the section entitled "habilitation."

The definition for residential supports is as follows:

"Habilitation, training and instruction are coupled with elements of support, supervision and engaging participation to reflect the natural flow of training, practice of skills, and other activities as they occur during the course of the person's day. This service is distinctive in that it includes active treatment, habilitation and training activities. Interactions with the person are designed to achieve outcomes identified in the Plan of Care. Support and supervision of the person's activities to sustain skills gained through habilitation and training is also an acceptable goal of Residential Supports. This service is provided to individuals who live in licensed community residential settings, foster homes, or alternative family living homes as well as unlicensed alternative family living homes that serve one adult. This service also provides assistance, support, supervision and monitoring that allow individuals to participate in home or community activities."

This definition is very different from personal care services and focuses on habilitation and training. Individuals with significant disabilities, like my son, have been approved for personal care services and have been living in alternative family living homes for years. It seems to me that the service is being changed based on where they live and not based on what they need. In addition, in Appendix B-2 of the waiver application, a comment is indicated regarding staff training for enhanced personal care and enhanced respite. However, neither of these services is mentioned in the service section of the waiver application. As I read this I couldn't help but wonder what the bureaucracy was up to. Red flags were popping up everywhere as I read this document.

I spoke with the executive director of The Arc of North Carolina shortly after the notes from the CAP coordinator appeared on my e-mail. The executive director had a conversation about the restrictions with the assistant director of the Division of DMH. According to the executive director of The Arc of North Carolina, the assistant director had assured him that the changes would be reversed. However, when the draft document finally appeared on the DMH Web site, the restrictions remained as indicated in the e-mail notes provided by the CAP coordinator.

During the DD consortium meeting on September 13, 2004, the division project manager for the waiver was present to answer questions regarding the proposed new waiver. It was evident in the discussion that took place that the executive director of The Arc of North Carolina, the CEO of Easter Seals/UCP, and the executive director of the North Carolina Council on Developmental Disabilities, all present at the meeting, did not review the draft waiver posted to the DMH Web site on August 23 and therefore were unaware that the restrictions had not been removed. I questioned the division project manager about the limitations for personal care services. She and the CEO of Easter Seals/UCP stated that the CAP MR/DD waiver was for individuals who required habilitation services and if an individual did not require habilitation, the Division of Medical Assistance would question if the individual was on the correct waiver. This was a direct threat to those individuals with significant disabilities presently served on the waiver. Not to mention it was also, first and foremost, a direct threat for me to shut up and stop messing up their meeting.

There is nothing in the present waiver or in the draft waiver that states individuals must require habilitation. The only requirement is ICF/MR level of care. Many recipients of the CAP MR/DD waiver who have significant disabilities have been ICF/MR eligible for years. Why should that change now? Many individuals with significant disabilities do not qualify for habilitation services. What most people with significant disabilities need to live in the community is an extensive amount of personal care services. Many of these individuals, because of their extensive needs, do better in a one-on-one community setting. An alternative family living home is one example of a one-on-one community setting. The draft waiver does not offer any other service comparable to personal care services. All other services, except respite services, are habilitation services. The division is trying to sell residential supports as a "blended service." But if an individual with significant disabilities does not require habilitation services, what is there to blend? The Social Security Law, section 1915(5) states the definition of *habilitation services* as follows: "services designated to assist individuals in acquiring, retaining, and improving the self-help, socialization, and adaptive skills necessary to reside successfully in home and community based settings." This definition does not apply to many individuals with significant disabilities. The draft waiver limitations on personal care services limit where an individual with significant disabilities can live. This is a violation of the individual's civil rights.

On September 30, 2004, without any changes made, the application was submitted by the director of the Division of DMH to the director of the Division of Medical Assistance. The good news was that the waiver had not yet left the state.

Shortly after, The Arc of North Carolina distributed its response of the Draft CAP MR/DD waiver.

"The Arc of North Carolina has read the proposed draft waiver and offers the Division the following thoughts, questions and issues for consideration. The waiver is the foundation by which supports and services are delivered to CAP eligible recipients. As the foundation, it is very important for the Division to consider how policy based on broad generalizations can negatively affect individual people.

"The Arc recognizes that many problems people currently encounter with the waiver are due more to interpretation of the waiver, than the actual waiver itself. Therefore, some of the feedback below may not necessarily apply to actual needed changes in the proposed waiver but may assist the Division as the policy manual is being written.

"Historically, the variety of interpretations of the waiver and service definitions has created unequal access to services and supports across the state. It is for this reason that The Arc of North Carolina strongly urges the Division to write a clear, concise manual that does not leave itself so open to individual interpretations.

"The Arc has concerns about the proposed limitations on Personal Care as stated on page 19....Broad generalizations about people and policy based on them can lead to inadvertent harm. The Arc recognizes that many individuals living in these settings will not need additional Personal Care Services (PCS) however, some people, particularly those with significant disabilities, will need to have PCS provided that goes beyond the basic personal care that is provided through residential placements. Failure to provide this additional personal care will result in high support need individuals not being accepted in many community settings. This will place people with significant needs at increased risk of institutionalization and result in out of community placement...

"On page 22 from the definition of Residential Supports:... Residential Supports by proposed definition includes training and instruction. That fact, coupled with the proposed limitations on Personal Care may well bring about the unintended consequence of forcing people to receive a higher level of support then what is actually needed. People living in AFLs, Group Homes, etc. who need additional assistance, may instead be forced to receive Residential Supports, a more intensive service than Personal Care that will no longer be an option for them due to the Personal Care limitations being proposed...

"On page 44 and 45 (in both Personal Care and Respite) within the 'Other Standards' column: *Staff providing enhanced personal care (also respite) have additional training/instruction specific to the medical and/or behavioral needs of the consumer.* The Arc is assuming that this is indicating that there will be two levels of Personal Care and Respite Services. What are the requirements needed to be met to receive enhanced services? Will this be addressed in the manual?"

It was encouraging to see The Arc of North Carolina step forward with the very same concerns. However, it was the only state nonprofit advocacy organization I knew of that did so. As a board member of the North Carolina TASH organization, I approached the board requesting that a letter be sent to the division director outlining the same concerns. Unfortunately many of the board members of the North Carolina TASH organization were also state employees and were reluctant to take a stand. As a result, no letter was sent by the North Carolina TASH organization on behalf of people with significant disabilities.

In addition to The Arc coming forward with these same concerns, families began sending e-mails to CMS to alert them on how this new waiver would impact the lives of their children. On September 20, 2004 a family from the western part of the state sent an e-mail to the deputy director of CMS outlining concerns with the proposed waiver and the impact it would have on her daughter.

The response received from the deputy director of CMS was as follows:

"Thank you for your comments concerning the North Carolina waiver. I will forward those comments to CMS Central Office and Regional Office staff responsible for review of that waiver.

"If your daughter is denied services under the North Carolina waiver which you believe are necessary for her to remain in the community, you should request a Medicaid fair hearing on that decision. In addition, you may also continue to work with the Office of Civil Rights."

This particular mom knows firsthand that there is nothing fair about a Medicaid hearing. The response from the deputy director confirms the inability of this bureaucracy to be proactive in supporting people. Why wait until you are backed into a corner with a waiver that is not meeting the needs of people with significant disabilities? Why not address the concerns of individuals with significant disabilities before you approve the waiver?

This same mom sent an e-mail to the North Carolina waiver point of contact person at the Division of Medical Assistance again outlining her concerns with the proposed waiver and its impact on her daughter.

The response received from the Division of Medical Assistance staff:

"All comments regarding the waiver will be reviewed by DMA and DMH together before the final version of the waiver is submitted to CMS. I do not have the authority to make decisions independently. I report the joint recommendations to my Assistant Director and to the Division Director for a final decision."

In the middle of the waiver battle, a letter was sent from CMS to all state Medicaid directors, dated August 17, 2004. Several issues were addressed in this letter. One of the issues presented was the self-directed waiver model. As I read the attachments to this letter regarding agency of choice, fiscal intermediaries, individual budgets, and employers of record, I recognized the innovation and pioneering spirit of the PCSS business model. While the federal CMS agency was trying desperately to convince North Carolina and other states that self-directed services were the way to go, CAP MR/DD waiver recipients in North Carolina were able to participate as co-employers with a person-centered operating budget through the PCSS business model. I've learned through these many years of battles that it is best to be innovative and creative with the system that exists rather than wait for permission to act.

As I moved through this waiver battle, I constantly researched and read over and over anything I could find on the waiver from CMS.

Several documents were obtained on the CMS Web site.

Home and Community-Based Services Waiver Program

How to Obtain Approval

- To receive approval to implement HCBS waiver programs, State Medicaid agencies must assure CMS that, on an average per capita basis, the cost of providing home and community-based services will not exceed the cost of care for the identical population in an institution. The Medicaid agency must also document and assure that necessary safeguards are in place to protect the health and welfare of beneficiaries. Additional federal requirements for states choosing to implement a HCBS waiver program include:... Ensuring that services are provided pursuant to a plan of care.
- An application...must be submitted by the State Medicaid agency to the Centers for Medicare and Medicaid Services for review and approval...
- Initial HCBS waivers are approved for a three-year period. Waiver may be renewed for five-year intervals.

Program History

- ...The HCBS waiver program recognizes that many individuals at risk of being placed in these facilities can be cared for in their homes and communities, preserving their independence and ties to family and friends at a cost no higher than that of institutional care.
- ...The initial legislation offered home and community-based services to individual who absent the waiver would require skilled nursing facility or intermediate care facility services including ICF/MR...

Program Design

- The home and community-based services (HCBS) waiver program, section 1915 (c) of the Social Security Act (the Act) is the Medicaid program alternative to providing long-term care in institutional settings.
- ...States can make home and community-based services available to individuals who would otherwise qualify for Medicaid

only if they were in an institutional setting…

- …States may use an HCBS waiver program to provide a combination of both traditional medical services (i.e., dental services, skilled nursing services) as well as non-medical services (i.e., respite, case management, environmental).

- …There is no limit on the number of services that can be offered under a single waiver program as long as the waiver retains cost-neutrality and the services are necessary to avoid institutionalization.

Program Guidelines

- Federal law implementing the home and community-based services waiver program – Section 1915 (c) of the Social Security Act.

- Federal regulations providing operating parameters for the home and community-based services waiver program – (42 Code of Federal Regulations Part 441.300)

- Policies governing the home and community-based services waiver program – State Medicaid Manual (Section 4440 of the State Medicaid Manual)

- State Medicaid Director letters providing States assistance in developing and implementing home and community-based services waiver programs.

As I went through old files, I found that exactly one-year prior, on September 22, 2003, I had received an e-mail from a state employee in the budget department of the Division of DMH stating, "Based on the billings for FY 2003, the State average ICF-MR rate is $264.12. This equates to an annual figure of $96,403.80." The maximum dollar amount in the present waiver was $86,058. However, the new proposed waiver would implement aggregate funding, meaning there would be no maximum amount. However, in the spirit of cost neutrality, the $96,000 figure was an important figure to keep in mind when deciding on services.

Not only were the service definitions important in the review of the proposed waiver, the rates for each of the services were just as important. Finally on October 19, 2004, a memo was posted on the website from the DMH and DMA directors outlining the rate structure for each of the services. Once again, simple math was an incomprehensible concept for the division staff.

The residential supports rates listed on the proposed fee schedule were as follows:

Residential Supports – Level 1	$ 86.00 per day
Residential Supports – Level 2	$125.45 per day
Residential Supports – Level 3	$145.17 per day
Residential Supports – Level 4	$164.90 per day

As a result of the October 19 memo, I sent the following e-mail on October 29 to the directors of DMH and DMA.

"In reviewing your letter dated October 19, I present the following concerns as a parent of a young adult on CAP MR/DD since 1995 and as a provider of CAP MR/DD services...

"In April 2001, all area program Directors received a letter from the DMA Director at the time informing them of the increase in the cost limit for CAP MR/DD to 'the average ICF/MR cost of $86,058.' If the average in 2001 was $86,058, what is it now?

"In an e-mail from (DMH budget staff) on September 22, 2003, the following was stated, 'Based on the billings for FY 2003, the state average ICF MR rate is $264.12. This equates to an annual figure of $96,403.80.' (The DMH budget staff) further stated, 'The CAP MR/DD service does not include Room and Board, but the ICF/MR rate does include Room and Board.' Without Room and Board calculated in the average cost, it would seem to me that the average cost of ICF MR is probably the same - $86,058 annual and $235.77 daily. If this is still the case, then why is the proposed rate for the highest level of care of Residential Support at $164.90?

"On page 3 of the waiver application it states, 'Through the implementation of aggregate funding versus slot funding individuals will receive the waiver funding that they need.'

"The waiver funding needed for many individuals with significant disabilities has already been determined through the SNAP assessment, MR2, and Plan of Care. Many individuals with significant disabilities – like my son – are already maxed out on their cost summaries solely with CAP MR/DD services at $86,058. However, if the services they receive transfer to Residential Supports, the most they can receive for services is $60,188.50 ($164.90 times 365 days per year). This is significantly lower than what has been determined necessary for them to live in the community.

"There is no indication in the information we have received so far to show there will be a restriction in the number of Personal Care hours an individual can receive. However, because of the restriction to the Personal Care definition, individuals with significant disabilities cannot receive Personal Care services while living in an AFL (Alternative Family Living home). Many individuals with significant disabilities presently live in an AFL. Therefore, their services under the new waiver would be redefined as Residential Supports. At the proposed daily rate of $164.90, these individuals will receive $25,869.50 less services under the new waiver than they are presently receiving.

"As you know, it is the responsibility of the Medicaid agency to provide assurances to CMS regarding the health and welfare of individuals served on the waiver and to ensure quality of services furnished under the waiver.

"Please share how you propose to protect the health and welfare of individuals served on this waiver and ensure quality of services that propose a reduction of over $25,000 in services."

One of the individuals copied on this e-mail was a member of the Easter Seals/UCP Leadership Team and board member of the North Carolina Provider Council. On October 27, after hearing no response from the division, I sent an e-mail to this individual asking if he heard anything. His response was as follows:

"Yes, ran some numbers on new rates and have some questions on why they reduced some of the active services we use the most. They did increase the Residential Supports rate a few $ per day, but I see no pattern on rationale...There was that big shift from residential rates to SL (Supported Living) periodic and PCS (Personal Care Services) and now looks like they are trying to shift back to a daily rate. Keep asking the questions and let the Legislative Oversight Committee know your service situation. (The Division Director) says they want to protect services, this will not."

In the meantime, the division released a document entitled, "Utilization Review Criteria" for the amount of services an individual could receive on the CAP MR/DD waiver. This "criteria" caused an up roar throughout the state. If the purpose of person-centered planning is to identify what an individual needs, then why do you need a "criteria" grid? The grid indicated a SNAP (Special Needs Assessment Profile) index score that was the result of an algebraic formula that began with the SNAP assessment score. The four levels identified on the grid listed the maximum amount of respite, personal care, and residential supports an individual could receive. There were two grids. The first was for individuals living in their own homes or with natural family and the second grid was for individuals living in AFL or provider-managed residences. Eventually, the "criteria" grid was changed to a "guideline." The guideline stated the following:

Individual living in their own home or with natural family

Respite	Level 1	576 hours per year
	Level 2	576 hours per year
	Level 3	576 hours per year
	Level 4	576 hours per year
Personal Care	Level 1	40 hours per month
	Level 2	80 hours per month
	Level 3	120 hours per month
	Level 4	180 hours per month
Residential Supports	Level 1	N/A
	Level 2	N/A
	Level 3	N/A
	Level 4	N/A

Home & Community Supports, Day Supports, Supported Employment

	Level 1	120 hours per month for any combination of these services
	Level 2	Same as above
	Level 3	Same as above
	Level 4	Same as above

Individual living in AFL or provider managed residences

Respite	Level 1	576 hours per year
	Level 2	576 hours per year
	Level 3	576 hours per year
	Level 4	576 hours per year

Personal Care	Level 1	N/A
	Level 2	N/A
	Level 3	N/A
	Level 4	N/A
Residential Supports	Level 1	Daily rate
	Level 2	Daily rate
	Level 3	Daily rate
	Level 4	Daily rate

Home & Community Supports, Day Supports, Supported Employment

	Level 1	120 hours per month for any combination of these services
	Level 2	Same as above
	Level 3	Same as above
	Level 4	Same as above

The division did their best to backpedal from the criteria idea to the guideline announcement. What was the real purpose of this document? It is my opinion that the real purpose of the document was its original purpose: to limit the number of services an individual can receive, thereby limiting the CAP MR/DD overall operating budget. When the division changed the grid from a set of criteria to a guideline, it announced at several meetings that if a consumer needed more than what was indicated in the guidelines, he or she could and should receive it. However, the grid was developed to contain cost. Even a new name could not prevent the document from fulfilling its original goal. Throughout the state I heard stories from families who were visited by their case managers with grid in hand. The case manager would announce to the family that, beginning with the new waiver, the maximum amounts of services allowed were indicated on the grid. Even if it meant a reduction in services, the grid was going to be followed. On several occasions I reported case managers to the state for following the grid and not the person-centered planning process. The state's response was always, "We do not condone this." But the mere existence of the grid itself proves that the state does in fact condone a limitation in services, regardless of the person-centered plan.

One night, in the middle of this waiver battle, I reviewed all that had transpired thus far in the hopes of identifying a winning strategy to pursue. I remembered what I learned about EPSDT. Five years prior to this waiver battle the maximum amount of the waiver was $68,000. The rates for each service were raised and all consumers at the $68,000 maximum were approached by case managers with instructions to cut something from the budget. It was perfect timing for families to question the cut in services, because the waiver was about to be renewed. When I spoke with the ADAPT attorney I was convinced our issue was related to Olmstead. Because Danny was under twenty-one years of age at the time, the attorney introduced me to EPSDT (early periodic screening, diagnosis, and treatment).

Two things happened in the EPSDT battle. One, the state was being bombarded with EPSDT questions like never before. Up until that point, it was successful in hiding the full array of EPSDT services from families and top CEOs throughout the state. Second, the waiver maximum had to be increased. Cost neutrality in the present waiver is based on a maximum cost that is comparable to the average cost of ICF/MR (Intermediate Care Facility for Persons with Mental Retardation). I further learned from the CMS (Center for Medicare & Medicaid Services) staff e-mail regarding case management that CMS will not only tell the state what needs to be done according to what they presently have in place, but it will also suggest an option that puts control back in the hands of the state. Thus, we have a proposal for targeted case management.

Five years ago there had been a conference call regarding EPSDT and the maximum allowable on the waiver between CMS Atlanta, CMS Baltimore, and North Carolina DMH staff. I do not know the specifics of what transpired in that meeting, but when it was over, area program directors across the state received a letter from the division stating the waiver limitation was being raised to $86,058— the average cost of ICF/MR care. I am willing to bet what also transpired during that conference call was CMS's suggestion that the state go to aggregate funding when it applies for the new waiver. I believe CMS further provided guidance as to how aggregate funding could help the state control the finances of the waiver. Although I do not have any written proof of this, the bureaucracy seemed to be following a pattern.

I also reviewed all the e-mail conversations with the directors of DMH and DMA. The responses to my e-mails were not really responses. These guys are not stupid. This is simple math and yet they were acting and responding in ignorance. I thought further about the list of people I've e-mailed waiver concerns to and their responses or lack. As I struggled to understand why the noose was being tightened around the necks of individuals with significant disabilities, I remembered something my husband said to me: "The needs of the many sometime outweigh the needs of the few." Although all the people receiving waiver services are ICF/MR level of care, there is a spectrum of need. There is a large average of people in the middle of the spectrum who receive $40,000 to $50,000 per year of services. Unfortunately my experience tells me that many of the individuals in the middle of the spectrum should be at the higher end of the spectrum. However, it takes knowledge of the waiver to get to that point. I have never seen an area program offer $86,000 to a family of a child/adult with significant disabilities. My thoughts immediately shifted to a thirty-three-year-old male PCSS serves in the Rocky Mount, North Carolina area. This young man had been on the waiver for many years with a budget under $44,000. The disabilities involved severe cerebral palsy and the needs included a new wheelchair, ramp, wheelchair-accessible transportation, more personal care services, etc. Because the area program believed this mother did not have the wherewithal to fight for more, it was comfortable throwing bones at the consumer—that is, until PCSS got involved.

On the higher end of the spectrum, there are individuals like my son, with significant disabilities who require more than the average $40,000 per year. The number of these individuals with extensive needs is quite low compared to the number of individuals in the low and middle part of the spectrum. In one of the e-mails from the DMH and DMA division directors, they alluded to budget constraints; something I knew had been driving their train all along. If there are budget issues and the general assembly is not responding to these issues, the needs of the many will outweigh the needs of the few. Thus are born schemes like the waiver guideline grid. Even though the division makes it very clear that it does not "condone" limiting individuals to the information outlined on the grid, it knows statistically that a certain percentage of case managers will go to families with grid in hand, limiting services. In addition, it also knows that a certain percentage of families will rely heavily on the word of the case manager and agree to a limited number of services, even if more hours are needed to sustain community living. Because of these statistics, savings in CAP services will be evident. The goal of the bureaucracy is to serve as many people as possible with a limited number of dollars. Numbers and dollars are important to the bureaucracy. What we have proven with the twelve-family project and now with the PCSS business model is that families and consumers are also interested in numbers and dollars but first and foremost seek a quality of life for their loved ones that is not at all considered by the bureaucracy.

My thoughts then went to the various allies in the DD world and their responses to the proposed new waiver issues.

The Arc of North Carolina took a stand and submitted its concerns to the division, but whether or not this would be enough to move the division remained to be seen. The North Carolina TASH organization hesitated to make any formal statement due to board officers' dual position as state employees. As a result of the North Carolina Provider Council's concern with the low residential support rates, the division conducted a provider assessment that raised the residential support rate from its original proposed rate of $164.90 to $175.35. I believe the division knew the amount would be $175.35 but low-balled it for the purpose of staging the provider assessment process. This way the division comes out looking like the good guy. After all, "we did an assessment and found out we were wrong and, therefore, will raise the rate by $10 to be fair." Fair my ass. But there you have it. AFL Providers are still going to have an annual reduction in pay by almost $25,000.

Up until this point, the deputy director of CMS Baltimore still had not answered my direct question, Will you approve a waiver that reduces services for people with significant disabilities? Although I pressed the "send" button several times on this e-mail, there was no reply. The division still had in its utilization tool guide, enhanced respite, and enhanced personal care services. In one of the e-mails from division staff, they stated that the enhanced services would provide more staff hours from "skilled" staff but they gave no indication what skills would be required. Were they talking about LPN or RN qualifications?

The ADAPT attorney located in Pennsylvania told me on several occasions he did not have time to address our waiver concerns and directed me to the protection and advocacy agency in our state. Since this agency is housed in state government, it is an absolute waste of time to pursue its support in any advocacy issues. Although The National Health Law Program has an office in the Chapel Hill, North Carolina area, it is very clear that it does not have funds available for cases in North Carolina. Yet when I approached the principal author of the primer "Understanding Medicaid Home and Community Services," he referred me only to the National Health Law Program located in Chapel Hill.

Fighting the bureaucracy is a full-time job on top of many other full-time jobs families endure, including raising children with and without disabilities. The bureaucrats are depending on the fact that we have our hands full with our children and do not have the time to devote to a battle that will obtain victory. I believe we won the increase in the waiver from $68,000 to $86,058 because it was perfect timing. The waiver was being renewed and the change could easily be attained. The division had no choice but to accommodate the request. But the waiver renewal battle was different. The bureaucracy had realigned itself to figure out a way to keep consumer budgets at the $68,000 limit through the passage of a "blended" service, known as residential supports, and the limitation of a basic service, known as personal care.

Not only did we have a flurry of e-mail conversations regarding the new proposed waiver, but my business partner and I also participated in several conference calls with division staff. It was during one of these conference calls that I realized this battle was lost. As we tried persistently to get the division to understand the reduction in services for individuals living in AFL settings, one of the division staff member asked outright, "Why are you so concerned about AFL settings? Is your home an AFL home?" Without thinking, we blurted out "yes!" The silence was deadly and I knew at that moment we were in trouble. After a long silence, the same division staff member asked, "How can your home be an AFL for your own son?" It was at that point that we began a discussion about a fundamental difference in philosophy. "My son," I explained, "is an adult. As an adult, his home is no longer my home. If he chooses to live in my home, it is an alternative to where he should be living, which is in a home of his own." Right away, the division staff clearly indicated that it was against the rules to do what we were doing. As I clearly train all families to do, I asked the division staff to show me in the North Carolina Administrative Code where it states that a parent's home of an adult consumer could not be an AFL home for his or her adult child. It took months before a response arrived from the division. Finally on March 31, 2005, Danny's twenty-third birthday, a letter arrived stating the following:

"We would like to address the issue of a natural or adoptive family being classified as an 'Alternative Family Living' program when the family provides care for their adult child in the family home. You are correct in your contention that 10 NCAC 27G.5601 does not specifically speak to that possibility. In fact, the rule is silent on the issue; it does not state that is not possible, but neither does it specifically permit it. We believe that a thorough reading of all of 10 NCAC 27G, including section .0103 in which the definition of a 'facility' is defined as having the same meaning as that outlined in G.S. 122C-3 supports our contention that an adult child, regardless of disability, living with their natural or adoptive family, is living in a family setting in the usual meaning of that term, not, as is the title of supervised living category, an Alternative Family Living arrangement."

All AFL (alternative family living) homes in North Carolina receive a difficulty of care payment according to IRS rule. The difficulty of care payment is a tax-free payment. Once again, division logic was discriminating against the family and what it termed the "natural support." The scenario is as follows: My son can live in my neighbor's home and the neighbor can receive a difficulty of care tax-free payment for the same services I provide to Danny in my home. The neighbor's home does not need to be licensed according to the North Carolina Administrative Code, which does not require licensing when only one adult lives in the AFL home. As an AFL provider for Danny, I used the difficulty of care tax-free payment to purchase items Danny needed, such as items for the construction of a ramp for our home, a bathtub in his room to allow privacy, alternative seating to be used in the home, a wheelchair Sure Lock system for his van, a specialized backing system for his wheelchair, alternative home seating systems…and the list goes on. All of these items could have been purchased with additional Medicaid dollars. Instead I maximized the Medicaid dollars allocated and received for Danny's services by using the tax-free payment to purchase the needed items. Now this will no longer be possible, because the bureaucracy sees the family unit as the natural support until either the consumer or the family dies, whichever comes first. The family is abused by the bureaucracy from the moment it enters the system. The abuse continues even after the consumer enters adulthood and the family ages into their fifties, sixties, and sometimes seventies. According to the bureaucracy, there is no end to the natural support providing free service. I wonder, however, if the shoe were on the other foot, would the bureaucrats consider it natural to walk away from their high-paying jobs and careers to care for their loved ones with no monetary compensation? PCSS has hired several grandmothers to care for their grandchildren with disabilities. These grandmothers walked away from full-time jobs. The salaries they receive from PCSS are the same, if not better, than their full -time positions. Are grandmothers a natural support? Grandmothers are the best support a child can receive. One of the children PCSS serves in the Rocky Mount, North Carolina area is a twin and a survivor of meningitis that occurred at two weeks of age. The relationship this child has with his grandmother is in part the reason for his many successes. Would he have been as successful in attaining goals if his staff member was a total stranger? I say probably not and certainly not with the speed and accuracy we have seen. Would the grandmother have been able to be his staff member without monetary compensation? Again I believe the answer is no. But the relationship is essential to this child's success. No rules are broken because of the arrangement. The grandmother is not the child's parent. In the same way, no rules are broken when an adult consumer is receiving services from his biological or adopted parent. As the division director noted in his letter, "You are correct in your contention that (the rule) does not specifically speak to that possibility. In fact, the rule is silent on the issue..." If the rule is silent on the issue, then why the heck aren't they silent on the issue? Unlike bureaucrats, parents of children and adults with significant disabilities are not taking extravagant vacations on monetary compensation of services provided. They are using monetary compensation to provide quality of care to their loved ones. They are purchasing equipment and supplies that take Medicaid too long to obtain. They are remodeling their homes to ensure their children have the privacy they need. I have banged my head against the wall a million times over this issue and I have watched PCSS families do the same. Despite families sending e-mails and letters to individuals throughout the chain of command, the bureaucracy was winning this waiver renewal battle. For the first time, families decided to bring out the big guns and file for a congressional investigation. Both Senators Dole and Burr accepted the letters from families and began pursuing their contacts at both the DHHS (Department of Health & Human Services) and CMS (Center for Medicare & Medicaid Services). However, what we learned from this strategy was that our congressional delegates are no different from most taxpayers. The waiver is something you learn about haphazardly once you are in need of the service. Although millions of state and federal dollars pour into the waiver program on a regular basis, the particulars of the waiver system are an unknown to those in positions to make a difference. The best we received from the congressional investigations was a three-month stall of the inevitable. As the waiver implementation date came closer, new bureaucratic schemes were unveiled.

The new proposed waiver would not have an individual consumer budget limitation; however, it would have a review process that involved three levels. If a consumer cost summary was under $50,000, the local approval specialist at the local area program/LME would review and approve/deny the plan of care. If the cost summary was under $85,000, a second-level review at the local area program/LME level would approve or deny the plan of care. All cost summaries in excess of $85,000 would be subjected to a state-level review for approval or denial. In the meantime, I started pushing for the definitions and staff qualifications of the enhanced personal care and enhanced respite services. Finally this information was revealed along with the rate for each service. The enhanced services targeted individuals with extensive medical or behavioral needs. The rate for each of these services was twenty dollars per hour. This was unbelievable and entirely out of character for this bureaucracy! At the time, Danny was receiving 466.5 hours per month of regular personal care services. The enhanced personal care service definition was the most appropriate service for Danny based on medical needs. Without a reduction in services, Danny's new budget, consisting of enhanced services, would total $111,960. Immediately I remembered my research on the average cost of ICF/MR care. The last figure I was able to attain was for FY 2003 at a little over $96,000. Would the bureaucracy conclude that Danny did not qualify for the waiver because it would cost more to serve him in the community than in an ICF/MR? As I pondered my options, I decided I was not willing to take this risk. Instead I opted to seek the dollar equivalent of the enhanced services with a cost summary budget of $5 under the $85,000 maximum. Because of the new review rules, all Danny's reviews were conducted at the local level. I also decided that if the area program/LME denied Danny's plan, I would, with staff support, take Danny to the Cumberland County Mental Health Center to meet with the director face to face. I would then ask the director to explain to Danny why his services were denied. Luckily, so far, there has been no need to implement this strategy. However, I witnessed parents engaging in head-to-head battles with the state when budgets exceeded the $85,000 limit. In the successful cases, the parent moved into the role of case manager and took the lead in fighting for services. When the parent did not have the skills to pursue the fight in the lead position, the family found itself in negotiation, sometimes in the presence of the attorney general's staff.

With the discrimination issue heavy on my mind, I decided on October 9, 2004 to submit a complaint to the Office of Civil Rights (OCR). Although I had filed an OCR complaint many years earlier with the Department of Education (DOE), this was different. The OCR office for this complaint was affiliated with the Department of Health and Human Services (DHHS). Unfortunately the inadequacies of the DHHS OCR department replicated that of its sister Department of Education OCR department. The OCR complaint contained an extensive packet of information regarding the alleged discrimination of the proposed restrictions of personal care and residential services. I followed up with the OCR staff from Region IV on several occasions and finally left it to rest. Much to my surprise on January 12, 2006, sixteen months after the complaint was submitted, I received a phone call from the OCR staff member. "I'm just calling, Mrs. Mercado, to see how things are going." I wanted so badly to slam the phone down on this guy. Where the hell was he for the past sixteen months? Instead I took a deep breath and thanked him for not being there for us and explained as calmly as possible that because he did nothing, the waiver went through without any corrections. He wanted to know if I knew of anyone who was placed in an institution as a result of the residential supports definition. Because I did not know anyone who was moved from his or her alternative family living home to an institution, he concluded that the waiver was not detrimental to community life. "Do you want to pursue this any further, Mrs. Mercado?" he asked. "Too much time has lapsed to pursue this any further," I said in disgust. This was a very special kind of bureaucrat! It didn't matter what consumers, families, and AFL providers had to go through during this battle or how their lives were transformed upon the approval of this new waiver. On January 17, 2006 I received a letter from the OCR/Region IV regional manager.

"…You spoke on January 12, 2006 with….my staff when he called to get an update on details of your complaint. It is my understanding that you stated that you were no longer interested in pursuing this complaint because of the time that has passed since your filing of your complaint and the information you felt that you would have to obtain to pursue it.

"We will keep your case open for another two weeks in case you change your mind. If we do not hear back from you by the end of the month, I will close this matter, as you directed. Of course, you are welcome to file another complaint with our office in the future, should you feel the State or other health and human services agency has violated the American's with Disabilities Act, or any of the other civil rights statutes that we enforce."

The new CAP MR/DD waiver was to begin on July 1, 2005. However, it is my belief that the congressional investigations prolonged the start date until September 1, 2005. In a last-ditch effort to try to understand the AFL/Difficulty of Care issue imposed upon the biological and adopted families of adult consumers, I contacted the IRS Office of Chief Counsel in Washington, DC. After a brief discussion with an attorney in this office, I was faxed an eight-page document on a court case that, according to the attorney, sets a precedent for a similar situation. The court case is entitled "Dorothy E. Bannon, Petitioner v. Commissioner of Internal Revenue, Respondent." The case was filed on July 20, 1992. Excerpts from the court case are as follows:

"During 1986, Petitioner received payments from the State of California to provide non-medical care to her totally disabled adult daughter pursuant to the State's in-home supportive services program. Petitioner did not report these payments as income on her 1986 Federal income tax return. Respondent determined that the payments are includable in gross income under section 61 as compensation for services. Petitioner contends that the payments were made in the public interest and constitute nontaxable welfare benefits. Held: Under California law, Petitioner's daughter was the welfare recipient under the program and was 'intended to be the ultimate beneficiary' of the welfare payment. Petitioner was employed to provide supportive services. The payments were not nontaxable welfare benefits to Petitioner and are includable in the Petitioner's gross income."

The court case is important to our dilemma because it clearly acknowledges the biological parent as paid staff without justification or negotiation. The petitioner in this particular case, however, believed that the nontaxable welfare payment made to her adult daughter was transferable to her as the parent and legal guardian. The court clearly states this is not so. The nontaxable welfare payment is made to the adult daughter. The parent as paid staff must adhere to all tax income rules like any other employee. However, this case does not address the specific IRS rule regarding the tax-free difficulty of care payment and its relationship to the AFL setting and the biological parent as the AFL provider. After many long, hard battles with this bureaucracy, I became overwhelmed at the mere thought of what it would take to file a complaint with the United States Tax Court on this specific issue. I decided to leave this battle to the next soldier, the next parent, who may have more energy than I do at this particular time.

After yet another barrage of e-mail newspaper articles, I received on March 2, 2006 the following e-mail from the executive director of a nonprofit organization in Raleigh. The e-mail included a letter sent to the North Carolina governor about the reform efforts of our North Carolina mental health/developmental disabilities/substance abuse system.

"The storm clouds are gathering over the state of North Carolina, and no one seems to be paying attention. As the March 20 implementation date for mental health 'reform' looms nearer, the levees protecting our most vulnerable citizens are straining and the people in charge are turning their backs.

"If you talk to anyone in your local community who works at a local mental health center or anyone who receives treatment there, you'll find precisely the same assessment: the Department of Health and Human Services has constructed a new way of delivering services to people with mental illness, developmental disabilities, and substance abuse that creates obstacles and firewalls, serpentine bureaucracy and endless confusion.

"The Department issues a new memo every couple of weeks announcing more revisions to rates, services, procedures, operations. How this 'reform' is actually going to be delivered is, well, as clear as mud. Ask anyone who's supposed to be providing services to our citizens and they'll tell you that with one month to go before the new system is supposed to be launched, the bosses themselves don't know what is going on or how it's supposed to proceed from here. They talk about keeping care local so it's most responsive to the needs of a community, and then they decide to centralize operations. They talk about providing a broader choice to consumers, and then they curtail the availability of some fundamentally essential services.

"If this were going on in the private sector, shareholders would— at the very least— clean house. They might even insist on an investigation into the administration that has allowed this level of chaos— maybe even ineptitude—to ensue over the past couple of years. They'd probably figure it would be wiser to investigate now, before someone (maybe a young child? maybe a disabled adult?) is caught in the tidal wave when the floodgates open.

"What's it going to take for someone in this state to stand up and say, 'Emergency!' Maybe we'll just have to wait for our own Katrina to hit."

Chapter 19

We've Been Transformed

During our battle for independent case management, John and I met with The Arc of North Carolina representatives for coffee prior to a meeting with the Cumberland County mental health area director. As we discussed our strategies and concerns, one of The Arc representatives looked at me and said, "Don't they realize they created you?" For a brief moment there was silence and then we laughed. But the truth of the matter is we all have been created and transformed through our experience with the bureaucracies.

The special education law written in 1975 opened the door for children with disabilities to receive a free, appropriate public education. Although the law has been revised throughout the years, it has never really been fully implemented. In July 2005, PCSS began serving a school-aged child in the western part of North Carolina with severe cerebral palsy. In February 2006, while reviewing the Medicaid documentation, I noticed the following comment on the back of the form written by one of the staff.

"(Consumer's) bottom is constantly raw and unclean after coming home from school. We have had to start checking everyday to make sure sores do not develop. They refuse to help him wipe at school and say that is not something he needs help with. Mother has begun applying medication."

I immediately called the mother and listened as she vented her frustration of the constant battles with the school system on a daily basis.

I gave her contact information for an organization that could help but also advised her to identify the chain of command all the way up to the secretary of education. "Get their names, titles, phone numbers, and e-mail addresses." This has been my chant to every parent I speak with. "Know your chain of command and use it! Begin sending e-mails starting from the bottom of the chain but always copying one or two supervisors." I followed up with the mom several months later to learn that after initiating a barrage of e-mails and meeting with several local and state officials, life at school for her son was a little better. This unfortunately is not an uncommon story in the lives of our children. Despite the written law, children with disabilities do not receive the support they need to attain an appropriate education. Children with disabilities continue to be educated in separate buildings, separate wings of buildings, and huts in the back of buildings. They sometimes are expected to arrive at school after it has begun and leave before it is over. When families learn the law and the entitlements for their children, the battles begin.

On July 26, 2004 a news release was issued by the United States secretary of Health and Human Services regarding the fourteenth anniversary of the Americans with Disabilities Act (ADA). Excerpts from the release are as follows:

"The ADA is an instrument of fairness and equity: it was enacted to help ensure that people with disabilities should not face unnecessary and counterproductive barriers...."

On August 17, 2004 a news release was issued by the Center for Medicare & Medicaid Services (CMS) entitled, "CMS Encourages States to give Medicaid Beneficiaries More Control over the Long-Term Care Services They Receive." The following quote from the CMS administrator was noted in the release.

"There is growing evidence that states can enable more people to live in the community by giving the elderly and people with disabilities more control over how they get the Medicaid services they need. Because the concept of money following the person's own preferences improves satisfaction and may reduce Medicaid costs too, we intend to keep taking steps to remove barriers, real or perceived."

In April 2004, shortly before the above news releases, the North Carolina Office of the State Auditor issued a press release entitled "(Auditor) Questions $415.3 Million in Spending by State - $414 Million from Medicaid Division Alone." The press release ended with the following statement from the auditor:

"Of real concern to us was an attitude that obviously existed in the Division for several years that it could do whatever it wanted, regardless of federal rules and regulations. That attitude, which goes to the heart of many of the problems we uncovered, must be reversed. The very least that taxpayers expect is that agencies will follow the rules in how they spend the funds they are given."

Almost immediately, news articles were popping up in every newspaper and e-mail system statewide. One of the articles stated the following: "(Auditor) called it the most damaging review he had released since taking office in 1993 and said he has forwarded it to state and federal prosecutors." Several days later, a Raleigh newspaper reported an "unusually public political squabble" between the state auditor and the North Carolina secretary of Health & Human Services. The article stated, "He accused her of mismanagement. She came darn close to calling him a liar."

While the United States secretary of Health & Human Services states that "people with disabilities should not face unnecessary and counterproductive barriers...," and the administrator for the Center for Medicare & Medicaid Services intends "to keep taking steps to remove barriers, real or perceived," I can't help but wonder if the actions that led to the "unusually public political squabble" displayed by North Carolina officials could be identified as one of the major barriers.

Although the Raleigh newspaper referred to the North Carolina official's actions as an "unusually public political squabble," there have been many other political squabbles that may not have been so public but are in fact a major barrier for people with disabilities.

On May 23, 2006 I received an e-mail attachment of a letter sent by the executive director of the North Carolina Council on Developmental Disabilities (NCCDD) to the North Carolina governor.

"I am writing on behalf of the North Carolina Council on Developmental Disabilities (NCCDD) to thank you for making a decision that we believe will have significant implications for advancing full citizenship for North Carolinians with developmental and other disabilities. I refer to your intention to re-designate the state's Protection and

Advocacy (P&A) System from the Department of Administration to the private sector. **For some fifteen years**, the NCCDD has advocated for the state's Protection and Advocacy system to join the vast majority of sister systems in the US – all established under the Developmental Disabilities Assistance and Bill of Rights Act (PL 106-402) in adopting the organizational structure most consistent with the P&A's federally mandated role of advocating for legal and human rights. The NCCDD commends to you the Disability Rights Center, which stands ready to accept a re-designation...."

My God, fifteen years! That was 1991 and the year our family moved to North Carolina.

In a previous letter from the same executive director dated December 9, 2005, the history of the re-designation issue was revealed.

- 1991: In a peer review of the GACPD (Governor's Advocacy County for Persons with Disabilities), the National Association of Protection and Advocacy Systems (NAPAS) states that it "strongly recommends that GACPD re-examine questions of conflict of interest largely stemming from the location of GACPD within a state agency which can hinder the independent functioning of Council members and staff." NAPAS went on to say that "the agency is compromised for its current placement."

- 1996: In a second peer review, NAPAS states that "organization within state government necessarily impairs the agency's ability to independently pursue certain advocacy initiatives." The report went on to cite examples of "impediments to independent advocacy resulting from GACPD's organization within state government." The report closed by stating that "determination must be made early on whether key state officials, including the Governor, will support, oppose or take no position on a move to leave state government, as any strategy will depend upon this factor."

- 1997: GACPD executive director produces a "rationale for privatization," concluding that "services can be more effectively provided in the private sector without sacrificing quality."

- 1998: The GACPD board votes to re-designate, approves a re-designation document, and seeks a meeting of its "presentation committee on re-designation" with the governor. The presentation committee secures the support of key statewide advocacy leaders from, e.g., the North Carolina Psychological Association, National Alliance for the Mentally Ill (NAMI), United Cerebral Palsy (UCP) of North Carolina, The Arc of North Carolina, Mental Health Association of North Carolina, North Carolina Council on Developmental Disabilities, and Carolina Legal Assistance for Persons with Disabilities.

- 2000: GACPD board member and director of the governor's Alcohol and Drug Council urges the GACPD to keep re-designation "a working priority."
- 2001: United States Administration on Developmental Disabilities (ADD) hosts public forums in the state on consumer satisfaction with the performance of NCCDD and GACPD. Public comment overwhelmingly favors re-designation of the P&A to the private sector.
- 2003: NCCDD and GACPD formally endorse by vote the re-designation of the P&A to the private sector.
- 2004: In a letter to NCCDD chair, the governor's senior assistant for government affairs states that the governor will give "careful and thoughtful consideration of re-designation" and is "committed to the decision that is best for the disability community."
- 2004: The Disability Rights Center of North Carolina is formed for the purpose of serving as the state's re-designated protection and advocacy system, in a process involving active dialogue with the governor's office.
- 2005: NCCDD writes the governor, reiterating its position in support of re-designation. This letter is among a number from NCCDD to the governor over a decade and a half, all stating NCCDD's support for re-designation.
- 2005: The director of Carolina Legal Assistance posthumously wins North Carolina Justice Center's Defender of Justice award. Her efforts to re-designate the protection and advocacy system to the private sector were among the contributions acknowledged by the legal and justice communities.

No one truly understands the sense of urgency like people with disabilities and their families. The director of Carolina Legal Assistance was a parent of a CAP MR/DD waiver recipient. Parents fight hard and fast because they know deep down they have a limited amount of time. Most of the time we have a sense of urgency because we recognize the narrow window of opportunity for growth and learning in the early years of our children's lives. A sense of urgency is also recognized when our children have significant disabilities that force us to face the reality of a shorter lifespan than most. But our lives as parents of children with disabilities are not guaranteed. As parents we are not exempt from illnesses and accidents. In many cases, because of the added stressors of dealing with the bureaucracies, we may be more prone to heart attacks, strokes, and other debilitating illnesses. Life happens to everyone. It is absolutely absurd and unacceptable that fifteen years of discrimination and torment continued throughout North Carolina for people with disabilities while committees and meetings were held to discuss re-designation. It seems to me that the North Carolina political process has been a definite barrier for North Carolinians with disabilities.

During one of our many trips to the emergency room with our son, I had an unusual experience that I believe uncovers yet another barrier for people with disabilities. While waiting for nursing staff to track down Danny's physicians, a doctor introduced himself to us. First, he asked Danny's age. At the time Danny was eighteen years old. He then shared information about his new granddaughter born with severe brain damage. As I talked with this doctor I realized he had no information on how to advise his son and daughter-in-law on where to get help to care for their child. The doctor and his wife were beginning to deplete their savings and retirement fund to help with therapy and supplies needed for their new granddaughter. At the time his granddaughter was eleven months old. I asked the doctor if his granddaughter had an IFSP. Upon hearing this acronym, the doctor had the same blank look on his face as most parents do when you begin talking about services. But this was a doctor, someone who comes in contact with people with disabilities on a regular basis. If he doesn't know how to direct members of his immediate family, what can he possibly say to his patients? I immediately pulled out one of my business cards and on the back of the card wrote the acronym, "IFSP." I explained it stood for "individual family service plan." This was part of the special education law that covers children with disabilities birth to three years of age. Shortly after meeting this doctor, I had the opportunity to speak with his daughter-in-law. After a brief conversation, she was on her way to obtaining an IFSP for her daughter. I want very much to believe that the doctor I spoke with in the emergency room at Womack Army Medical Center shared our conversation with his colleagues. But whether or not this information is shared with other families remains to be seen. Lack of knowledge of services available is an unnecessary barrier that must be overcome in order for people with disabilities to achieve quality of life. The medical profession can help us by being informed of the services available and directing patients to reliable sources. Decades ago, the medical profession was very aware of the institutions available for people with disabilities. Doctors and nurses of decades ago praised many institutional settings and encouraged families to admit their children to the institutions. Just as doctors and nurses of years ago were keenly aware of the institutional settings, they must be equally aware of the community opportunities for people with disabilities and their families and they must share this information with their patients.

In April 2006 our private insurance company questioned Danny's enrollment as a hospice patient. After all, he had been on hospice since 2002! As a result of the insurance company's inquiry, our family physician wrote the following statement:

"I met Daniel Mercado In July 2003 when he came to see me for an initial new patient evaluation because I was assuming his medical care. He is a 24 year old man who at the age of 6 months contracted meningitis and developed neurological sequela to include cerebral palsy. He is faced with multiple medical problems that arise each day. He was recently hospitalized in 2002 for pneumonia, which was thought to be aspiration. Since there was concern for recurrent episodes of aspiration, Daniel takes nothing by mouth and all of his nutrition is through his g-tube. He requires 24 hour medical attention and frequent assessments by medical personnel to evaluate his vital signs, breathing status, and oxygen saturation. Daniel has been on hospice for a long period of time and has far outlived his life expectancy with his current medical conditions. His mother and father are very dedicated to his every day needs, but they cannot do this alone. His demanding medical conditions to include: his skin care issues, bowel/urinary incontinence, severe mental retardation, severe scoliosis, and wrist and ankle contractures require attention from multiple disciplines. It would be in Daniel's best interest for him to have continued hospice care because he is a very terminally ill young man with a life expectancy of less than 6-12 months. Daniel is a success story who at the same time also is very sick. He enjoys the outdoors, music, movies, and shopping. These are things that people his age enjoy. I highly recommend that he have continued home care. If you have any further questions, please do not hesitate to contact me at …"

In 2004, while Danny was a patient on hospice, we discovered Danny had blood in his stool. We immediately contacted the hospice RN. After consulting the doctors, it was decided a scoping procedure would be performed to identify the source of the blood. Before Danny entered the treatment room for the procedure, John and I kissed him and once again watched the gurney as it made its way slowly to the treatment room. No less than ten minutes into the procedure, the alarms went off throughout the hospital and a voice announced "code blue." Immediately doctors and chaplains came from all directions. John and I held onto each other with tears flowing uncontrollably. We both knew in our heads what was happening, but no matter how much you plan, no matter how prepared you try to be, your heart is never prepared to say goodbye. I felt myself double over and my back tightened with fear. One of the doctors finally came to us and told us Danny was okay. "It was a very long couple of seconds," he said, "but he's okay." As they tried to sedate Danny, he became choked by his secretions. His small airways made it difficult for them to clear the airway. He stopped breathing for several very long seconds but then on his own took a breath. The doctors concluded that because of his condition, he can never undergo any form of sedation. For this reason we are very careful to ensure the G-tube is well taken care of and replaced on a regular basis. If Danny's G-tube becomes dislodged, the opening in the stomach would close within hours. The only way to put the G-tube back in place would be through a procedure similar to scoping, and this would require sedation. Without a G-tube, Danny would die of starvation. Sound familiar? As I watched the TV news about Terry Shiavo, I thought of God's tears. What were we thinking? The greatest nation in the world pulls the feeding tube from a person with a disability and tries to call it humane!

Another major barrier for individuals with disabilities is the bureaucracy's insensitivity to the emotional, physical, and spiritual connection to our children. There must be an understanding for all that families go through before you can ever provide adequate and sufficient services. The only way a bureaucracy can understand the many responsibilities of the family unit is by meeting families where they are instead of requiring them to go to the bureaucracy.

The year John and I were married (1978) "Mom" and Aunt Dorothy left St. Mary's Boys Home in Syosset, Long Island and moved to Brooklyn. At first they converted a vacant convent into a group home for former residence of Willowbrook institution. After almost ten years, they then moved to a separate part of Brooklyn known as Red Hook, where they lived in a home in a very rundown part of town. In the true spirit of nunhood, these two women revitalized the neighborhood in so many ways. They held protests. They organized groups and rallies, concerts, plays, and parades. One Easter, to prepare for a celebration with their CCD class, they went into a local bar with dozens of hardboiled eggs. "We hear from the neighbors that most of you are artists," they announced. "Well, we have eggs that need to be decorated for the local children." They didn't leave the bar until all the eggs were decorated and everyone present helped. At one point, they organized a group of senior women, borrowed meeting space from a local merchant, and had a widescreen TV donated. These senior women, led by Sister Mary Olivia and Sister Dorothy, met on a weekly basis for line-dancing sessions. John and I truly enjoyed their stories, but we worried about their safety as they traveled throughout Brooklyn day and night and arrived home to their small house on Dykeman Street. One day I asked if they would consider moving to the mother house in Brooklyn and then visiting Red Hook on a daily basis. My thought was that they would at least be safe at night in the convent. Without hesitation Mom replied. "If you want to help people, you have to live with them and among them." Wow! What a profound statement filled with truth. It is a basic Christian value. Jesus didn't help those in need by calling a town meeting and inviting them to Nazareth. He went to them and met with them where they lived. The bureaucracy needs to understand that in order to serve, you must have a servant's attitude. Danny has been on the CAP MR/DD waiver since 1995. Local, state, and federal officials have reviewed, approved, and denied services for Danny without ever meeting him. Children with disabilities congregate in the school system, but the Medicaid bureaucracy is no where to be found. The Medicaid bureaucracy sits on a hill and expects the person with the disability and his or her family to first find the hill and then climb the hill, no matter how steep it may be. Even after services are provided, the bureaucracy maintains its distance by holding audits in conference rooms and reviewing papers and files on consumers, but it never takes the time to meet the consumer and the family in their home, where they live. For these reasons, obtaining services can be compared to strategic battle planning.

As we look at the American Civil War, one of the decisive battles was Gettysburg. For the first time the Union forces were defending their land. Never before had Confederate forces come as far north as Pennsylvania. Most of the Civil War battles were fought in the south and the Confederate forces won most of those battles. But this time it was different. Imagine a local approval specialist from the local LME sitting in your living room with your son or daughter, discussing the plan of care. This would be no different than the Confederate forces trying to attack Pennsylvania. They would come into your home with their clipboards and papers in hand, thinking that they had the upper hand and would settle this once and for all. However, it would be difficult to deny services with Danny sitting in his wheelchair with oxygen and a suction machine close by. It would be difficult to deny bathroom modifications or other home modifications as they observed obvious small doorways throughout the home. I have been in homes of children with autism. Holding a conversation with a parent as the child moves aimlessly throughout the room while getting into everything is difficult to do. Many times our conversation involves a strategic plan on how to get additional services. If it were the local approval specialist in the home of the family instead of me, I imagine the specialist with the clipboard in hand would say, "Does he do this all the time?" I would expect the parent to say, "Yes, do you still question why I need more respite than the state guidelines allow?"

The bureaucracy may very well argue that it does come to the family through case management services. However, the case manager is not the deciding factor in the approval or denial of a plan. The case managers also do not develop the local and state budgets associated with services and supports needed. The case managers simply lead the team meeting and develop the plan of care. Once the plan of care gets into the hands of the approval specialist, if there are any questions, the specialist should go directly to the consumer and family. This unfortunately is not what occurs.

For as long as this civil war continues, parents will fight hard and fast to get what they need for their children. In Hickory, North Carolina, parents of a twelve- year-old with significant disabilities are fighting to change a major barrier involving the Office of Administrative Hearings (OAH). After receiving documentation from doctors and physical and occupational therapists regarding the medically necessary equipment needs for their daughter, they were denied all equipment requests by the local LME. The family filed for an OAH. The judge overturned seven of the eight denials. However, as we have learned many years earlier, the final decision rests with the division director, not the OAH law judge, even if the judge finds the LME to be **arbitrary, capricious, and erroneous** in their actions.

Parents join the ranks of the disability army in many different capacities. The officers and noncommissioned officers of this unique army are identified every day. On April 16, 2006 I received the following e-mail from a natural leader gaining rank and prestige in the disability army.

"I have much documentation regarding the head of our mental health agency and his workers denying request after request that are 'no brainers.' We have one family who has had every request for their daughter since her last CNR (Continued Needs Review) denied right down to her diapers. They appealed and the judge overturned seven of the eight denials, but the county is appealing his decision. It is crazy. I have another family who has requested a handicapped bathroom for their adult daughter. The parents are now in their sixties and can't lift her and care for her like they once did, but they have been turned down three times over a span of eighteen months. We have complied with every request made and still haven't gotten an approval. (The division director's) office said that this request should have never been denied. I have another young man whose parents adopted him in Catawba County. Their home has always sat on the Catawba County/Lincoln County line, but once the young man who is deaf and mentally retarded turned fifteen, Catawba County decided to stop his benefits, Medicaid included. The only reason the county has given me is that his bedroom is in Lincoln County. Lincoln County has never been responsible for this young man, and to get him into Lincoln County's system would take forever, and they are talking about the waiting list, etc. This is absolutely ridiculous. He has been without benefits for more than two years now while his adoptive parents are still paying taxes in North Carolina and Catawba and Lincoln counties. These are just a few examples of what is taking place here. I have come into the good graces of a few 'anonymous' individuals working within the mental health department who have given me some very disturbing news. First, I was told that the director told them to 'deny, deny, deny because 85 percent will never say a word and the other 15 percent they could deal with.' On another occasion, a family was denied a one-on-one for their daughter when she qualified for that assistance very easily, and they asked me to call the director. He told me to call one of his workers, name specified, and have her set up a meeting that would work with everyone's schedule. He told me that she could be sure that he would have no conflicts and would be there. I sent an e-mail to her naming all the individuals that we wanted at this meeting and all she had to do was to call me and the family, give us the time, and we would make arrangements to be there. When we arrived for the meeting, we went in and the director was not there. I asked where he was and was told that he didn't think it necessary for him to be there. I was later told by a source that he had made the comment that he had to show me that he was in control of his department and not me. Earlier, I had sent him an e-mail asking for specific costs on programs so that I could better judge the cost of client's attending this program rather than having care at home. He e-mailed me back and said point blank, 'That is none of your business.' I politely replied to him that since it was my tax dollars it is my business, so he e-mailed me with a three word statement. Recently, I was told by (the Division Director's) office that this mental health center is the only county in the state that constantly operated in the black month after month. It seems that every other county goes into the red for at least a few months during the year and has to make up the difference, but this mental health center always seems to have plenty of money in their budget. That, obviously, is because he has mandated a denial of every needed benefit, but I don't understand exactly what benefit he gets from it. Does he get more money if he spends less, or is there something else that I do not know about? I am very curious because I need to not be blind sided Thursday evening. *(This parent was preparing to speak to the LME Board of Directors on Thursday.)* We are also having the problem with denial of parents of children under age 18 being compensated for their care. It is plainly stated on the state website that this practice is not prohibited as long as the parent/guardian is qualified by the rules of the manual. When I spoke to the assistant about this and pointed this policy out, I was told that she didn't care what the manual said that they were going to do what they thought was right. When a parent can't keep a worker, they have to provide the care which means that they cannot hold down a job. This makes the household budget very strained at best. These are just a few things that I have been dealing with, so any help that you can give would be greatly appreciated."

And the battles continue....

During the case management battle in 2003, I sent an e-mail to one of the many North Carolina consultants inquiring about the consumer's right to choose case management agencies. Impressed with my direct questions, he sent the following e-mail on January 14, 2003:

"Denise, Denise, Denise...Can we clone you and put you to work in forty-nine other states? And five US Territories?"

The cloning process has already taken place. God has taken the hearts of mothers and the bonding relationship of mother and child and exposed the injustices across this country. What I've experienced in North Carolina is no different than what others experience throughout this country. On March 26, 2006 I had an e-mail reunion with a colleague in California.

"Denise, this is nothing short of amazing that I would hear from you. I was just talking about you two days ago to a client's sister. There has been an absolute nightmare of a situation going on with her two siblings—both disabled, parents deceased and she and her husband are the two family members that are actively involved in her siblings' life. The case management system here in California is as messed up as it could get and she has just begun to battle them.

"I don't know if I ever told you how grateful I am to you for making a change in the system. I hope you realize that what you did in North Carolina 'set the wheels in motion' for change on a national scale. There hasn't been any progress such as you've made there and I'd really like to see change happen…

"They talk about client rights out here, but they don't really care about it. After sixteen years of working in this profession, I hear a lot of hollow words. Case managers have taken on such an ominous role in a client's life that if a client wants to change, they can, but they're still within the exact same system. It makes no sense and it doesn't really give any client a solid choice…Change is needed and monopolies, certainly in the matters of case management services are simply not good.

"There is a desperation in some of these situations that demands more than one case management agency. They are not good at 'self-policing.' They are not good at being objective. What has been allowed to exist is a network of friends and buddies that do things that are best suited to their professional needs. Rarely, if ever, is the client involved in the decision-making process. I could go on and on, but what you did was exactly what was needed…It was great to hear from you and I certainly haven't forgotten you. I am very glad I have the same e-mail address. Regards…."

Throughout these past twenty-four years, I have grown in many ways. The growth that has taken place has been tremendous at all levels and continues on. I have learned so much about myself and my abilities. For so long I questioned who I was and whether I was competent to handle all that was put before me. But my source of strength is truly from above. Thank God I am not on this journey alone.

I think very often about Danny and his purpose in life. There is nothing like a child to motivate the heart of a mother. Our children make us do things we never knew we were capable of doing. As parents, we overcome our fears in meetings with officials if we know the meeting is to benefit our children. We change our sleeping habits and get up at the crack of dawn and stay up beyond midnight to study special education law and to read the Social Security Act because we know what we will learn will help us fight for services for our children. We overcome our fear of computers and become e-mail savvy in order to fight and win battles with bureaucrats who sometimes resemble demigods but in reality are nothing more than vultures picking at defenseless prey. Sometimes parents, like me, decide it is time to put pen to paper and tell their story. I have spent the last two and a half years writing this book.

Many families, including my business partner, provided encouragement to complete the book and get it published for all to read. On Danny's twenty-fourth birthday, my business partner gave Danny a birthday card with the following saying:

"God is writing a book about you. The pages tell of your life and the lives you were created to touch. No one else will take exactly the same path as you, meet the same people, or have a chance to show the love of God in the same way. You are unique and so is your story…and it's one of the Author's favorite reads."

I do not know how much longer Danny will be with us. I cherish every day and love him beyond words for all that he has done and for all that he represents. This is a young man who has never spoken a word; however, his mere presence speaks volumes.

God speed my precious son.

Glossary of Acronyms

PCSS, LLC   Person Centered Support Services, LLC

A

ADA	Americans with Disabilities Act
AFL	Alternative Family Living
ALJ	Administrative Law Judge

B

C

CAP MR/DD	Community Alternative Program for Persons with Mental Retardation/Developmental Disabilities
CCMHC	Cumberland County Mental Health Center
CFAC	Consumer & Family Advisory Committee
CM	Case Management
CMS	Center for Medicare & Medicaid Services
CNR	Continued Needs Review
CP	Cerebral Palsy

D

DD	Developmental Disabilities
DDTI	Developmental Disabilities Training Institute
DHHS	Department of Health & Human Services
DOA	Department of Administration

DOC	Difficulty of Care
DOD	Department of Defense
DOE	Department of Education
DPI	Department of Public Instruction
DSS	Department of Social Services

E

EC	Exceptional Children
ELP	Essential Lifestyle Planning
EOR	Employer of Record
EPSDT	Early Periodic Screening, Diagnosis & Treatment
ESY	Extended School Year

F

| **FI** | Fiscal Intermediary |

G

GACPD	Governor's Advocacy Council for Persons with Disabilities
GAO	Government Accountability Office
GS	General Statute

H

| **HCBS** | Home & Community Based Services |
| **HCFA** | Health Care Finance Administration (now known as CMS) |

I

ICF/MR	Intermediate Care Facility for People with Mental Retardation
ICM	Independent Case Management
IDEA	Individuals with Disabilities Education Act
IEP	Individual Education Plan
IFSP	Individual/Family Service Plan

J

K

L

LEA	Local Education Agency
LME	Local Management Entity
LRE	Least Restrictive Environment

M

MR2	Mental Retardation Form (completed by physician or case manager)
MRA	Mental Retardation Association
MRC	Mental Retardation Centers

N

NAPAS	National Association of Protection & Advocacy Systems
NASMD	National Association of State Medicaid Directors
NC Division of MH/DD/SAS	North Carolina Division of Mental Health/Developmental Disabilities/Substance Abuse Services
NC DMA	North Carolina Department of Medical Assistance
NCAC	North Carolina Administrative Code
NCCDD	North Carolina Council on Developmental Disabilities

O

OAH	Office of Administrative Hearings
OBRA	Omnibus Budget Reconciliation Act
OCR	Office of Civil Rights
OHI	Other Health Impaired
OSEP	Office of Special Education Programs
OSERS	Office of Special Education & Rehabilitative Services
OT	Occupational Therapy

P

P&A	Protection & Advocacy
PCP	Person Centered Planning
PCS	Personal Care Services
PIP	Partners In Policymaking
PL 94-142	Public Law 94-142
POC	Plan of Care
PT	Physical Therapy

Q

QDDP	Qualified Developmental Disabilities Professional

R

S

SB	Support Brokerage
SL	Supported Living
SLP	Speech/Language Pathology
SMC	Smoky Mountain Center
SNAP	Special Needs Assessment Profile
SNEC	Special Needs Education Center
SOP	Standard Operating Procedure
SSA	Social Security Administration
SSI	Social Security Income
STOMP	Specialized Training of Military Parents

T

U

UCP	United Cerebral Palsy
UR	Utilization Review
US ADD	United States Administration on Developmental Disabilities

Appendix A

- Thomson/Medstat Statistics – Expenditures FY 2000 through 2005
- Overall Satisfaction with Services – Area Program Summary by Clients' Primary Disability
- HCFA Progam Issues Transmittal Notice – Region IV – SUBJECT: Monetary Cap on Services Provided under the Early and Periodic Screening, Diagnosis, and Treatment (EPSDT) Program
- North Carolina 1998 Annual EPSDT Participation Report
- Utilization Review Guidelines – North Carolina CAP MR/DD Manual 2005

STATE	Institutional LTC Services		Community-Based Services		TOTAL LTC Expenditures
	Expenditures	% of Total Medicaid LTC Dollars	Expenditures	% of Total Medicaid LTC Dollars	
Arizona[1]	$0	n/a	$0	n/a	$0
Alaska	$0	0.0%	$66,320,549	100.0%	$66,320,549
Oregon	$0	0.0%	$303,626,385	100.0%	$303,626,385
Vermont	$944,808	1.0%	$93,730,942	99.0%	$94,675,750
New Hampshire	$2,348,269	1.8%	$129,373,461	98.2%	$131,721,730
Rhode Island	$7,067,988	3.6%	$191,203,527	96.4%	$198,271,515
Michigan	$20,778,960	5.0%	$397,130,103	95.0%	$417,909,063
New Mexico	$21,123,412	8.1%	$239,136,221	91.9%	$260,259,633
Hawaii	$8,605,505	10.0%	$77,393,107	90.0%	$85,998,612
Alabama	$27,248,061	12.3%	$195,035,545	87.7%	$222,283,606
Maryland	$63,085,684	15.0%	$357,903,837	85.0%	$420,989,521
Minnesota	$171,455,673	17.0%	$838,064,158	83.0%	$1,009,519,831
Montana	$12,350,308	17.1%	$60,030,419	82.9%	$72,380,727
Wyoming	$18,335,225	19.3%	$76,593,348	80.7%	$94,928,573
Colorado	$58,726,134	20.1%	$232,982,576	79.9%	$291,708,710
South Dakota	$21,296,554	22.3%	$74,284,039	77.7%	$95,580,593
West Virginia	$55,100,628	22.5%	$189,563,974	77.5%	$244,664,602
Maine	$55,769,276	22.9%	$187,672,392	77.1%	$243,441,668
Kansas	$66,999,732	23.7%	$215,962,833	76.3%	$282,962,565
Massachusetts	$213,106,263	24.9%	$642,246,937	75.1%	$855,353,200
Washington	$126,200,726	26.7%	$347,277,731	73.3%	$473,478,457
Georgia	$100,254,754	29.4%	$240,981,965	70.6%	$341,236,719
Wisconsin	$197,374,367	32.0%	$420,385,734	68.0%	$617,760,101
Delaware	$25,821,497	32.5%	$53,603,630	67.5%	$79,425,127
Nebraska	$59,443,762	32.7%	$122,274,755	67.3%	$181,718,517
Florida	$301,190,366	32.7%	$619,286,347	67.3%	$920,476,713
Connecticut	$219,690,073	33.9%	$428,887,905	66.1%	$648,577,978
Utah	$57,513,532	33.9%	$112,076,753	66.1%	$169,590,285
Nevada	$26,472,598	35.6%	$47,981,582	64.4%	$74,454,180
Oklahoma	$121,544,040	35.6%	$219,685,238	64.4%	$341,229,278
Pennsylvania	$577,222,902	35.7%	$1,039,396,059	64.3%	$1,616,618,961
California[2]	$649,831,934	38.2%	$1,050,006,600	61.8%	$1,699,838,534
Kentucky	$107,747,087	41.1%	$154,428,570	58.9%	$262,175,657
Tennessee	$289,361,481	43.2%	$380,075,322	56.8%	$669,436,803
Virginia	$228,819,663	44.0%	$291,768,427	56.0%	$520,588,090
New York	$7,710,066,847	44.7%	$9,399,061,000	55.9%	$19,181,111,111
Indiana	$318,265,018	45.2%	$386,151,992	54.8%	$704,417,010
Missouri	$256,706,484	46.8%	$292,275,546	53.2%	$548,982,030
South Carolina	$161,433,481	47.0%	$182,399,186	53.0%	$343,832,667
Idaho	$54,588,955	52.6%	$49,149,206	47.4%	$103,738,161
North Dakota	$65,278,839	52.9%	$58,068,712	47.1%	$123,347,551
Iowa	$248,752,217	53.5%	$216,333,966	46.5%	$465,086,183
New Jersey	$565,546,561	57.2%	$422,511,983	42.8%	$988,058,544
North Carolina	$446,972,145	61.0%	$286,101,708	39.0%	$733,073,853
Arkansas	$140,908,587	61.6%	$87,972,571	38.4%	$228,881,158
Illinois	$688,155,342	62.2%	$418,648,223	37.8%	$1,106,803,565
Louisiana	$425,679,479	63.3%	$246,677,702	36.7%	$672,357,181
Texas	$805,708,216	65.6%	$422,256,285	34.4%	$1,227,964,501
Ohio	$1,005,053,573	67.5%	$483,963,481	32.5%	$1,489,017,054
Washington DC	$79,196,025	88.7%	$10,135,846	11.3%	$89,331,871
Mississippi[3]	$209,110,070	100.0%	$0	0.0%	$209,110,070
United States	$12,103,242,101	41.6%	$17,024,072,941	58.4%	$29,127,315,042

Institutional services include ICF-MR services

Community-based services include HCBS waiver services for people with mental retardation and developmental disabilities.

[1] Arizona data does not include spending for most long-term care, which is provided through a managed care program.

[2] California's reported expenditures will likely increase as the state submits more prior period adjustments. For the MR/DD waiver, FY2001 through FY2004 expenditures were $200 - $500 million greater than the amount originally presented. For ICF/MR, adjustments increased expenditures by about $100 million each year after data were originally presented.

[3] Mississippi did not submit waiver-specific expenditures reports in FY2005, so community-based expenditures are not known.

Source: CMS 64 data, Office of State Agency Financial Management   July 7, 2006

TABLE H

HCBS WAIVERS MR/DD

Rank 2005	Rank 2004	State	FY 2000 Expenditures	FY 2001 Expenditures	Percent Change 00-01	FY 2002 Expenditures	Percent Change 01-02	FY 2003 Expenditures	Percent Change 02-03	F* 2004 Expenditures	Percent Change 03-04	FY 2005 Expenditures	Percent Change 04-05	FY 2005 Expenditures Per Capita
1	2	Rhode Island	$143,250,035	$145,069,687	1.3	$157,406,341	8.5	$175,830,428	11.7	$185,472,226	5.5	$191,203,527	3.1	$177.70
2	1	New York	$1,827,812,584	$2,070,065,739	13.3	$2,390,494,190	15.5	$2,806,080,787	17.4	$3,302,734,838	17.7	$3,365,055,563	1.9	$174.76
3	3	Minnesota	$405,156,441	$512,817,576	26.6	$711,469,196	38.7	$806,933,306	13.4	$811,967,693	0.6	$838,064,158	3.2	$163.27
4	4	Wyoming	$44,641,541	$365,098	-99.2	$54,505,220	14828.9	$68,039,300	24.8	$71,983,911	5.8	$76,593,348	6.4	$150.48
5	6	Vermont	$64,394,913	$70,664,068	9.7	$75,143,452	6.3	$79,627,787	6.0	$87,807,600	10.3	$93,730,942	6.7	$150.45
6	5	Maine	$114,111,227	$128,964,859	13.0	$155,499,692	20.6	$186,790,814	20.1	$196,984,207	5.5	$187,672,392	-4.7	$141.96
7	8	New Mexico	$117,266,492	$137,571,078	17.3	$166,439,525	21.0	$185,829,200	11.6	$200,875,481	8.1	$239,136,221	19.0	$124.03
8	7	Connecticut	$358,327,517	$358,856,015	0.1	$328,884,351	-8.4	$345,391,320	5.0	$461,241,082	33.5	$428,887,905	-7.0	$122.19
9	14	West Virginia	$85,751,079	$103,696,763	20.9	$126,985,317	22.5	$144,538,596	13.8	$147,261,348	1.9	$189,563,974	28.7	$104.33
10	11	Massachusetts	$432,871,686	$460,833,905	6.5	$518,841,183	12.6	$577,122,380	11.2	$554,774,091	-3.9	$642,246,937	15.8	$100.37
11	12	Alaska	$32,434,353	$44,671,283	37.7	$52,517,049	17.6	$61,237,980	16.6	$56,880,732	-7.1	$66,320,549	16.6	$99.88
12	9	New Hampshire	$112,550,780	$114,267,785	1.5	$124,459,836	8.9	$116,786,264	-6.2	$124,446,115	6.6	$129,373,461	4.0	$98.76
13	10	South Dakota	$50,719,469	$55,572,002	9.6	$59,694,938	7.4	$63,506,215	6.4	$67,962,295	7.0	$74,284,039	9.3	$95.73
14	13	North Dakota	$39,806,923	$43,368,700	8.9	$46,878,372	8.1	$48,738,896	4.0	$54,548,616	11.9	$58,068,712	6.5	$91.16
15	15	Pennsylvania	$659,318,641	$800,525,109	21.4	$888,105,157	10.9	$993,658,430	11.9	$996,547,970	0.3	$1,039,396,059	4.3	$83.62
16	16	Oregon	$227,196,908	$261,545,752	15.1	$285,437,475	9.1	$286,057,489	0.2	$287,755,411	0.6	$303,626,385	5.5	$83.39
17	17	Kansas	$168,836,234	$179,905,423	6.6	$192,430,242	7.0	$197,030,196	2.4	$198,329,721	0.7	$215,962,833	8.9	$78.67
18	18	Wisconsin	$299,459,798	$294,630,485	-1.6	$319,146,815	8.3	$374,762,706	17.4	$394,395,664	5.2	$420,385,734	6.6	$75.94
19	25	Iowa	$87,688,597	$105,048,019	19.8	$123,742,876	17.8	$138,164,972	11.7	$170,697,151	23.5	$216,333,966	26.7	$72.94
20	19	Nebraska	$52,908,946	$104,703,801	97.9	$133,373,602	27.4	$108,271,226	-18.8	$125,061,216	15.5	$122,274,755	-2.2	$69.51
21	23	Montana	$34,602,222	$37,677,438	8.9	$42,684,900	13.3	$50,220,936	17.7	$55,897,102	11.3	$60,030,419	7.4	$64.14
22	20	Maryland	$167,801,112	$207,008,326	23.4	$197,211,754	-4.7	$434,575,664	120.4	$344,828,039	-20.7	$357,903,837	3.8	$63.91
23	33	Tennessee	$196,148,510	$178,425,944	-9.0	$261,634,791	46.6	$170,406,412	-34.9	$252,100,842	47.9	$380,075,322	50.8	$63.74
24	24	Delaware	$34,124,354	$35,709,014	4.6	$40,069,982	12.2	$46,766,424	16.7	$51,036,253	9.1	$53,603,630	5.0	$63.51
25	21	Oklahoma	$158,773,988	$195,054,643	22.9	$225,102,394	15.4	$212,160,802	-5.7	$218,054,698	2.8	$219,685,238	0.7	$61.92
26	22	Indiana	$88,949,300	$120,013,602	34.9	$158,309,729	31.9	$263,005,971	66.1	$369,527,150	40.5	$386,151,992	4.5	$61.57
27	26	Hawaii	$18,422,414	$28,646,412	55.5	$35,162,092	22.7	$46,013,345	30.9	$66,812,034	45.2	$77,393,107	15.8	$60.70
28	31	Washington	$209,082,516	$227,279,626	8.7	$240,896,798	6.0	$248,060,984	3.0	$282,567,895	13.9	$347,277,731	22.9	$55.23
29	28	Louisiana	$103,401,161	$130,460,366	26.2	$148,287,290	13.7	$173,845,112	17.2	$221,918,667	27.7	$246,677,702	11.2	$54.53
30	30	Missouri	$202,371,195	$218,352,774	7.9	$253,367,800	16.0	$256,652,312	1.3	$275,515,824	7.3	$292,275,546	6.1	$50.39
31	27	Colorado	$215,153,012	$228,602,539	6.3	$243,749,371	6.6	$238,782,437	-2.0	$242,156,622	1.4	$232,982,576	-3.8	$49.94
32	29	New Jersey	$291,038,279	$234,531,851	-19.4	$297,405,388	26.8	$338,240,160	13.7	$424,406,132	25.5	$422,511,983	-0.4	$48.46
33	32	Utah	$75,896,263	$83,546,056	10.1	$96,324,086	15.3	$104,919,649	8.9	$103,574,481	-1.3	$112,076,753	8.2	$45.38
34	34	South Carolina	$100,068,135	$127,639,870	27.6	$182,172,656	42.7	$179,488,876	-1.5	$172,034,064	-4.2	$182,399,186	6.0	$42.87
35	36	Alabama	$95,750,764	$104,572,600	9.2	$126,413,978	20.9	$150,484,422	19.0	$176,308,232	17.2	$195,035,545	10.6	$42.79
36	35	Ohio	$184,447,084	$198,375,602	7.6	$238,310,663	20.1	$407,280,700	70.9	$459,737,437	12.9	$483,963,481	5.3	$42.22
37	37	Michigan	$296,628,688	$226,803,347	-23.5	$334,151,145	47.3	$337,368,306	1.0	$384,952,089	14.1	$397,130,103	3.2	$39.24
38	41	Virginia	$149,962,364	$181,522,927	21.0	$214,035,306	17.9	$255,903,735	19.6	$244,013,269	-4.6	$291,768,427	19.6	$38.56
39	40	Kentucky	$64,502,432	$81,496,823	26.3	$91,875,929	12.7	$108,946,111	18.6	$137,016,621	25.8	$154,428,570	12.7	$37.01
40	38	Florida	$271,020,760	$419,070,922	54.6	$487,447,294	16.3	$552,473,675	13.3	$598,464,752	8.3	$619,286,347	3.5	$34.81
41	42	Idaho	$18,295,522	$28,217,858	54.2	$30,717,900	8.9	$36,698,083	19.5	$44,614,955	21.6	$49,149,206	10.2	$34.39
42	43	North Carolina	$190,496,958	$235,232,775	23.5	$254,035,290	8.0	$263,186,889	3.6	$269,303,718	2.3	$286,101,708	6.2	$32.95
43	45	Illinois	$136,721,645	$211,829,431	54.9	$249,652,970	17.9	$252,514,368	1.1	$351,663,999	39.3	$418,648,223	19.0	$32.80
44	46	Arkansas	$35,424,698	$47,104,650	33.0	$55,331,114	17.5	$62,656,304	13.2	$71,155,071	13.6	$87,972,571	23.6	$31.66
45	39	California	$556,376,630	$717,820,018	29.0	$889,552,300	23.9	$801,923,980	-9.9	$1,191,586,102	48.6	$1,050,006,600	-11.9	$29.06
46	44	Georgia	$77,909,835	$83,494,732	7.2	$147,772,799	77.0	$110,708,930	-25.1	$272,891,478	146.5	$240,981,565	-11.7	$26.56
47	49	Nevada	$13,651,627	$19,975,232	46.3	$24,860,705	24.5	$27,810,666	11.9	$21,656,952	-22.1	$47,981,582	121.6	$19.87
48	47	Texas	$266,536,528	$272,436,224	2.2	$303,161,000	11.3	$347,635,582	11.3	$379,583,642	9.2	$422,256,285	11.2	$18.40
49	48	Washington DC	$0	$403,180	100.0	$1,424,524	253.3	$3,353,453	135.4	$5,651,087	68.5	$10,135,846	79.4	$18.40
50	51	Arizona	$0	$0		$0	0.0	$0	0.0	$0		$0	0.0	$0.00
51	50	Mississippi	$3,464,496	$13,854,025	299.9	$26,210,130	89.2	$30,421,046	16.1	$3,069,037	-89.9	$0	-100.0	$0.00
		United States	$9,581,526,056	$10,888,301,954	13.6	$12,808,786,607	17.6	$14,276,903,586	11.5	$15,189,825,612	13.4	$17,024,072,941	5.2	$57.43

TABLE B

ICF-MR

RANK 2005	RANK 2004	STATE	FY 2000 EXPENDITURES	PERCENT CHANGE 00-01	FY 2001 EXPENDITURES	PERCENT CHANGE 01-02	FY 2002 EXPENDITURES	PERCENT CHANGE 02-03	FY 2003 EXPENDITURES	PERCENT CHANGE 03-04	FY 2004 EXPENDITURES	PERCENT CHANGE 04-05	FY 2005 EXPENDITURES	FY 2005 EXPENDITURES PER CAPITA
1	1	Washington DC	$70,280,093	10.9	$77,914,495	2.0	$79,480,032	-1.4	$78,338,985	3.2	$80,808,512	-2.0	$79,196,025	$143.73
2	2	New York	$2,129,387,466	1.4	$2,159,385,111	14.5	$2,472,622,451	5.5	$2,608,036,033	1.3	$2,642,385,675	2.9	$2,719,055,847	$141.21
3	4	North Dakota	$49,980,530	-3.7	$48,134,972	13.6	$54,683,268	-6.5	$51,152,406	4.8	$53,586,849	21.8	$65,278,839	$102.48
4	3	Louisiana	$347,438,513	2.3	$355,268,229	2.0	$362,343,106	1.7	$368,331,056	13.7	$419,201,757	1.5	$425,679,479	$94.09
5	5	Ohio	$558,612,234	40.9	$787,065,753	18.4	$931,910,322	5.7	$985,165,085	-10.7	$879,995,156	14.2	$1,005,053,573	$87.67
6	6	Iowa	$191,252,400	6.1	$202,856,281	-4.9	$192,996,276	21.2	$233,929,703	-3.3	$226,181,218	10.0	$248,752,217	$83.87
7	8	Mississippi	$158,201,464	7.6	$170,211,742	4.6	$178,042,983	3.3	$184,000,113	1.4	$186,534,891	12.1	$209,110,070	$71.59
8	10	New Jersey	$380,579,725	10.7	$421,459,378	9.8	$462,968,767	-7.9	$426,296,020	20.3	$512,838,236	10.3	$565,546,561	$64.87
9	7	Connecticut	$230,624,610	-0.1	$230,489,160	-7.4	$213,455,475	15.7	$246,911,096	3.1	$254,582,505	-13.7	$219,690,073	$62.59
10	9	Illinois	$649,195,470	3.0	$668,984,334	7.8	$720,940,905	-6.3	$675,562,611	14.5	$773,363,350	-11.0	$688,155,342	$53.92
11	12	North Carolina	$396,863,370	0.8	$400,129,463	4.1	$416,422,558	0.5	$418,470,495	6.2	$444,541,825	0.5	$446,972,145	$51.48
12	11	Indiana	$258,454,594	14.9	$296,849,846	14.2	$339,070,244	-2.3	$331,408,679	4.4	$345,888,129	-8.0	$318,265,018	$50.74
13	29	Arkansas	$121,239,605	-20.6	$96,255,399	-69.9	$28,958,296	-39.1	$17,643,095	304.2	$71,321,403	97.6	$140,908,587	$50.70
14	20	Tennessee	$234,719,370	-0.8	$232,818,131	8.5	$252,512,375	1.3	$255,674,647	-11.0	$227,494,079	27.2	$289,361,481	$48.53
15	17	Pennsylvania	$496,918,629	-2.2	$486,148,847	4.1	$506,212,065	1.1	$511,953,415	-1.1	$506,187,585	14.0	$577,222,902	$46.44
16	14	Missouri	$164,291,907	12.3	$184,558,123	24.7	$230,168,835	0.8	$232,091,638	10.8	$257,065,690	-0.1	$256,706,484	$44.26
17	13	Maine	$35,306,066	27.0	$44,841,108	12.3	$50,370,111	20.3	$60,571,420	0.4	$60,794,291	-8.3	$55,769,276	$42.19
18	18	Idaho	$53,210,529	14.7	$61,011,544	-5.4	$57,714,097	-6.0	$54,266,274	2.2	$55,442,698	-1.5	$54,588,955	$38.20
19	15	South Carolina	$171,931,801	-1.6	$169,106,468	3.4	$174,843,154	-4.1	$167,696,107	4.3	$174,884,240	-7.7	$161,433,481	$37.94
20	26	Wyoming	$16,054,327	-7.5	$14,856,367	4.6	$15,542,906	1.7	$15,807,889	7.0	$16,908,396	8.4	$18,335,225	$36.02
21	16	Wisconsin	$254,700,314	-19.2	$205,681,098	9.9	$226,014,485	-1.7	$222,180,663	1.7	$226,054,638	-12.7	$197,374,367	$35.65
22	19	Texas	$728,986,838	-0.6	$724,584,981	12.0	$811,721,857	6.3	$862,672,801	0.8	$869,659,629	-7.4	$805,708,216	$35.25
23	25	Oklahoma	$103,178,346	10.6	$114,123,962	-1.6	$112,292,158	3.4	$116,157,674	3.8	$120,545,148	0.8	$121,544,040	$34.26
24	23	Nebraska	$48,861,869	-2.2	$47,765,756	-0.2	$47,671,206	3.0	$49,091,766	23.7	$60,734,502	-2.1	$59,443,762	$33.79
25	22	Minnesota	$208,714,012	4.3	$217,662,491	-4.5	$207,841,249	-6.3	$194,709,417	-7.1	$180,916,065	-5.2	$171,455,673	$33.40
26	21	Massachusetts	$210,037,470	0.9	$211,838,811	-6.5	$198,022,895	11.3	$220,310,836	3.6	$228,163,817	-6.6	$213,106,263	$33.30
27	24	Delaware	$32,544,972	-5.1	$30,869,844	1.1	$31,219,292	-8.7	$28,514,265	-0.2	$28,453,879	-9.3	$25,821,497	$30.59
28	27	West Virginia	$47,088,484	1.4	$47,763,206	-0.5	$47,513,217	11.6	$53,018,568	2.3	$54,248,872	1.6	$55,100,628	$30.33
29	28	Virginia	$183,139,808	2.3	$187,411,959	15.3	$216,052,352	1.6	$219,531,091	-1.9	$215,435,405	6.2	$228,819,663	$30.24
30	30	South Dakota	$17,999,207	2.8	$18,503,152	-0.3	$18,447,709	-1.5	$18,165,553	3.5	$18,793,990	13.3	$21,296,554	$27.44
31	31	Kentucky	$83,523,742	12.9	$94,311,899	3.8	$97,888,453	15.7	$113,264,181	-5.7	$106,755,738	0.9	$107,747,087	$25.82
32	33	Kansas	$66,924,380	3.0	$68,926,147	-4.4	$65,862,911	-13.2	$57,154,770	18.3	$67,637,569	-0.9	$66,999,732	$24.41
33	36	Utah	$53,199,473	1.9	$54,230,152	1.2	$54,883,090	-0.4	$54,664,369	-1.3	$53,977,353	6.6	$57,513,532	$23.28
34	34	Washington	$133,127,030	-1.9	$130,662,490	-2.2	$127,817,207	-11.1	$113,673,603	6.6	$121,232,112	4.1	$126,200,726	$20.07
35	37	California	$387,213,341	8.4	$419,725,174	58.2	$663,954,138	8.0	$716,923,618	9.3	$783,902,135	-17.1	$649,831,934	$17.98
36	35	Florida	$281,143,157	3.3	$290,508,354	6.8	$310,393,230	1.8	$316,110,930	-2.2	$309,107,343	-2.6	$301,190,366	$16.93
37	41	Montana	$22,839,812	-6.5	$21,363,372	-34.2	$14,061,080	-18.4	$11,480,253	68.1	$19,298,626	-36.0	$12,350,308	$13.19
38	40	Colorado	$17,985,707	-10.9	$16,034,098	19.8	$19,202,441	68.9	$32,424,912	38.0	$44,751,475	31.2	$58,726,134	$12.59
39	38	Maryland	$58,820,123	-0.7	$58,419,284	5.5	$61,628,216	-6.5	$57,640,025	4.4	$60,164,534	4.9	$63,085,684	$11.27
40	42	Georgia	$110,219,342	1.6	$111,980,166	-1.2	$110,659,329	-6.3	$103,659,336	41.0	$146,169,254	-31.4	$100,254,754	$11.05
41	39	Nevada	$28,496,213	1.5	$28,912,477	4.8	$30,309,013	-18.1	$24,825,043	-10.6	$22,196,769	19.3	$26,472,598	$10.96
42	45	New Mexico	$27,815,226	-33.8	$18,412,417	3.2	$18,993,063	3.7	$19,693,560	16.5	$22,940,983	-7.9	$21,123,412	$10.96
43	44	Hawaii	$7,975,547	0.3	$8,000,357	7.1	$8,572,313	-13.2	$7,444,198	0.2	$7,461,592	15.3	$8,605,505	$6.75
44	43	Rhode Island	$6,292,079	12.8	$7,094,523	2.1	$7,244,449	-3.7	$6,979,980	10.1	$7,686,159	-8.0	$7,067,988	$6.57
45	46	Alabama	$63,946,199	-3.5	$61,714,388	-1.9	$60,516,473	-13.5	$52,358,441	-34.3	$34,397,853	-20.8	$27,248,061	$5.98
46	47	Michigan	$27,883,649	11.9	$31,213,716	-11.4	$27,647,769	3.5	$28,612,200	-3.4	$27,629,687	-24.8	$20,778,960	$2.05
47	48	New Hampshire	$1,660,413	29.3	$2,146,914	-9.0	$1,952,826	-4.5	$1,865,866	22.7	$2,290,044	2.5	$2,348,269	$1.79
48	49	Vermont	$1,661,352	-2.0	$1,628,446	0.1	$1,630,657	-6.2	$1,528,774	-45.7	$829,376	13.9	$944,808	$1.52
49	50	Alaska	$0	0.0	$0	0.0	$0	0.0	$0	0.0	$0	0.0	$0	$0.00
50	51	Arizona	$0	0.0	$0	0.0	$0	0.0	$0	0.0	$0	0.0	$0	$0.00
51	32	Oregon	$24,519,621	-54.3	$11,216,811	1.2	$11,346,249	-23.8	$8,643,411	-100.0	$0	0.0	$0	$0.00
		United States	$9,955,040,629	4.0	$10,351,051,240	9.7	$11,352,617,557	2.5	$11,637,806,871	3.4	$12,031,441,032	0.6	$12,103,242,101	$40.83

Overall Satisfaction with Services
Area Program Summary By Clients' Primary Disability

This table summarizes the overall levels of satisfaction for area programs by clients' primary disability.

Overall, most clients in all three primary disability groups surveyed in area programs indicated they were satisfied with services with the largest variation being in substance abuse. However, in all area programs, the overall satisfaction for substance abuse clients was 71% or higher.

Consumers Surveyed October 2001	Overall Satisfaction with Services			
	Average Percent of Consumers Indicating Overall Satisfaction			
	Mental Health	Substance Abuse	Developmental Disability	Primary Disability Not Reported
Alamance-Caswell	89%	87%	91%	85%
Albemarle	90%	88%	N/A	83%
Blue Ridge	88%	94%	97%	88%
Catawba	90%	93%	N/A	84%
Centerpoint	89%	83%	N/A	85%
Crossroads	90%	81%	100%	92%
Cumberland	86%	86%	N/A	85%
Davidson	87%	73%	N/A	N/A
Duplin-Sampson	92%	90%	85%	96%
Durham	88%	82%	80%	81%
Edgecombe-Nash	88%	90%	100%	84%
Foothills	88%	88%	N/A	88%
Guilford	86%	71%	87%	81%
Johnston	82%	89%	N/A	79%
Lee-Harnett	95%	100%	N/A	85%
Lenoir	95%	88%	N/A	92%
Mecklenburg	83%	85%	92%	83%
Neuse	89%	88%	98%	91%
New River	91%	86%	97%	89%
Onslow	85%	N/A	90%	79%
OPC	91%	94%	N/A	86%
Pathways	93%	87%	N/A	93%
Piedmont	87%	74%	N/A	84%
Pitt	88%	90%	N/A	80%
Randolph	90%	90%	90%	89%
Riverstone	95%	N/A	96%	94%
Roanoke-Chowan	93%	90%	98%	80%
Rockingham	95%	85%	N/A	95%
Rutherford-Polk	84%	85%	100%	88%
Sandhills	89%	85%	81%	84%
Smoky Mountain	92%	81%	N/A	94%
Southeastern Center	87%	96%	N/A	93%
Southeastern Regional	91%	88%	N/A	85%
Tideland	88%	88%	96%	95%
Trend	88%	93%	N/A	92%
VGFW	89%	80%	100%	91%
Wake	Not Reported	Not Reported	Not Reported	Not Reported
Wayne	83%	83%	N/A	78%
Wilson-Greene	91%	94%	96%	86%
All Area Programs	**89%**	**87%**	**93%**	**86%**

N/A indicates that there were less than ten responses so the data is not shown for the area program.

HCFA PROGRAM ISSUANCE
Transmittal Notice
REGION IV

T-8

DIRECTOR'S OFFICE
SEP 21 1990

DATE: SEP 18 1990   PROGRAM IDENTIFIER: MCD-90-90

TO: All Title XIX State Agencies

SUBJECT: Monetary Cap on Services Provided Under the Early and Periodic Screening, Diagnosis, and Treatment (EPSDT) Program

This is to disseminate a recent policy clarification we received from our Central Office on the issue of placing a monetary limit on the services provided under the EPSDT program.

After April 1, 1990, the effective date of Section 6403 of the Omnibus Budget Reconciliation Act of 1989, States must provide any medically necessary service to a child if the service is found to be needed as a result of EPSDT screening services. A monetary cap, or putting a dollar limit on a set of services, has the same effect as putting a limit on quantity. Cash limits are precluded in the current EPSDT program, which requires provision of any medically necessary Medicaid service, whether or not it is covered under the State's Medicaid Plan.

A State may set payment amounts for specific services, or reimburse providers by capitation or fees for time. A State may employ a combination of thresholds and prior authorization procedures as a part of the program's financial management. Overall monetary limits or caps may not be set which could prevent the provision of medically necessary services under EPSDT. After April 1, 1990, whether or not a cap was included in the Medicaid State Plan, the State would be liable for payment for necessary services provided under EPSDT.

Questions or comments may be addressed to Cathy Kasriel at (404) 331-5028 or Mal Williams at (404) 331-5889.

George R. Holland
Regional Administrator
Health Care Financing Administration

categorically *neat*

evidently *neat*

```
              ANNUAL EPSDT PARTICIPATION REPORT              09/07/2000
                 NORTH CAROLINA  FY: 1998                   PAGE 1 OF 2
========================================================================
                          CAT.      TOTAL      <1      1-5     6-14    15-20
========================================================================
1.  NO. OF INDIVIDUALS    CN      663,862    88142   209861   251360  114499
    ELIG FOR EPSDT:       MN        8,512      155     1259     3847     3251
                          TOTAL   672,374    88297   211120   255207  117750

2.  RATIO OF RECOM.       CN                          6.00     1.20     0.56     0.50
    INIT OR PERIODIC:     MN                          6.00     1.20     0.56     0.50
    SCREENING SERV        TOTAL                       6.00     1.20     0.56     0.50

3   AVG PERIOD            CN         0.75     0.58     0.75     0.74     0.66
    OF ELIGIBILITY:       MN         0.41     0.33     0.41     0.41     0.41
                          ALL        0.75     0.62     0.78     0.79     0.70

4.  ADJ RATIO OF          CN                          3.48     0.90     0.41     0.33
    REC. INIT. OR         MN                          1.98     0.49     0.23     0.21
    PER. SCREEN SERV      ALL                         3.72     0.94     0.44     0.35
    PER AGE GROUP:

5.  PRO.OF ELIG           CN                          1.00     0.90     0.41     0.33
    WHO SHOULD RECIEVE    MN                          1.00     0.49     0.23     0.21
    AT LEAST 1 INIT OR    ALL                         1.00     0.94     0.44     0.35
    PER. SCREENING SERV:

6.  NO.  OF ELIGS         CN       417,860    88142   188875   103058    37785
    WHO SHOULD RECEIVE    MN         2,340      155      617      885      683
    AT LEAST 1 INIT       ALL      420,200    88297   189492   103943    38468
    PER SCREENING SERV:

7.  NO. OF ELIGS          CN       228,840    68796   100716    50349     8979
    RECEIVING AT LEAST 1  MN          817       43      316      338      120
    INIT OR PERIODIC      TOTAL    229,657    68839   101032    50687     9099
    SCREENING SERV:

8.  PARTICIPANT RATIO:    CN         0.54     0.78     0.53     0.49     0.24
                          MN         0.34     0.28     0.51     0.38     0.18
                          ALL        0.54     0.78     0.53     0.49     0.24

9.  EXPECTED NO. OF       CN       636,452   306734   188875   103058    37785
    INITIAL AND PERIODIC  MN         2,492      307      617      885      683
    SCREENING SERVICES:   ALL      638,944   307041   189492   103943    38468

10. ACTUAL NO. OF         CN       379,063   187914   129095    52670     9384
    INITIAL OR PERIODIC   MN          959       96      395      345      123
    SCREENING SERVICES    ALL      380,022   188010   129490    53015     9507

11. SCREENING RATIO       CN         0.59     0.61     0.68     0.51     0.25
                          MN         0.38     0.31     0.64     0.39     0.18
                          ALL        0.59     0.61     0.68     0.51     0.25
```

**LINE 6 AND LINE 9 HAVE BEEN ROUNDED USING STANARD ROUNDING CONVENTIONS

	CAT.	TOTAL	<1	1-5	6-14	15-20
12. NO. OF ELIGS	CN	5,805	1323	2812	1413	257
REFERRED FOR	MN	21	6	8	5	2
CORRECT. TREATMENT:	ALL	5,826	1329	2820	1418	259
13. NO. OF ELIGS	CN	234,151	68848	101346	54041	9916
RECEIVING VISION	MN	902	43	325	385	149
ASSESSMENTS:	ALL	235,053	68891	101671	54426	10065
14. NO. OF ELIGS	CN	111,874	42	27159	69277	15396
RECEIVING DENTAL	MN	1,018	0	138	558	322
ASSESSMENTS:	ALL	112,892	42	27297	69835	15718
15. NO. OF ELIGS	CN	229,099	68801	100807	50486	9005
RECEIVING HEARING	MN	819	43	316	340	120
ASSESSMENTS:	ALL	229,918	68844	101123	50826	9125
16. TOTAL NO. OF	CN	0	0	0	0	0
ELIGS ENROLLED IN	MN	0	0	0	0	0
CONTINUING CARE	ALL	0	0	0	0	0
ARRANGEMENTS:						

APPENDIX M. UTILIZATION REVIEW GUIDELINES

Utilization Review Guidelines for CAP-MR/DD Recipients Residing at Home

Home = own home or with natural family _____

Service	LEVEL 1 SNAP Index 24-44	LEVEL 2 SNAP Index 45-78	LEVEL 3 SNAP Index 80-92	LEVEL 4 SNAP Index 95-230
Respite	576 hours/year	576 hours/year	576 hours/year	576 hours/year
Personal Care	40 hours/month	80 hours/month	120 hours/month	180 hours/month
Residential Supports	N/A	N/A	N/A	N/A
Home and Community Supports, Day Supports, Supported Employment	120 hours/month for any combination of these services	120 hours/month for any combination of these services	120 hour/month for any combination of these services	120 hours/month for any combination of these services

- Individuals at level 3 or 4 are eligible for Enhanced Respite and Enhanced Personal Care Services
- Hours of Home and Community Supports, Day Supports and Supported Employment can be exchanged for additional Personal Care hours, if indicated on the person centered plan

Utilization Review Guidelines for CAP-MR/DD Recipients in Residential Placements

Residential = alternative family living or provider managed residences

Service	LEVEL 1 SNAP Index 24-44	LEVEL 2 SNAP Index 45-78	LEVEL 3 SNAP Index 80-92	LEVEL 4 SNAP Index 95-230
Respite	*576 hours/year	*576 hours/year	*576 hours/year	*576 hours/year
Personal Care	N/A	N/A	N/A	N/A
Residential Supports	Daily rate	Daily rate	Daily rate	Daily rate
Home and Community Supports, Day Supports, Supported Employment	120 hours/month for any combination of these services	120 hours/month for any combination of these services	120 hours/month for any combination of these services	120 hours/month for any combination of these services

- *Only available to individuals residing in alternative family living homes
- *Individuals at levels 3 and 4 are eligible for Enhanced Respite services
- Individuals in residential placements are only eligible to receive the community component of Home and Community Supports

Appendix B

Website Information

Team Daniel, LLC
> www.teamdaniel.info

Person Centered Support Services, LLC
> www.pcssllc.net

Partners in Policymaking
> www.partnersinpolicymaking.com

Project Leadership – SABE (Self-Advocates Becoming Empowered)
> www.sabeusa.org/leadership

United States Department of Education
> www.ed.gov/index.jhtml

- OSERS (Office of Special Education & Rehabilitation Services)
- OCR (Office of Civil Rights)

United States Department of Health & Human Services
> www.hhs.gov

- Click on the icon "All HHS News" to receive news releases via email.

United States General Accounting Office
> www.gao.gov

- Reports & Testimonies
- Go to "Keywords or Report #" in the upper right-hand corner.
  - o Enter "GAO-01-749" for GAO Report on EPSDT dated July 2001.

Social Security Administration
>   www.ssa.gov
> - Social Security Act – Section 1915
>   http://www.ssa.gov/OP_Home/ssact/title19/1915.htm
>   - o Enter into search engine "Social Security Act Section 1915"

Center for Medicare and Medicaid Services (CMS)
>   www.cms.hhs.gov
> - Medicaid
> - EPSDT
> - Medicaid Waiver & Demonstration Projects
> - Icon at top of page. "Newsroom"
>   - o Press Releases
>   - o Fact Sheets

National Association of State Medicaid Directors (NASMD)
>   www.nasmd.org
> - Waivers
> - State Medicaid Director Letters

National Health Law Program
>   www.healthlaw.org
> - Medicaid
> - EPSDT
> - GAO Reports

Human Services Research Institute
>   www.hsri.org

TASH
>   www.tash.org

The Arc of United States
>   www.thearc.org

The Clearinghouse for Community Living Exchange Collaborative
>   www.hcbs.org

Appendix C
The Fayetteville Observer Articles

The Fayetteville Observer

(C) Copyright

Monday, October 18, 1993

Page 1A

MONDAY, OCTOBER 18, 1993

Parents Push For Including Handicapped

By Suzanne Walker
Staff Writer

Denise Mercado wants her son to have the same opportunities to learn as any other child in Cumberland County.

The problem is that only select classrooms in Fort Bragg and Cumberland County schools are equipped to handle children like her mentally retarded son Danny, who has cerebral palsy and is confined to a wheelchair.

As a result, the 11-year-old has been separated from normal children most of his life. The boy now attends Bowley Elementary School, where he is in a class for children with severe handicaps.

Mercado hopes to change that. She is one of 25 representatives chosen to participate in Partners in Policymaking, a statewide organization aimed at helping parents improve services for handicapped children.

The group meets once a month in Raleigh, where parents learn about educational laws, employment opportunities for handicapped people and the Americans with Disabilities Act. The sessions started in June and will end next month.

Mercado's goal is to make sure that by next fall handicapped students are included in the classroom activities of normal students and are given extra help so they can work at their own pace. This approach is called ``inclusion.''

The Americans with Disabilities Act specifies that children have the right to be educated in the ``least restrictive environment.''

We have some mainstreaming in Cumberland County and Fort Bragg, but there is a difference between mainstreaming and inclusion,'' Mercado said.

Mainstreaming involves placing students in handicapped classes for part of the day and putting them in regular classrooms for subjects such as art, music and physical education.

Inclusion, she said, involves mixing handicapped children with normal students while providing them extra help, such as instruction by teachers' assistants.

Mercado admits that inclusion isn't as easy as it sounds. The regular classrooms aren't equipped to handle emergencies that can arise with handicapped children. The teachers aren't properly trained and few classes have a full-time teacher's assistant.

In Cumberland County Schools, handicapped children face similar problems.

At Douglas Byrd Junior High, for example, three deaf students spent a week without an interpreter, while at Sherwood Park Elementary School one teacher and a part-time teacher's assistant are responsible for nine handicapped students with medical problems.

Patricia Barnes, a Sherwood Park parent, pleaded with county school board members recently to hire a full-time assistant for her son's class.

``The exceptional children's program at Sherwood Park Elementary needs a full-time teacher's assistant,'' she said during the meeting.

She said she fears for the safety of her son because the teacher can't be attentive to all the students. When the teacher leaves the class to escort one student to a bus, she said, the class is left with a teacher from another class who isn't trained to handle handicapped children.

``The teacher cannot devote one-on-one right now.''

Dr. James McKethan, director of the county schools' Exceptional Children's Program, said those problems keep schools from mixing handicapped children with normal students.

Cumberland County has 4,700 handicapped students. Fort Bragg has 419.

McKethan said he believes handicapped children should be given the chance to learn with their non-handicapped peers. He said inclusion and mainstreaming help them learn how to interact with people and develop social skills.

He knows first-hand what inclusion can do for handicapped children. His handicapped son attended regular classes at Seventy-First High School.

``He felt included there and the people pretty much accepted him there. I think sometimes having a disabled person in mainstream classes is a reality check for us. I can say that generally, based on my experience, children are accepting, given the opportunity. Our experience in school was a success,'' he said.

McKethan said Cumberland County has made some progress.

Two years ago, children classified as trainable mentally handicapped were sent to Walker-Spivey School. Now, McKethan said, there are programs for those students at Anne Chesnutt and Reid Ross junior high schools. The system plans to start another program in a high school next year.

``There will always be some separate classes. We're making a lot of progress. We know we've got a ways to go, but we're continuing to develop and enhance what we've got,'' he said.

``We believe we need to provide the opportunities for youngsters who will benefit from being in a regular environment. I do believe in educating disabled children in the least restrictive environment possible based on the individual needs of the children. Over the years, we probably removed more children from the regular educational setting than we should have, but now we're beginning to see more children having their needs met in a regular setting.''

In the meantime, Mercado said she's hoping to mainstream her son in art classes next month. If he's successful, they will try music and physical education classes.

``I feel like my son Danny has a lot inside that needs to come out. In reality, I don't know if Danny will ever be academic -- reading, writing and arithmetic -- but you don't know that unless you let him try.''

The Fayetteville Observer

(C) Copyright
Monday, February 21, 1994
Page 1A
Monday, February 21, 1994

DANNY HAS A SPARK

AH HANDICAPPED BOY ADDS LAUGHTER, LEARNING TO CLASS

By Suzanne Walker
Staff writer

Denise Mercado wants what's best for Danny.

Until a few months ago, she was sure that the best thing for her 11-year-old handicapped son was to spend his days in a class for children with severe disabilities.

That was before she got involved in Partners in Policymaking, a statewide program aimed at helping parents improve services for their handicapped children.

The group met once a month from June to November. Parents learned about education laws, employment opportunities for handicapped people and the Americans with Disabilities Act.

Until she got involved in the program, Mercado was content to leave her son in handicapped classes. Then, on a visit to a school at Camp LeJeune, she saw what ``inclusion'' and ``mainstreaming'' can do for children like Danny.

Inclusion involves having handicapped students participate in the classroom activities of normal students. The handicapped students are given extra help so they can work at their own pace.

Mainstreaming involves placing students in handicapped classes for part of the day and putting them in regular classes for subjects such as art, music and physical education.

Armed with new information about programs for handicapped students, Mercado persuaded Fort Bragg school officials to put Danny in art and P.E. classes with regular students at Bowley Elementary School.

Danny is mentally retarded and has cerebral palsy. He can't speak and is confined to a wheelchair.

``I feared him being with other children. I really bought into him being separate, but after 11 or 12 years I'd had enough. I just couldn't see him being separate any more,'' Mercado said.

Danny takes P.E. and art classes once a week. He spends the rest of the time in a class with five other handicapped boys.

While the other students practice somersaults in the P.E. class, teachers Joan Montgomery and Darcy Iles flex Danny's muscles using a blue rubber wheel.

CLASSMATES HELP

Students fight over who will be the helpers, a problem the teachers solved by setting up a rotation.

On a recent Monday afternoon, 10-year-olds Amanda Pearce and Priscilla Gizoni had their turn.

The work is hard, but the girls don't mind.

``It's fun,'' Priscilla said. ``I like when he laughs. He laughs a lot.''

The girls said they were worried at first about having Danny in their class, but they quickly got used to him.

``I was sort of scared at first, now I'm not because I got to know him. I'm used to him now,'' Amanda said.

Barbara Thomas, a Bowley substitute, was so impressed with the way the students reacted to Danny that she wanted her sons to get involved. Mike, 7, and Tony, 9, now read to Danny every Saturday.

``It was selfish on my part. I wanted them to see him so when they grow up they're not going to turn their head away. I thought the boys could benefit as well as Danny,'' Thomas said.

``Other kids are neat, but Danny has a spark. There's something cooking inside.''

Thomas said it took her sons a while to get used to Danny's habits. He sometimes interrupts the stories they read with loud noises and laughter.

Tony and Mike said they wait until Danny settles down, then continue with the stories.

REACTION TYPICAL

Barbara Jones, director of the system's exceptional children's program, said the students' reaction to Danny is typical.

``It humbles them, it makes them think,'' Jones said. ``It helps them to be sensitive to other folks who are not as fortunate as they are. This is the age to start it.''

Jones said it could be years before students like Danny are fully included in school programs, but the system is working toward that. In January, the system appointed a task force to study inclusion.

Mercado's goal for next year is to move Danny into a middle school, where he will be around children his own age. She hopes he can be mainstreamed into reading and math classes.

For the time being, Mercado is satisfied.

``He's always had great teachers and therapists, but now he has friends.''

The Fayetteville Observer

(C) Copyright
Monday, June 27, 1994
Page 1B
Monday, June 27, 1994

DISABLED CHILD'S TRIP TO CAMP MAY OPEN DOORS FOR OTHERS

By Suzanne Walker
Staff writer

ROCKFISH -- Danny Mercado couldn't run with the other children at Camp Rockfish.

The 12-year-old has cerebral palsy and is mentally retarded. He is confined to a wheelchair, cannot speak and is fed through a tube in his stomach.

But with a little help from the Easter Seal Society of North Carolina, he was able to spend last week at the camp canoeing, swimming, and riding horses.

Officials with the society, which helps people with handicaps, hope that Danny is the first of many children with severe disabilities to go to camp with children who aren't handicapped.

Karen Hamilton, Easter Seal recreation director, said Danny's camp trip is the first of its kind in the state.

``We've been helping children go to camp for about three years. Our specialty is children with physical disabilities,'' Hamilton said. ``But Danny is a pilot project this summer. We're seeing what it would take to help a student with those disabilities go to camp during the summer.''

Hamilton said the society has sent about 300 handicapped children to camps throughout North Carolina. Most of the children have had either physical or mental handicaps. Danny has both.

During his week at Camp Rockfish, Danny slept, ate and played with other children. His mother, **Denise Mercado**, said the week was just what he needed and deserved.

Mercado has struggled for years to have her son included in school and other activities offered to children without handicaps. In August, Danny started taking physical education and music classes at Bowley Elementary School on Fort Bragg. He will go to a junior high school on post this fall.

Mercado said it took about six months to arrange the trip to Camp Rockfish. The Easter Seal Society paid for Andrea Anderson, a certified nursing assistant, to feed, bathe and dress Danny. Mercado was responsible for the regular camp fees.

As camp counselors helped Danny participate in activities, Anderson stayed close by to tend to his needs.

``What we wanted to show is that even people with severe disabilities can be included, that children with and without disabilities can go to camp together and that everyone benefits when children with disabilities go to camp,'' Hamilton said. ``They are learning from each other.''

Camp counselor Kelly Woodlief said the 10 children in Danny's group went out of their way to include him in activities.

``They just love him,'' she said. ``I was a little worried at first because they haven't been exposed to handicapped children, but when he got here, they ran up to Danny and practically fight over who will push his wheelchair.''

311

The Fayetteville Observer

(C) Copyright
Monday, April 24, 1995
Page 1D
Monday, April 24, 1995

MENINGITIS

By Bonnie Carlson
Staff writer

Curtis Jones was fine the afternoon of April 5, laughing and talking with friends at Westover High School.

The next night he was at Womack Army Medical Center, his health failing fast. By April 7 he had been taken by helicopter to Duke University Medical Center, where he is still in intensive care.

The diagnosis: Neisseria meningitidis, a deadly form of bacterial meningitis.

The bacteria attacked every organ in Jones' body, leaving him in a coma, a ventilator helping him breathe. He was in fair condition over the weekend, according to Renee Twombly, a Duke spokesman. She would not say what his prognosis is, saying only that ``we can't give that in these situations.''

DIFFERENT TYPES

Dr. Charles Ellenbogen of the Fayetteville Area Health Education Center has studied meningitis and other infectious diseases for 30 years. There are different varieties of the disease and people recover differently.

Viral strains of the disease generally cause flu-like symptoms ranging from fever to body aches, and often come and go without ever being diagnosed, he said.

Bacterial strains are more serious, progressing rapidly and inflicting serious and often fatal damage.

Ellenbogen first saw Neisseria meningitidis in the 1960s when he was working with military recruits at the Air Force teaching hospital in San Antonio, Texas.

As in Jones' case, it often attacks all organs of the body and causes bleeding under the skin, leaving a red or purple rash.

``It is one of the most rapidly progressive diseases we know,'' Ellenbogen said.

He was a senior resident at the Air Force hospital in San Antonio when a young airman came in with symptoms of the illness.

Ellenbogen and an assistant examined the man and drew spinal fluid to be tested for the meningitis bacteria. They circled with ballpoint pens the few red and purple splotches on the man's skin to chart how quickly the bleeding was spreading.

``I go out to the nurses station for 10 or 15 minutes to make the notes on his chart. I come back in to see him and he's got multiple small spots that rapidly expand to big spots before my eyes and he's going into shock,'' Ellenbogen said. ``It was one of my little lessons on just how quickly this disease progresses.''

Bob Howard, a spokesman for the National Center for Infectious Disease at the Centers for Disease Control in Atlanta, said about one in 50 people carries the meningitis bacteria without contracting the disease.

ODDS IMPROVING

For most people, meningitis is not a threat, but it can be deadly for some. And doctors don't know why.

Not so long ago, Howard said, 70 percent of people who contracted bacterial meningitis died. Today the disease is fatal in only about 10 percent, but it can leave people with brain damage, hearing loss, mental retardation or other disabilities.

Denise Mercado knows about the lasting effects of meningitis. Her 13-year-old son, Danny, was 6 months old when he became ill with Haemophilus influenza, the biggest cause of meningitis in young children.

It started with an ear infection. Twenty-four hours later, despite taking antibiotics for the infection, Danny was panting for breath, arching his back and vomiting. Mercado, who lived at Fort Lewis, Wash., at the time, called an ambulance.

From the military hospital at Fort Lewis, Danny was taken to a children's hospital in nearby Seattle. During a month in the hospital, Danny had a stroke and multiple seizures.

``It pretty much wiped him out,'' Mercado said. Danny has severe brain damage. He is unable to speak or do even the simplest things for himself.

When he was 5 or 6 years old, he outgrew the stroller his parents had pushed him around in since he left the hospital. ``We realized he needed a wheelchair,'' Mercado said. ``That's when we realized that this was Danny for the rest of his life. Until then, my husband and I felt, `He's a baby, he'll grow out of this.' ''

Although it is still the most common cause of meningitis in children, Haemophilus influenza is not as common as it was in 1982 when Danny got sick. About 10 years ago, the federal Food and Drug Administration approved a vaccine against the disease. Now, the HiB vaccine, as it is called, is routinely given to youngsters along with the polio vaccine and other immunizations. But Howard said there are still 11,000 to 12,000 cases reported each year.

A vaccine against Neisseria meningitidis was developed in the early 1970s and is given to military recruits, according to Ellenbogen of the Fayetteville Area Health Education Center. The disease, once epidemic among groups of recruits, is uncommon now in the military population.

Although Neisseria meningitidis is the most common form of bacterial meningitis in adults, Howard said, the vaccine is not available to the general public because the disease is not a serious threat to most people.

``It's not as contagious as something like influenza, and it's not spread by casual contact,'' he said. ``However, if you do live in close proximity to someone who has this, you can develop that through intimate contact.''

Still, he said, even among those with close contact to someone with the disease, only one in 100 develops it.

Symptoms usually develop within 10 days of infection, health officials said.

Why it strikes some people down while others are unaffected is a mystery, Howard said.

``It does not appear to have a geographic proclivity, although we do believe that we see more of it in the springtime."

The disease usually strikes young people, probably because they come into contact with more people through school than most adults encounter during an average day.

``We think probably more important than that, though, it relates to the immunity that they have built in their body or have not built up in their body," Howard said. ``It's a combination of environment, lifestyle and immunity."

Doctors at a regional office of the Centers for Disease Control in Oregon are studying a new drug-resistant strain of meningitis, Howard said. The disease has not become widespread, but could pose a dangerous threat if doctors don't find a way to fight it.

Because some forms of the disease are so deadly, people tend to panic when they hear the word ``meningitis," health officials said.

Dr. Jesse Williams, director of the Cumberland County Health Department, said his phones have been tied up for two weeks with calls from people who have a child at Westover, where Curtis Jones goes to school, or people who are worried that they may have come into contact with the disease.

Health Department nurses gave antibiotics to prevent the disease to about 60 to 65 people who had come into close contact with Jones, said Shirley Mozingo, a spokesman for the Cumberland County Health Department.

But Williams said many people who don't understand the disease are calling to ask for the antibiotic and are being turned away or told to call their private doctor.

``Most people just do not need to worry about this," Williams said.

Ellenbogen agreed: ``The vast majority of cases of meningitis are ones that are not bacterial, and the risks of injury to the brain and death are very much less. I worked face-to-face with meningitis patients, and I have never taken a microgram of antibiotic and I have never had the vaccine because I wasn't in danger."

If someone has a slight fever, headache, stiff neck and other discomforts that drag on for several days, Howard said, there is nothing to worry about.

When people should be concerned, he said, is when symptoms develop suddenly and worsen quickly.

``If it happens quickly and it appears to be progressing quickly, you want to get to a doctor as fast as you possibly can," he said.

*

WHAT ARE THE SYMPTOMS?

Meningitis is a contagious infection of the three thin layers, the meninges, that cover the brain and spinal cord.

VIRAL MENINGITIS:

* Fever

* Stiff neck

* Headache

* Irritability

* Eyes sensitive to light

* Vomiting

* Confusion, lethargy and drowsiness

BACTERIAL MENINGITIS:

* Sore throat or other signs of respiratory illness

* Fever, chills and sweating

* Stiff neck

* Headache

* Irritability

* Eyes sensitive to light

* Vomiting

* Confusion, lethargy and drowsiness or unconsciousness

* Red or purple skin rash caused by bleeding under the skin (resembles

bruising)

About the Author

Denise Mercado was born in Brooklyn, New York. Shortly before her sixteenth birthday, she moved to Plainview, Long Island with her family. At twenty-one years of age, Denise married and began a life as a military spouse. In 1982 Denise gave birth to her second son, Danny. Life took a sharp turn after Danny suffered a severe bout of meningitis. As a result, Denise embarked on an advocacy journey that has uncovered numerous injustices throughout the bureaucratic systems that support people with disabilities.

Denise is an honors graduate of Campbell University. She is also a graduate of the first North Carolina Partners in Policymaking Program (1993) and the national Project Leadership Program (2002). Denise has held several positions throughout the disability world, including project manager for one of the North Carolina Self-Determination Projects, executive director of The Arc of Cumberland County, and co-director of the Special Needs Education Center. Denise is presently co-owner of a North Carolina Medicaid provider agency that shifts control of Medicaid dollars to individuals with disabilities through fiscal intermediary and employer of record services. Denise and her husband, John, have also established Team Daniel, LLC in honor of their son, Danny, who continues to inspire them both to stand up for what is right.